0024458

D1366832

DATE DUE

© THE BAKER & TAYLOR CO.

LIFE AFTER POSTMODERNISM
Essays on Value and Culture

For Victoriana

LIFE AFTER POSTMODERNISM
Essays on Value and Culture

Edited and introduced by
John Fekete

St. Martin's Press
New York

First published in the United States of America in 1987

Printed in Canada

ISBN 0-312-00833-3 (cl.)
ISBN 0-312-00834-1 (pbk.)

Library of Congress Cataloging-in-Publication Data

Life after postmodernism.

(CultureTexts)
Bibliography: p.
Includes index.
1. Values   2. Postmodernism.   3. Aesthetics.
4. Hermeneutics.   5. Philosophy, Modern — 20th century.
I. Fekete, John. II. Series.
BD232.L53   1987   121'.8   87-20565
ISBN 0-312-00833-3
ISBN 0-312-00834-1 (pbk.)

CONTENTS

Acknowledgements

This book was conceived as a companion volume to *The Structural Allegory (1984)*. Since *The Critical Twilight (1978)*, I have been occupied with the question of value, and the massive shift in the forms of thought in this century whose result has been a downgrading of attention to value in favour of a foregrounding of all the categories of structure. I have been convinced that, not only is the change of emphasis in some important respects disabling (though also productive), but that there is in any case an ineluctable connection between structure and value that has to be made again more visible. This book issues from that conviction and I hope that its evidence, in turn, provides support for it.

When I began to work on the text four years ago, with the intention of stimulating a collaborative project to complement the earlier book in the form of a (set of anticipations of a) retheorization of the value question, I learned rapidly just how deeply the whole issue had been buried, even in the midst of a lively proliferation of (related) concerns and methods. The one intellectual current that addressed it at all with a contemporary flavour — one section of the heirs of Nietzsche — spoke to it only to denounce and put an end to the discourse of value, in the extravagant belief that the latter, especially in its reductive acceptance as in effect *moral* value, was completely under the deathly hegemony of the pathologies of Christianity, or modernity, or both. It was very difficult, even among friendly colleagues, to make intelligible a post-axiological, more-than-ethical, perspective on value, fit for a post-modern and post-scarcity prospect.

Now, at the end of that period, I think that a change is coming. As it becomes clearer that we are living after the onset (in some unperspicuous yet unavoidable sense) of postmodernity, it seems also strategically desirable to more people to think about life beyond the horizons of the more nihilistic and paralyzing aspects of postmodernism. Ultimately, it turns out to be possible to think *with* the question of value, and this book is offered as a kind of early testimony and invitation to that possibility.

I am particularly grateful to Barbara Smith, who invited me to think out loud about value at the MLA, and who has herself been effectively campaigning at the frontiers of a renewed discussion of value. I want to express my appreciation to Charles Levin, Andrew Wernick, Ian McLachlan, and Costas Boundas, friends and colleagues, who encouraged my interest, read manuscripts, and generally provided the loosely supportive milieu in which the project could be personally sustained. As often before, I am thankful to Suzan Wheeler, who has help fully given of her time to provide the index. I want to thank Arthur and Marilouise Kroker, who have not only been always generous, but who have been prepared to take risks to back up their intellectual commitments. Finally, I want to acknowledge that, without the untiring attention and many-sided engagement of Victoria de Zwaan, my task would have been harder beyond calculation.

I want to thank everyone who has contributed, collaborated, or helped. In particular, I want to acknowledge the financial support of the Social Sciences and Humanities Research Council of Canada, whose leave fellowship helped with the earlier stages of this project, and Trent University which, with some support within its modest means, helped to complete it.

J.F.

INTRODUCTORY NOTES FOR A
POSTMODERN VALUE AGENDA

John Fekete

We may be on the threshold of a new round of theoretical value discussion in cultural studies, opening to a radical reconstruction and revaluation of the modern fact-value discourse. The essays in this volume are characteristically postmodern probings into the wilderness of looming interdisciplinary agendas. Grouped together in a text, their coordinated inscription may be read as playing on the critical and creative hinges between deconstruction and deconstriction.

Not to put too fine a point on it, we live, breathe, and excrete values. No aspect of human life is unrelated to values, valuations, and validations. Value orientations and value relations saturate our experiences and life practices from the smallest established microstructures of feeling, thought, and behavior to the largest established macrostructures of organizations and institutions. The history of cultures and social formations is unintelligible except in relation to a history of value orientations, value ideals, goods values, value responses, and value judgements, and their objectivations, interplay, and transformations. Yet it is no exaggeration to say that the oceans and continents of value, though much travelled, remain almost entirely uncharted in any way suitable to the navigational contingencies of postmodern itineraries.

We live our intellectual lives transitionally, in the interval between an onto-epistemological tradition that has been losing currency and a value-theoretical tradition that is just beginning to be coined and released into exchange and circulation. The gap yawns through both the everyday and the social-political levels of life and, without a viable value discourse, we are obliged to negotiate a commotion of disorientational crises amidst unadjudicated claims of validity and diverse experiences of evaluation (ranging from the most automatized to the most conflicted). Among professional academics, value inquiry has been by and large fragmented and specialized into sub-specialities of economics and philosophy, confirmed in their respective proprietorships by the distinction that the Dewey system of classification makes between "value" and "worth". References to value, where they are not confined narrowly to disciplinary subject-matter, tend to be either casual and colloquial (as in the remnants of traditional humanist discourse, including literary criticism), or literally censored from the theoretical agenda, exiled from theory-formation, and censured in discursive practices (as in the post-Northrop Frye cornucopia of interpretative frameworks for literary theory).

In other words, the fields of value lie fallow, even within the specialist social sciences and humanities. Further, both interdisciplinary value-theoretical inquiry and, equally importantly, a metatheoretical discourse (on the analogy of the philosophy of science) that would be concerned with specialist discourses related to value, validity, and valuation, today have only the standing of as yet unarticulated promises that are already, as I shall argue, on postmodern paradigmatic horizons. The anticipatory observation of the Cornell value-study group in 1949, that "value is a potentially bridging concept which can link together many diverse specialized studies — from the experimental psychology of perception to the analysis of political ideologies, from budget studies in economics to aesthetic theory and philosophy of language, from literature to race riots"[1] is, in effect, programmatically implied for an emerging theoretical enterprise. This latter will have absorbed the ineluctable contemporary impact of anti-epistemological neo-pragmatism, deconstruction, and the post-rationalist structural allegories (that have already brought the regulative metaphors of the humanities and social sciences into familial relations with those categorical reconfigurations that have been effected by the paradigm shifts in contemporary physical and biological sciences).[2] Such new field theories and metatheories of value may come to provide invaluable guidance for linking the professional intellectual discourses, the lifeworld of orientational background assumptions, and the systems of institutional social organization.

Emphasizing the revaluation of value inquiry that can be expected from postmodernism necessitates some thoughts on the shape of this revaluation. A look at the trajectory of modern axiology suggests that both the neglect, censorship, or exile of value inquiry in some quarters, and its disciplinary and subdisciplinary confinement (and evisceration) in others, are results of the exhaustion of a particular tradition of value that has dominated the heritage of Western Enlightened modernity: the positivist-modernist tradition, with its antinomic 'fact-value' structure, within which value inquiry underwent both its heroic rise and scandalous reduction and decline in the span of roughly a century and a half. By this I mean that

ii

the methodological narrowing, the substantive dead ends, and the thinning credibility that mark the late fate of this whole region of discourse are all paradigm-dependent, with the effect that the postmodern paradigm shift may place value-theoretical interventions into positions of far greater esteem. (Naturally, within the sketchy schematism of a brief account, I cannot provide a social-theoretical or social-phenomenological accounting for rationality structures and paradigm shifts; I can only acknowledge these through the inner logic of the foregrounded tradition of value discourse.)

The modern axiological project has been shaped by British and Austrian empiricists, German Kantians and neo-Kantians, American pragmatists and realists, and logical empiricists around the world. In brief, it has been built on a secular world picture that accepts the characteristically modern division between two stable terms: a world of objects and a world of representations; entities that are object-constrained and entities that are subject constrained; facts and values. These are, of course, polar terms, but the mode of intellectual articulation, as could be expected from the antinomic reproduction of such binary categories, is occupied with establishing relationships (dialectical, hierarchical, causal, semantic, syntactic, pragmatic, etc.) between the poles. (Indeed, the pre-occupation with the subject-object relationships becomes so obsessional that, when the modern paradigm is given its postmodern flip, the polar terms are retranslated as mere effects of the relationality that remains foregrounded and methodologically foundational).

The point is that a general, autonomous value inquiry (into value as an autonomous kind of entity) is from the start a product of this paradigm, emerging from the pre-modern subordination of value study to metaphysics, and from the correspondingly metaphysical subordination of value to its metabolism with being. Modern axiology, in a significant sense, constituted the emancipation of value from its immediate ties to ontology; but, accordingly, as a modern cognitive venture, it was also to face the persistent demand within the secularized onto-epistemological paradigm that it should justify and ground values objectively in relation to existence or else consign them to the status of a diminished reality. In other words, the validity or significance of values was no longer a metaphysical given, entailed in the nature of being, but rather a *demonstrandum*. The effect and pathos of the positivist-modernist approach is that the realm of fact is hypostatized without validation, while the realm of value is left floating in indeterminate relation to it; but now that both are free of the metaphysical symbiosis, the realm of value is under pressure to reconnect itself with the realm of fact (being) and to find secular supports (grounding) to guarantee this connection, on the analogy of the former metaphysical supports. This problem haunts all action orientations and cognitive inquiries from within, including the newly autonomous inquiry into value. The problematic of foundation is thus organized around the gap between the positive terms, the secular abyss, the interval of uncertainty, the absence of transcendental guarantees. In its comic mask, the triumphalism of this onto-epistemic configuration is known in philosophy as positivism; in its tragic mask, its pathos is known in literary culture as modernism.

It is important that the first specific value theories outside the religious-metaphysical world views (where the stratifications of being and value directly coincided, descending from such onto-axiological peaks as the Good, or God) were formulated in the field of economics. Value in the modern economic tradition has been customarily tied to the various costs of producing goods for exchange in the market, particularly the costs of labour (power) as measured by the costs of its (physical) reproduction. This labour theory of value, from Cantillon to Smith, Ricardo, and Marx, dis-tinguished value in use from value in exchange, increasingly stressing the latter, particularly when under challenge from theorists of "marginal utili-ty" (Gossen) who emphasized the priority of the former. It matters less to us here which of these two abstractions serves the other better as its phantom grounding or alibi. We are concerned to note that in either case, and in all the variations (including the Mercantilist issues of supply and demand), the question of value was being raised by economic theorists within a specific subsystem of explicitly human activity, at a distance from metaphysical considerations. It was also being raised, we may note, from the *object* side, in derivation from empirical elements.

General value theories, however, that could encompass all areas of hu-man valuing, remained to be attempted from the *subject* side. In England, Hobbes, Hume, and Bentham all derived value from affect — the Bentha-mite utilitarian calculus of pain and pleasure, summing to the 'greatest-happiness principle,' being perhaps the first general model of a value the-ory. (I shall return to utilitarianism below.) The most sustained and self-conscious intervention in this area, however, was that of Austrian axiolo-gists (Brentano, Meinong, von Ehrenfels, Marty, Kraus, and Mally), often called the "Second Austrian School of Values." Theirs was a deliberate move to generalize a unified value theory beyond the concerns and scopes of economic value theorists — even the original utilitarian "First Austrian School of Values" (Menger, Wieser, Böhm-Bawerk), whose work they con-sidered superior to that of the labour theorists of value. The axiologists' argument was that the derived value of the utility theorists (not to men-tion the cost-accounting of their opponents) would not address the problem of unmediated values, that the economic concern with the ob-ject side could not account for subject-variant valuation, and that, in any case, the subject, *presupposed* in the economic discussion, was the key to the value problem.

In general, on this *relational* account, value *phenomena* are encoun-tered solely in value *experience*, and can be described only with reference to the affective-conative responses of subjects, with the result that a psy-chological value theory alone is capable of offering a unified account of value across the range of our interests and actions in economics, ethics, and other areas. Within the broad framework of value-hedonism, members of the school then divided, on psychological grounds, as to whether the source of value was to be found in feelings (Meinong) or desire (von Ehrenfels). They also divided, on epistemological grounds, as to whether the relationship between the objects valued and the psychological experience of value was objective (Brentano, Meinong) or subjective (von Ehrenfels): that is 1) whether value had an objective basis in the characteristics of the object, such that it was valued (correctly) because it was valuable, the value experience thus disclosing the value of the object (a phenomenological line that goes from Brentano and Meinong to Husserl, Scheler, and Nicolai Hartmann); or 2) that an object was valuable because it was actually or potentially valued, the value experience thus conferring value on the object (the line from von Ehrenfels to the most influential American subjectivist value theorist before the Second World War, Ralph Barton Perry: 'x is valuable = interest is taken in x').[3]

These disagreements are well documented and need not concern us here.[4] I want to note only that the epistemological objectivists and subjectivists in the Austrian psychological school of axiology both agreed that, whether value was the capacity of an object to command psychological attention or whether value sprang from psychological attention, it was not an independent but a derivative characteristic, arising out of a relationship between stable, self-possessed entities, i.e., between integral objects and the unitary self-conscious experience of integral subjects. But implicit in this relationship (as it was constructed within the disabling framework of the onto-epistemic subject-object fixation) was the characteristic axiological question, always identified in different branches of the continental tradition, but never quite resolved (nor resolvable within the antinomic framework).

The question of the validity of values — validity across a number of different subjects and a range of differing situations — is posed in the following way. If something is valu*able* or desir*able*, as opposed to *merely* subjectively valu*ed* or desir*ed*, or, put differently, if not every experience of pleasure or striving is *ipso facto* a value experience — if, that is, there is a real, non-arbitrary, and not merely terminological connection between the object and the value response, so that the recourse to the concept "value" is to do some real work — then the concepts "valuable" or "desirable" (as opposed to "valuing," "desiring") involve an aspect that refers to some quality that makes the object *worthy* of desiring or valuing. What is at issue here is a closely related further dimension pertinent to the valuing experience and beyond the purview, strictly speaking, of psychology or sociology, because it touches on whether we *ought* to value or on the demand to *be* valued — it touches, in other words, on a normative relation between subject and object, exceeding the preferred boundaries of the naturalist inquiry into value as valuation. In short, the validity question was the form in which value theory attempted to raise the question of value to a second order inquiry into the *value of value*. Implicit in this move is the strategy of establishing at this second level of value that objectivity (or that universality) which always remained elusive at the first level. Contemporary forms of rationalism continue to pursue this tack, and they continue to be resisted by contemporary forms of naturalism, behaviorism, and pragmatism.

This aspect of the problem was most sharply developed in the 19th century by Rudolf Hermann Lotze, generally credited with founding axiology, and by the South German school of value theorists at Baden (Windelband, Rickert) whom he influenced. Lotze and the neo-Kantians write openly in the tradition of Kant's decisive distinction between problems of existence and problems of value, and with the corollary certainty that the latter are not derivable from (and hence not reducible to) the former. To protect a realm of humane significance from the militant imperialism of scientific naturalism, Lotze stresses a double-realm conception (fact and value), systematically working the Humean 'is-ought' dichotomy into an axiological framework. In a characteristic humanist posture, he polemically counterposes value rationality to cognitive-instrumental rationality. Values, on his account, have no being, only validity, which is not to be identified with actual valuations or *de facto* value judgements. This is the validity problem (including the relation between validity and the realization of value in actual practice) that the neo-Kantians (with Kant's *a prioristic* dichotomization of rational being and natural being) elaborated in sharp contrast to Austrian psychological naturalism, and to both empirical and non-empirical historicism (e.g. Dilthey, Hegel, Ranke, Mannheim), on the grounds that these failed to establish the significance of value positing and to provide for universal validity and value continuity.

Once again, looking past the problematical elements in the way that the questions and attempted solutions were posed — for example, in Scheler's project to theorise absolute values as *prior* to the world of objects and the representational contents of experience, within the realm of which they would have only relative subject-dependent validity — what we can see is that autonomous value inquiry has reproduced the paradigmatic antinomies that gave birth to it in the first place. From the naturalist side, the question of validity is left unanswered; from the rationalist side, the foundations for values fade into transcendence. Thus value is either dissolved in (empirical, experiential) fact or severed from it.

It remained for yet another current spreading out from Vienna, riding the waves of the linguistic turn in philosophy, to draw the consequences of these axiological impasses and to marginalize the axiological project of developing a unified field theory and phenomenology of value. Logical empiricism (Schlick, Carnap, *et al.*) of course had its own unification project: to purify and link the sciences on the basis of analytically clarified empirical propositions. The effect of their reduction of axiology and their classification of its inventory of utterances and key terms as mere emotive expressions was to strip evaluative expressions of propositional status and of any pretentions (such as the early empiricists and rationalists had entertained) to offering cognitive meaning or descriptive information about either the value objects or the value experiences.

With the consolidated support of philosophers like Russell, Stevenson, and Ayer, and with incursions into other value fields like literary theory (where I.A. Richards' concept of artistic "pseudo-statements" for a time broadened the hegemony of this much reduced axiology), a widely in-fluential logical empiricism succeeded in delegitimating and marginalis-ing theoretical value inquiry. To be sure, as empiricists and pragmatists all agreed, valuation behaviour could remain a proper object of empirical study in a variety of disciplines (psychology, sociology, anthropology, his-tory, medicine, education, etc.). At that level, it has remained to varying extents a continuing humanist concern. But as a significant autonomous theoretical discourse, axiology had no further place in the dominant positivist-modernist tradition.

This separation of value from cognitive validity converged in its cul-tural impact with the effects of a theoretical approach with precisely the opposite cognitive intention: the effects of the realist theory of intrinsic value as a non-natural property advanced by G.E. Moore in England at the turn of the century. This effort to resist instrumentalism could expect sup-port from the substantialist position lodged in the everyday belief that the grammatical structure of value judgements is a logically correct emblem of the propositional content asserted. But Moore's position that value was an unanalysable, non-natural, pure property of a natural state of affairs, to which the only securely assured cognitive access was by intuition, reversed the intended meaning, and had the practical effect of determining value through the expression of entirely personal preferences that were to stand as unguided and unjustified choices of the will.

Split by the dichotomy on which it was founded, the axiological project thus self-destructed, leaving the situation of value disarray that Alasdair MacIntyre has analyzed: "To a large degree people now think, talk and act *as if* emotivism [the doctrine that all evaluative judgements and more spe-cifically all moral judgements are *nothing but* expressions of preference, expressions of attitude or feeling, insofar as they are moral or evaluative in character] were true, no matter what their avowed theoretical stand-point may be. Emotivism has become embodied in our culture."[5]

Out of the modern axiological tradition, then, in the context of the dynamic processes of a cognitively-instrumentally biased culture, the gener-ic concept of value (as it was finally instituted) has the relational features of ungrounded subjective apprehension or taste: value in the mind of the beholder. At the professional level, meanwhile, more recent analytic philosophy has softened somewhat on the question of the rationality of value judgements. By and large, therefore, what is being developed from the modern axiological heritage is a formal theory of preference, equipped with axioms and rules, and quantitative methods for value measurement. The remnants of axiology now serve chiefly as technical links between the traditions of logic, mathematics, and economics.[6] Value inquiry, once considered as an epic adventure of cross-disciplinary unification, has just barely retained professional credibility by cutting itself down to the procrustean measure of a narrow specialty. Founded as a general theory in order to forestall the colonization of value discourse by economists, it is now chiefly of use as a technique in economic calculation. Hard-headed positivism has fashioned value inquiry in its own image.

It is pertinent in this respect that remnants of the Austro-German heritage (since Brentano concerned with naturalistic psychological preference) have been readily reabsorbed into utilitarian value theory. First on the scene, it has carried on as the major value theory of a general character with wide legitimacy and is, even today, seeking to adapt and gain influence within shifting paradigms. Although utilitarianism is a theory of personal morality as well as a theory of public choice, its domain of investigation has been primarily economic, as have been its basic categories. As a theory of preference-based valuation, modern utilitarianism analyses the choice of actions in terms of consequences and evaluates the consequences in terms of the satisfaction of needs and desires and the advancement of general welfare. This is a program for rationalising action in cost-benefit terms, and it presupposes goal-oriented behaviours that can be motivated through a (value) conception of benefit, interest, pleasure, desire, and the like.[7] In other words, as an axiology, utilitarianism collapses the *analysis* of value into the *criterion* of value and endorses the concept of 'utility' (being desired, giving pleasure, etc.) as the sole criterion and measure of value.

Modern utilitarianism, like naturalist psychologism, begs the whole issue of how the importance of something may be related to or differ from the extent of the desire for it or the satisfaction it generates. In a critical vein, this would be described as utilitarian *reductionism*, i.e. "the device of regarding all interests, ideals, aspirations, and desires as on the same level, and all representable as preferences, of different degrees of intensity, perhaps, but otherwise to be treated alike."[8] This is in effect to treat utility theory as the kind of approach to the value question that processes information only at the level of a motivational pattern, and to claim that, however appropriate that may be to psychological explanation, it is not (or less) appropriate to, say, moral-practical justification, criticism, and deliberation — i.e. that it sidesteps the neo-Kantian validity questions. From the view point of this criticism, it is customary to press the point that, in basing valuation on choice, rather than choice on value, utilitarianism inverts the order of priority between them, and that its descriptive motivational commensurations cannot accommodate a moral language of rights and incommensurability. In the classic format of the debate, utilitarianism responds that (in effect) these claims urged upon it are transcendentally formulated and become pertinent only within the empirical framework of the demands of experience and their calculable consequences.

The point I want to highlight about utility theory is that its conception of utility as a standard of value is based on the teleological concept of action (to the point of the exclusion or subordination of other conceptions), and draws its paradigmatic force as a notion of autonomous value from the modern autonomisation of the cognitive-instrumental rationality that underwrites it within the onto-epistemological paradigm. Utility, as an instrumentality of life practices, is the evaluative orientational criterion of purposive rationality. But in the utility conception of utilitarianism, precisely purposive rationality itself is hypostatized as an end value (instead of appearing as one among alternative rationality structures),[9] with the effect that only utilities pertinent to aim achievement are entered into the measurement of value and the assessment of validity claims. It is this narrowing that leads rights theorists to claim that the norm-conformative claims pertinent to moral-practical action are squeezed out or reductively reprocessed according to utilitarian criteria. A similar complaint could be raised on behalf of aesthetic validity claims.

It is also this selective entrenchment of a particular value-theoretical bias with respect to rationality structures (instrumentalism) that is the subject of George Grant's lament that the liberal-utilitarian endorsement of value plurality with respect to end values (especially with respect to the *summum bonum*) at the level of the individual actor-calculator really provides only for a motivational pluralism subordinated to the hegemonically monistic social value of technological instrumentalism as itself the governing, co-ordinating end value operating in modern social formations.[10] This is the same picture that MacIntyre characterizes as bifurcated between emotivism at the private level and unscrutinisable technological ends at the organisational-bureaucratic level.[11]

In other words, utility theory at this level is dependent on a paradigmatic *hypostatization of subjects counterposed against environments* by means of representations and action orientations designed to satisfy their aims and desires. Actions organized to *posit* and maintain *values* and to *set* goals are then assessed, if at all, only according to the instrumental dimension of *aim achievement* on the above model, that is, according to the criteria of purposive rationality into which the criteria of value rational action are dissolved.[12] It is worth drawing these distinctions because the notion of utility is sure to stay with us at least as long as this social formation persists; indeed, it is already being reinscribed into the pragmatist structuration of postmodernist formulations. What it need not do is to remain bound to the onto-epistemological paradigm on which the positivist-modernist theories of value have depended. Inscribed in a postmodern value language, the utility concept may come to play a different function; indeed, one way to assess its performance within particular formulations would be to inquire into its paradigmatic affiliations.

A preference-based utilitarian theory, it has been noted, is already in effect post-hedonist, in that it cannot simply *discover* and measure pleasures and satisfactions; it must first get involved with the utilities people *set on* things in the course of their *construal* of preferable alternatives.[13] Indeed, under pragmatist influence, utilitarian consequentialism as the criterion of choice shifts to a contextualism to provide the choice variables. But the expansion of the pertinent variables and the differential possibilities for the construal of aspects of situations mitigates the closure of the system on the side of the object or environment, and already introduces evaluative elements at the stage of representing the contextual or consequential elements pertinent to the value decision. From the other side, as well, utilitarian theory can volatilise the subject, describable as the site at which such activities as pleasuring, desiring, preferring and the like take place, and thus open a formerly closed subjectivity to transactions with a whole circuit of formative influences, introducing evaluative elements at the stage at which such activities are performed and are represented to the subject.

It may be that, even modified, a utility theory will take too narrow a view of persons and continue to exclude or to transform information that could be expected to contribute to a fuller view.[14] Evidently, revised utility conceptions will have to be assessed against the most telling critique of the utility concept of value: that it addresses necessary but not sufficient conditions for value, and that the teleological concept of action to which it has been tied is a necessary concept but not a sufficient theory of social and personal action. To say this, of course, is to claim a value for, and to assume responsibility for, a more differentiated world view and a more differentiated value language, or, put differently, for a postmodern pluralism of images and narratives of action, rationality, and value, within the frame of a commitment to foreground with richer density the play of value in the practice of life.

Such a world view and such a value language is emergent and can be glimpsed in the proliferation and dissemination of contemporary intellectual models. In the past generation alone, the unparalleled wealth of theoretical effort invested in post-empiricist and post-rationalist formulations — primarily a result of a linguistic-structural turn — has significantly altered the humanities and social sciences. I have tried to characterise the importance of the new structural allegories (and their ambiguous self-presentation) elsewhere, as have others, and will be very brief here.

What appears to be decisive to the emergent postmodern configuration is the committal to do without foundational, asituational, representational, and hypostatising-stabilising closures, objectivist or subjectivist. It is possible to put a skeptical or nihilistic construction on this, but to insist on it, I venture to say, would amount to settling for a limited outlook on a larger prospect. Notwithstanding continual theory-regressions and paradigm-regressions, unsurprising in the light of the immense challenges of resituating the social-cultural heritage, I think we can identify as post-modern *a certain value-rational opening to the human world* — inclusively, to all of it, and to everything related to it — *as home*, though a home whose plan we do not have and which we have never quite (and will never quite) finish building and fitting to ourselves, just as we who build it and for whom it is to be fit change with every alteration of it, with every bit of construction and deconstruction. I put it this way to acknowledge that the postmodern ethos has a certain continuity with the projects and horizons of secularising and historicising modernity, but also to suggest its difference from the ethos of modernism.

The latter I have tried to present as tied to positivism and marked by the stigma of the wound left in reality by the amputation of The Standard. A delusional euphoria and an obsessional depression, settling into the culture from a persisting phantom Standard effect, are antinomic polarities articulating the modernist structure of feelings. By contrast, postmodernism may be at last ready — or may, at least, represent the transition to a readiness — unneurotically, to get on without the Good-God-Gold Standards, one and all, indeed without any capitalised Standards, while learning to be enriched by the whole inherited inventory once it is transferred to the lower case. However, there is no need to get sentimental about this, as all the problematic situations will not thereby have vanished. Indeed, there are great dangers here, especially in the possibility of un-critical, craven embrace of every kind of manipulation as equally holy (without privilege). We need to believe and enact the belief that there are better and worse ways to live the pluralism of value. To see all cows as the same colour would truly amount to being lost in the night. But the prospect of learning to be at ease with limited warranties, and with the responsibility for issuing them, without the false security of inherited guarantees, is promising for a livelier, more colourful, more alert, and, one hopes, more tolerant culture that draws enjoyment from the dappled relations between meaning and value. (I am prepared to use a deliberately upbeat vocabulary in order to place my bets on the upbeat possibilities.)

I want to sketch only two anticipatory remarks about the place of value in the postmodern paradigm, without wishing at this juncture to make hypotheses about the shape of postmodern value theories. The first is that the renewal of value discourse seems to be indicated as the ineluctable order of the day by the convergence of a number of theoretical currents important in the formation of a postmodern outlook. The post-empiricist analytic theory of science (Mary Hesse, et al.), in the wake of the substantial revaluations following Kuhn's structural analyses in the history of science, is now identified with the proposition that, in all the sciences equally, data description is theory dependent and theoretical languages are paradigm dependent. Although the position is framed in terms of successive levels of dependency on interpretations, it is pregnant with the discovery that interpretations are value dependent and that descriptive languages and evaluative languages have an analytic relation.

Moreover, stressing the methodological role of communicative experience in the social sciences, Habermas and Giddens argue that below the threshold of theory construction and description, already at the level of *obtaining* social scientific data, the observer necessarily brings into the encounter with the symbolically prestructured information in the object domain the unanalysed pretheoretical knowledge of his/her own life world, i.e. a set of background convictions.[15] Since these are saturated with value elements, including basic value orientational categories, it is not necessary to adjudicate the dispute between Habermas-Giddens (pro) and Hesse-Rorty (con) — as to whether there is or not an ontological and hence a methodological difference between the social and natural sciences — in order to see that both positions subvert the fact-value separation and point to an inquiry into the character and implications of the value-dependency of cognitive-interpretive articulation and the value-rationality of paradigm formation.

In cultural philosophy, the neo-pragmatist anti-epistemological moves comprise an insistence that the pattern of all inquiry is a deliberation concerning the relative attractions of various concrete alternatives. It is proposed, moreover, that there is no fixed nature of things and no truth of correspondence, no linguistic picture and no literary imitation for any inquiry to discover or decode — and, therefore, that both propositions and narratives simply offer alternative images of ourselves.[16] In effect the neo-pragmatist argument invites commentary on the valuations implicit in such activities and on the nature of their circulation in cultural discourse. The powerful Wittgensteinean language paradigm and the textualist claim arising in the new literary culture — to the effect that all problems, topics, and distinctions in cultural discourse are results of the choice of a vocabulary and the conventional rules of the language game — again draw attention to the value dimensions that underpin and follow from such choices and from the moves that they warrant. Indeed, the popular theoretical language of strategic moves, textual strategies, and the like — although these are currently articulated within the programmatic structural allegories as addressing the *structural warrants* for such moves which arise from the pertinent institutional conventions and contextual contingencies — can equally be regarded as a *choreography of valuations* and value-related orientations and rationalities.

It is a matter worthy of analysis that the growing post-empiricist interest in the patterns of cultural practices was taken up first, and insistently, from the side of structure and not simultaneously (and still not) from the side of value. The great impact of deconstruction has been to restore methodologically the dynamic historical character of temporary stabilizations. Its method has been to denaturalise whatever presents itself, by tracing its empirical features back to a process of emergence from alternatives of a construction/structuration/closure related to the contingencies of a local context of social and cultural practices. Deconstruction, however, has itself prepared the ground for putting an end to the censorship of value — i.e. for the programmatic revaluation of the procedures of deconstruction, and of the closures in orientation that are its targets, as moves in a historical field of value relations. There is here an intriguing cultural loop in circulation. It was Nietzsche's passionate call for a revaluation of values that immediately preceded the rise and fall of positivist-modernist axiology. Now, it has been once again the heirs of Nietzsche, the structural deconstructors, who, without entering explicitly the realm of value discourse, precede and prepare for the emergence and dissemination of the postmodern discourse of value.

One needs to note as well the evidence of cultural sociology, particularly the Kantian line from Weber to Habermas and the study of emergent structures of rationality and action orientations in the frame of the problem of modernity and the mental division of labour that results in the differentiation of relatively autonomous spheres of cultural value (science and technology, law and morality, art and criticism). Even a short list of salient considerations — the relations between concrete and changing value contents within these spheres; the tensions and complementarities among the spheres; the relations between such cultural value formations and the normative value formations of societal institutions in the economy and polity; the contingencies of transformations in these value relations, including the contingent character of this particular perspective on the specializations of values; and the relation of such specialization to rationality questions and to a decentered view of the primary reference systems that shape, structure, and orient the modern sense of reality — helps to flesh out with social theoretical depth the agenda of a renewed value inquiry.

In this connection, it is of particular interest, from the point of view of an increasingly prominent literary culture, that the autonomy of the aesthetic sphere from religion and ritual, then from patronage, and finally, under market relations, from morality and the everyday conventions of knowledge and action, is now under growing challenge, a result of both the contemporary conditions of reception in mass mediatized culture and also the intertextual anti-aesthetic conventions of reception in the current literary criticism. If, moreover, we embrace Richard Rorty's image of modern literary culture as a complex, luxuriant phenomenon — one that the Enlightenment could not have anticipated, that does not fit into Kant's threefold division of possible human activities (science, morality, aesthetic free play), and that has become the presiding sphere in culture, the successor to philosophy and spiritually superior to science,[17] — then we shall also have to shift from a predominantly cognitive to a predominantly orientational domain for the leading reference points of our postmodern discursive engagements.

We may find in the latitudes of that space the warrant for a freely paratactic commentary on cultural discourses, guided less by a preoccupation with doctrines and their foundations than by an interest in the implications of value relations and orientations — meaning by this, of course, not at all a monistic reduction, but, on the contrary, an opening to a spectrum of the colours of human value creation and value maintenance, including the cultural value question of the postmodern personality: how to accommodate and value the incommensurabilities that Weber, in his essays on art and science, had already identified as endemic to modern cultural life — that is, the discontinuity of a rich variety of possibly incompatible goals, virtues, standards, and values — without excluding the value-languages of "qualitative contrast"?[18]

I have been arguing that with the shift toward what looks like an emerging postmodern cultural framework, the prospects for the renewal of value discourse are compelling and stimulating. I am not talking of a unified axiology, of a single discipline, of an abstraction from specialised studies. What is at issue is an emerging intertextual discursive field in which the point of view of value orientation may disseminate, in which value commentary may take the form of an intervention, and in which a value-theoretical approach may hold greater attractions than the representations of the onto-epistemological tradition.

My second anticipatory remark, then, is that there can be no question, of course, of a discursive field being occupied by a single unified theory, and, therefore, that it comes as no surprise that the anti-foundationalist, anti-transcendentalist discourse of value has not been evacuated of tensions. The most interesting of these for me, at this time, is the tension between the neo-pragmatist post-liberal current and a kind of post-Marxist, post-existentialist current that I can only characterize, for lack of a better name, as "pragmatism plus."

Very schematically, and slightly sharpened, it would appear that this latter wishes to be preoccupied with what it refutes less than does pragmatism, i.e. it wishes to emancipate its imaginative energies from a negative bondage to foundationalism. By the same token, it wishes to deconstruct in a way that is less formal than the stories of deconstructionists; it wishes to do more and other than re-enact in reverse, in a permanent repetition loop, the closures of the world; it wishes to make a difference rather than to make points. It is a little more inclined to take a risk and intervene in order to deconstrict as well as deconstruct, making attempts at reconstruction while minimising as best it can the inexorable reconstriction, or at least the rate at which it sets in. It is more inclined to an ecological position, to complementarities and ecumenical inclusions, to critical meliorism; and less attracted to utilitarian formulations on their own. It is less impressed with the regulative analogies of the market and economic liberalism. It is more sanguine about employing the species category "humankind" as a regulative ideal for which it is prepared to take responsibility (at a time of global dangers, pressures, opportunities, options) because such a universalist value concept may help to expand value discussion to include the question of what may be the most desirable predications of such species terms — i.e. what can be made of such universalisms if inscribed, not as avatars of a metaphysical conception harking back to frozen and loaded myths of origin, presence, and end, but instead as harbingers of an open-ended, polymorphous future for what may emerge, through its own practical self-institution, as a human family, announcing thereby a shape of the autonomisation of *human* history. By virtue of such risks, of course, the "pragmatist plus" position also risks methodological impurity: at any rate, at its best, it is a mixed position of deliberately and simultaneously substantive and formal value articulation. A certain tension between these two positions, or between certain aspects of such positions, may appear from time to time in the essays in this volume.

I turn now to a brief review of the eight original essays grouped together in this text. They are linked in their efforts to appropriate and dynamise the structural allegory and to reinscribe value discourse within relational, contextual, and interdisciplinary postmodern horizons. They do not, by any means, add up to a theory of value: nor has that been the project of the text. These essays are paradigm-related probings into the contexts of value, and in their implied interactions they contribute to the elaboration of an intertextual discursive field. They touch on the general economy and the specific interpretive, political, and anthropological dimensions of value and valuation, with particular reference to value relations in the cognitive, aesthetic, and moral spheres of culture, but also moving freely through diverse realms of simulation, from psychoanalytic representations to the literary and philosophical metatheory of culture, from the postmodern visual arts to the outlaw practices of graffiti, from metaphysics to sexual politics. Readers will find certain affinities in the groupings and placements of essays within the order of the text; but the discursive frame of the book does not require that the essays be read in sequence.

Barbara Smith, to whose work a number of essays in this volume refer, has played a leading role, through her writings and her organizing (including a major session on the question of value at the 1982 annual meeting of the Modern Languages Association), in getting a renewed postmodern value discussion off the ground. Here, seeking a new account of aesthetic, moral, and cognitive value — in general, value without "truth-value" — she offers the fullest elaboration to date of her influential theory of the radical contingency of value as a function of the shifting state of an economy, and provides, through the use of a consistently and carefully interlaced network of economic metaphors and post-axiological communications theoretical concepts, one of the most elegant and challenging postmodern reformulations of value theory available to contemporary cultural studies.

The essays that follow explore divergent traditions, and call on psychoanalytic, literary theoretical, hermeneutic, philological, and grammatological modes of addressing the placement of value in the contexts of art and interpretation. They are all concerned with the contingency of value and the historicality of cultural practices. At the same time that they explore and elaborate these aspects of the postmodern discourse of value, the essays engage also in family quarrels with variant interpretive or evaluative currents. In this frame, Charles Levin's essay is a complex psychoanalytic reflection, in part by way of object-relations theory, on the radical contingency of symbolic process, and hence on the aesthetic resistance to the modern project of generating "paradigms" (whose function is to formalize and rationalize the symbolic). His observation that the paradigmatic climate of the postmodern structural allegories is linked with a sociologistic blindspot, resulting in the self-contradictory fixation on relationality, is a provocative critique of a disabling culturalist reality principle, from which Levin draws the salient axiological consequences. In particular, his argument for the aesthetic dimension as an indispensable emergence implies strategic pathways toward thinking "value" and "future" together.

In a related vein, my own paper offers an anthropological perspective on value orientation as a social fact and examines the cultural politics of the ambivalent contingency argument in the literary academy before attempting a postmodern but non-utilitarian reconceptualisation of aesthetic value in the *infinitive* mode, within the frame of a critique of the tendency to *vampirism* in the value-space of contemporary culture. The discussion draws on Heidegger as well as Barbara Smith, on Nietzsche and Ágnes Heller as well as Jean Baudrillard. The essay is committed to the future-oriented horizons of a renewal of value discourse, a renewal of the Western knowledge project, and a renewal of the autonomy discourse of art, personality, and society on the model of an (anthropologically significant) emergent reflexivity of value.

The alienation critiques of these two essays are even further foregrounded (and carried into the realm of art itself) in Jay Bernstein's discussion of the contemporary forgetting of value within a general disorder of our practices as a whole. He argues the need for a postmodern, post-aesthetic theory of art that will foreground the question of historicality, and thus the question of aesthetic alienation, i.e. the historical loss of the cognitive capacity of art, as is confirmed in the contemporary experience that the value horizons of art are not inhabitable. Through a sustained study of Heidegger, and through a reading of Adorno, Bernstein comes to situate the deferred praxis of the institution of peripheralised, autonomised art in the gap between linguistic community and social community, i.e. in the question of politics and a history not yet written.

Arkady Plotnitsky's study of the anti-logocentrist interpretative paradigm of Nietzsche, Heidegger, Derrida, and the implications of a thoroughgoing deconstructionist program for an anti-metaphysical approach to the theoretical problem of evaluation, likewise emphasizes the locality and historicality of all interpretations (including the interpretation of interpretation) and evaluations (including the evaluation of evaluation). The farthest reaching conclusion of his dense analysis is that where the interminability of interpretation arising from its "trace" structure is, in the practice of a specific interpretation, terminated and abandoned, where new chains of interpretations are begun, evaluation is always on the scene: i.e. that evaluation is the structure of this termination, the structural limit of interpretation — in other words, that interpretation is value-dependent, and also value-producing; or put differently, that there is an analytical relation between interpretation and evaluation. The scope of the implications for the deconstructionist tradition can be measured in Plotnitsky's suggestion, therefore, that the level at which the conceptuality of value and evaluation theoretically belongs is within a "general economy" accounting for *différance*, rather than a restricted economy of social, economic, and aesthetic value.

György Márkus also argues for the foregrounding of the radical contingency of historicality, in this case with respect to philosophy and interpretation, not art. Through the example of the transmission and interpretation of philosophical tradition in the totally unsatisfactory yet immensely influential history of philosophy of Diogenes Laertius in late antiquity, Márkus's intriguing and amusing essay shows that Gadamer's relativism of interpretation is not relativist enough. With respect to their objects, functions, and procedures, well beyond the question of perspectivism, interpretations are normatively regulated cultural performances integrated into the cultural practices of a given time, and therefore a general hermeneutics, ontologising what all interpretations share, is impossible.

The next two essays pursue axiological implications directly into the public arena. Susan Stewart's theoretical study of the phenomenology of the contemporary criminal act of graffiti, conceived as the other side of a crisis in the situation of the high art commodity, opens to the investigation of the axiological premises of both consumer culture (high and mass) and popular culture (deviant, outlaw). In a sparkling and informative essay, she analyses how these are played out within a system of axiological practices that become most intelligible, with the broadest frame of reference, around the fault lines or the sites of contradiction in the culture.

Arthur Kroker's passional meditation on value in modern culture is a fitting provisional termination of a text committed to the renewal of value discourse. This is not only because it deliberately hurls itself against the contradictions and paradoxes in the North American value calculus, but also because it does so in a language of pathographic intensity that approximates expressionist poetry — with a postmodern flip schooled in the metaphysical pain of Baudrillard and Bataille. As an heir of Nietzsche and George Grant, Kroker writes against the grain of the pragmatic and technical subordination of value to the *telos* of a fully realized technological society innocent of any understanding of technology as deprival. This is, of course, a reprise of themes from the history of axiological discussion, but framed in a tragic idiom that adds dimension to the agendas of a pluralistic value discourse. Kroker's critical scansions of Baudrillard, and his incandescent interrogations of the darkness in the art of Francis Bacon and Alex Colville — cast as they are in the high voltage end-of-the-world value language of deprival, burnout, decomposition, exterminism, and decay, and designed as they seem to be to turn value against value and to trigger the implosion of value discourse from within — describe, incarnate, and defer the postmodern discourse of value. Functioning partly as a coda to the text, Kroker's essay, not only reminds us of just how problematical is the world that shapes (and is to be refashioned by) the emerging postmodern ethos, but also, in place of a conclusion, opens the text directly into the emergencies of life after the onset of postmodernity.

Notes

1. Cited in Clyde Kluckhohn et al., "Values and Value-Orientation in the Theory of Action: An Explanation in Definition and Classification," in Talcott Parsons and Edward Shils, eds., *Toward a General Theory of Action* (Cambridge: Harvard University Press, 1982), p. 389.

2. For further elaboration, see John Fekete, ed., *The Structural Allegory: Reconstructive Encounters with the New French Thought* (Minneapolis: University of Minnesota Press, 1984), esp. the editor's Introduction: "Descent into the New Maelstrom," pp. xi-xxiv.

3. Ralph Barton Perry, *General Theory of Value* (first pub. 1926), 2nd ed. (Cambridge, MA.: Harvard University Press, 1950), p. 116.

4. See the invaluable W.H. Werkmeister, *Historical Spectrum of Value Theories: The German-Language Group*, (Lincoln, NE.: Johnsen Publishing Co., 1970). Also, Howard O. Eaton, *The Austrian Philosophy of Values* (Norman: University of Oklahoma Press, 1930); and the pertinent sections in Risieri Frondizi, *What Is Value? An Introduction to Axiology* (La Salle, IL.: Open Court Publishing Co., 1971), and Nicholas Rescher, *Introduction to Value Theory* (Englewood Cliffs, NJ.: Prentice-Hall, 1969).

5. Alasdair MacIntyre, *After Virtue: A Study in Moral Theory* (Notre Dame: University of Notre Dame Press, 1981), p. 21.

6. Cf. Rescher, pp. 59, 74.

7. Rescher is an influential recent example of this kind of philosophical conception. See esp. pp. 9-11.

8. See the "Introduction" in Amartya Sen and Bernard Williams, eds., *Utilitarianism and Beyond* (Cambridge: Cambridge University Press, 1982), p. 8. This "Introduction" offers a generally sharp and intelligent critique, although it does not express interest in the paradigm questions at issue here.

9. Jürgen Habermas touches on utilitarianism in the context of a discussion of Weber and the neo-Kantian distinction between interests and values. See *The Theory of Communicative Action: Reason and Rationalization of Society*, trans. Thomas McCarthy, I (Boston: Beacon Press, 1984), 172.

10. George Grant, *Technology and Empire: Perspectives on North America* (Toronto: Anansi, 1969), p. 119.

11. MacIntyre, p. 33.

12. Max Weber discusses the concept of value rationality in *Economy and Society*, ed., G. Roth and C. Wittich (New York: Bedminster Press, 1968), 3 vols.; Ágnes Heller discusses the concept and its differences from purposive rationality in *A Radical Philosophy*, trans. James Wickham (Oxford: Basil Blackwell, 1984).

13. See Frederic Shick, "Under Which Descriptions," in Sen and Williams, *Utilitarianism and Beyond*, pp. 251-60.

14. Cf. Sen and Williams, p. 4.

15. See Habermas, pp. 108-11. Also, Anthony Giddens, *New Rules of Sociological Method* (London: Hutchinson, 1976), p. 158.

16. See Richard Rorty, *Consequences of Pragmatism* (Minneapolis: University of Minnesota Press, 1982), *passim*, but esp. pp. 198-99, 164, and xliii.

17. Rorty, pp. 149-50.

18. Cf. Charles Taylor, "The Diversity of Goods," in Sen and Williams, *Utilitarianism and Beyond*, pp. 129-44.

1

VALUE WITHOUT TRUTH-VALUE[1]

Barbara Herrnstein Smith

Introduction

The varying conceptions of the relations between "the good" and "the true" — and, when their sometime companion, "the beautiful," is added, the combined and permutated identifications and distinctions among all three — form as long a chapter as any in the history of classical philosophy. No version of that chapter will be recited here, but contemporary critiques of those classical conceptions and alternate formulations of the relations in question are central concerns of the present paper. Specifically, I shall be exploring here certain implications, particularly for communications theory, of an account that I have developed elsewhere in which the value of artworks and works of literature — and indeed, all value — is seen as radically contingent.[2] Such an account bears, of course, on the question of the truth-value of aesthetic judgments, but not only such judgments; for, by this account, the value not only of any artwork or other object but that of any *utterance* is also contingent, and aesthetic judgments (in the sense here of overt verbal evaluations of artworks) are no different in this respect from any other type of utterance, including so-called factual or scientific statements.

I shall begin with a few general observations on value which, though a bit stark as presented here, will serve to introduce certain themes that recur in the subsequent discussion.

That which we call "value" may be seen as neither an inherent property of objects nor an arbitrary projection of subjects but, rather, as the product of the dynamics of some economy or, indeed, of any number of economies (that is, systems of apportionment and circulation of "goods"), in re-

[handwritten at top: S + O, Try to deny S + O + yet have a concept of S + O. Should instead affirm]

[handwritten: the dissociated S + O are derivative from]

lation to the shifting state of which an object or entity will have a different (shifting) value. In the case of exchange-value or "price," it is, of course, a function and effect of the dynamics of a market economy. In the case of use-value, or the utility of some object for a particular subject, it is a function and effect of that subject's personal economy: that is, the system — which is *also* an economic system — constituted by his/her needs, interests and resources (biological, psychological, material, experiential, and so forth), all of which are continuously shifting both in relation to each other and as they are transformed by the subject's interactions with his/her environment (physical, social, cultural, and so forth), which, of course, is itself continuously changing. *[handwritten: descriptive]*

The two kinds of economic system described here are, it should be noted, not only analogous but also interactive and interdependent; for part of our environment *is* the market economy (or, indeed, any number of market economies) and, conversely, any market economy is comprised, in part, of the diverse personal economies of individual producers, distributors and consumers. It should also be noted that any particular subject's "self" — or that in behalf of which s/he may be said to act with "self-interest" — is also variable, being multiply and differently configurable in terms of different roles, relationships and, in effect, identities, in relation to which different needs and interests will acquire priority under different conditions.

Two corollaries of the conception of value just outlined are of particular interest here. The first is that a verbal judgment of "*the* value" of some entity — for example, an artwork, a work of literature, or any other kind of object, event, text or *utterance* cannot be a judgment of any independently determinate or, as we say, "objective" property of that entity. What it can be, however, and typically is, is a judgment of that entity's *contingent* value: that is, the speaker's estimate of how it will figure in the economy of some subject or set of subjects under some implicitly limited set of conditions. *[handwritten: Contextual.]*

The second corollary is that no value judgment can have truth-value in the usual sense. The "usual sense," however, is no longer all that usual. When interpreted in accord with some version of the traditional telegraphic model of discourse in which communication is seen as the *duplicative transmission* of a code-wrapped message from one consciousness to another, "truth-value" is seen as a measure of the extent to which such a message, when properly unwrapped, accurately and adequately reflects, represents, or corresponds with some independently determinate fact, reality, or state of affairs. That model of discourse, however, along with the entire structure of conceptions, epistemological and other, in which it is embedded, is now increasingly felt to be theoretically unworkable. It has not, however, been replaced by any other widely appropriated model. There have been, of course, throughout the century, sophisticated demonstrations of precisely that unworkability; and there have also been attempts,

[handwritten at bottom: what is the cash value of modern dis ETc.?]

some of them quite painstaking, to rehabilitate the key terms, concepts and conceptual syntax of the traditional model.[3] What appears to be needed now, however, and is perhaps emerging, is a total and appropriately elaborated reformulation, and, in particular, one in which the various fundamentally problematic explanatory structures involving duplicative transmission, correspondence, equivalence and recovery are replaced by an account of the dynamics of various types of *consequential interaction*.

With respect to its epistemological component or what is traditionally referred to as "perception," "knowledge," "belief," and so forth, this would be an account of how the structures, mechanisms and behaviors through which subjects interact with — and, accordingly, constitute — their environments are modified by those very interactions.[4] With respect to what we now call "communication," it would be an account of the dynamics of the differentially constrained behaviors of subjects who interact with, and thereby act *upon*, each other, for better and for worse. I shall return to this latter suggestion below but, for the moment, it is enough to observe that, whatever its emergent shape or, more likely, shapes, an alternate account of our commerce with the universe *and* our commerce with each other is not yet available.

In the meantime, the telegraphic model of communication, along with its associated conception of truth as correspondence to an independently determinate reality, continues to dominate theoretical discourse, and the theoretical interest of the term "truth" itself continues to be reinforced by its numerous — and, it must be emphasized here, irreducibly *various* — idiomatic and technical uses. Indeed, the term appears to be irreplaceable and, economically speaking, priceless: for its rhetorical power in political discourse alone — and there is perhaps no other kind of discourse — would seem to be too great to risk losing or even compromising. Nevertheless, as already indicated, the theoretical value of the concept of truth-value has already been compromised. Indeed, the value of truth and of truth-value seem to be as contingent — as historically and locally variable — as that of anything else.

The question of the truth-value of value judgments has, of course, been debated endlessly and unresolvably in formal axiology, and the continued preoccupation of disciplinary aesthetics with corresponding debates over the logical status and cognitive substance of aesthetic judgments, typically posited and examined as totally unsituated (or, at best, minimally situated) instances, has no doubt contributed to its reputation for dreariness and perhaps to its terminal sterility as well. Other, potentially more productive projects, however, may be undertaken more or less independently of such debates. One, which cannot be pursued here, is the exploration of the institutional and broader cultural and historical operation of literary and aesthetic evaluations, verbal *and otherwise*. Another, to be outlined below, is the analysis of verbal value judgments considered not as a class of "propositions" identified through certain formal features but, rather, as a type of communicative behavior responding to and constrained by certain social conditions.

The latter sort of analysis makes apparent the theoretical impoverishment as well as fundamentally problematic dualism of more traditional "analytic" approaches. For, as will be seen, the classic dichotomies thereby produced (e.g., personal/impersonal, conditional/unconditioned, expressing personal preferences vs. making genuine judgments, speaking for oneself alone vs. claiming universal validity, trying to persuade and manipulate people vs. indicating the value of things, and so forth) have obscured not only the enormous range, variety, richness, and modulation of individual verbal judgments, but also the crucially relevant *continuities* between evaluative and other types of discourse and, most significantly, the social dynamics through which *all* utterances, evaluative and otherwise, acquire value.

The Value of Value Judgments

"The work is physically small — 18 by 13 inches — but massive and disturbingly expressive in impact."
"Brava, brava!"
"It's not up to his last one, but that's just my opinion."
"Yes, if you're looking for a teachable text; no, if you want the most current research."
"Absolutely beautiful, though not, of course, for all tastes."
"Go, see it, believe me, you won't be sorry."
"They gave it the Booker Prize in England, but I'll bet the Americans will pan it."
"Suggested Supplementary Readings"
"XXX"
"* * * *"

Value judgments appear to be among the most fundamental forms of social communication and also among the most primitive benefits of social interaction. It appears, for example, that insects and birds as well as mammals signal to other members of their group, by some form of specialized overt behavior, not only the location but also the "quality" of a food supply or territory. And, creatures such as we are, we too not only produce but also eagerly solicit from each other both, as it might be said, "expressions of personal sentiment" (*How do you like it?*) and "objective judgments of value" (*Is it any good?*). We solicit them because, although neither will (for nothing can) give us knowledge of any determinate value of an object, both may let us know, or — and this will be significant here — at least *appear* to let us know, other things that we could find interesting and useful.   *x probability. Worth trying.*

It is evident, for example, that other people's reports of how well certain things have gratified them, though "mere expressions of their subjective likes and dislikes," will nevertheless be interesting to us if we ourselves — as artists, say, or manufacturers, or cooks — have produced those objects, or if — as parents, say, or potential associates — we have an independently motivated interest in the current states of *those people* or in the general structure of their tastes and preferences. Also, no matter how magisterially delivered and with what attendant claims or convictions of universality, unconditionality, impersonality or objectivity, any assertion of *"the* value" of some object can always be unpacked as a judgment of its *contingent* value and appropriated accordingly[5]: that is, as that speaker's observation and/or estimate of how well that object (a) compared to others of the same (implicitly defined) type (b) has performed and/or is likely to perform some particular (even though unstated) desired/able functions[6] (c) for some particular (even though only implicitly defined) subject or set of subjects (d) under some particular (even though not specified) set or range of conditions.

Any evaluation, then, no matter what its manifest syntactic form, ostensible "validity claim," and putative propositional status, may be of social value in the sense of being appropriable by other people. The actual value of a particular evaluation, however, will itself be highly contingent, depending on such variables as the specific social and institutional context in which it is produced, the specific social and institutional relation between the speaker and his/her listener(s), the specific structure of interests that motivates and constrains the entire social/verbal transaction in which the evaluation figures, a vast and not ultimately numerable or listable set of variables relating to, among other things, the social, cultural and verbal histories of those involved and, of course, the particular perspective from which that value is being figured.

In the case of someone's verbal evaluation of an artwork, for example, the value of that *evaluation* would obviously be figured differently by (a) *the evaluator* himself, who, we should note, could be anyone from the artist's teacher, student, brother or agent to some casual gallery visitor, a Warburg Institute art historian or a member of a Committee for the Preservation of Cultural Standards and Ideological Purity, (b) *the artist* herself, whose interest in the evaluation would be different from that of the evaluator but whose evaluation of it would still depend on the latter's identity and/or relationship to her and/or institutional role, (c) any of various *specifically addressed listeners* or some interested *bystander or eavesdropper,* for example, a potential patron, a gallery-going reader of *Art News,* a fellow art historian, or someone who just likes to know what's going on and what other people think is going on. For each of these, the evaluation would be "good" or "bad" in relation to a different configuration of heterogeneous interests: interests that might be unique but might also be more or less shared by other — perhaps many other — people.

Who thinks value is 'in' the object?

We may take note here of the recurrent anxiety/ charge/claim — I shall refer to it as the Egalitarian Fallacy — that, unless one judgment can be said or shown to be more "valid" than another, then all judgments must be "equal" or "equally valid." While the radical contingency of all value certainly does imply that no value judgment can be more "valid" than another *in the sense of* an objectively truer statement of the objective value of an object (for these latter concepts are then seen as vacuous), it does not follow that all value judgments are equally valid. On the contrary, what does follow is that the concept of "validity" *in that sense* is unavailable as a parameter by which to measure or compare judgments or anything else. It is evident, however, that value judgments can still be evaluated, still compared, and still seen and said to be "better" or "worse" than each other. The point, of course, is that their value — "goodness" or "badness" — must be understood, evaluated and compared *otherwise*, that is, as something other than "truth-value" or "validity" in the objectivist, essentialist sense. I shall return to the point below.

The social value of value judgments is illustrated most concretely, perhaps, by the most obviously commercial of them, namely the sorts of assessments and recommendations issued by professional evaluators: film and book reviewers, commissioned art connoisseurs, and those who prepare consumer guides, travel guides, restaurant guides, racetrack tipsheets, and so forth. Such evaluations are not only regularly produced but also regularly sought and bought by the citizens of late capitalist society who live in what is, in effect, a vast supermarket, open 24 hours a day, with an array of possible goods that is not only enormous but that constantly increases and changes and, moreover, does so at a pace that constantly outstrips our ability to obtain current information about them and thus to calculate how they might figure in our personal economies. Indeed, if we were the "rational consumers" so beloved by economists — that is, consumers who, given total information about market conditions, always buy the best for their money — we would have to spend so much of our time acquiring that information that there would be little time left to buy, much less to consume, anything at all.[7]

The supermarket described here is, to be sure, a flagrant feature of contemporary Western society. It is not, however, as recent or as culturally unique as is sometimes suggested. For we always live in a market, always have limited resources — including limited time, energy and occasion to locate and sample for ourselves the entire array of possible goods in it — and therefore always find it economical to pay others to locate and sample some of those goods for us. Professional evaluations — reviews, ratings, guides, tips, and so forth — are only highly specialized and commoditized versions of the sorts of observations and estimates of contingent value commonly exchanged more informally among associates in any culture; and, though we do not always pay each other for them in hard coin, we do pay for them in coin of some sort, such as gratitude and good will, redeemable for return favors and future services.

It appears, then, that evaluations — of artworks, along with anything else consumable (and what isn't?) — are themselves commodities of considerable value, and this in spite of what is sometimes alleged to be their tenuous cognitive substance and suspect propositional status as compared with other kinds of utterances: "factual descriptions," for example, or "empirical scientific reports." Of course, the cognitive substance and propositional validity of aesthetic judgments have been strenuously defended. Indeed, the dominant tradition in post-Kantian aesthetic axiology has characteristically offered to demonstrate that such judgments *do* have truth-value, or at least that they can properly "claim" to have it under the right conditions — which, however, always turn out to be excruciating ones to meet and also rather difficult, or perhaps impossible, to certify as having *been* met. We are, however, approaching the issue from a different — in fact, reverse — direction, the procedure and objective here being not to demonstrate that value judgments have as much claim to truth-value as factual or descriptive statements but, rather, to suggest that, just as value judgments do not have but also do not need truth-value in the traditional sense, neither, it seems, do any of those other forms of discourse.

There is, to be sure, no way for us to be certain that our associates' reports of their personal likes and dislikes are sincere, or that the ratings and rankings produced by professional connoisseurs and local men and women of taste are, as we might say, "honest" and "objective." Indeed, we may grant more generally that any evaluation, aesthetic or otherwise, will be shaped by the speaker's own interests, both as a party to the verbal transaction in which the evaluation figures and in other ways as well. It may also be granted that, since value is especially subject-variable for certain classes of objects, among them artworks, the appropriability of value *judgments* of such objects may be correspondingly highly subject-variable. For these reasons, that is, because we do tend to learn that there is no such thing as an honest opinion and that one man's meat is the other's poison, we typically *supplement* and *discount* the value judgments we are offered "in the light," as we say, of knowledge we have from other sources: knowledge, for example, of the reviewer's personal and perhaps idiosyncratic preferences, or the connoisseur's special interests or obligations and thus suspect or clearly compromised motives.

Or, rather, knowledge we *think* we have. For there is, of course, no way for us to be sure of the accuracy, adequacy, or validity of this supplementary knowledge either, and we may therefore seek yet further supplementary information from yet other sources: some trustworthy guide to travel guides, perhaps, or a reliable review of the reliability of film reviewers, or an inside tip on what tipsheet to buy. It is clear, however, that there can be no end to this theoretically infinite regress of supplementing the supplements and evaluating the evaluations, just as there is none to that of justifying the justifications of judgments, or grounding the grounds of knowledge of any kind — though, in practice, we do the best we can, all things considered, at least as far as we know those things, or think we know them. We need not linger over the epistemological regress here. What is more pertinent to observe is that, *in all the respects mentioned*, value judgments are not essentially different from "descriptive" or "factual" statements, and that their reliability and objectivity are no more compromised by these possibilities — or, for that matter, any *less* compromised by them — than the reliability or objectivity of any other type of utterance, from a pathetic plea of a headache to the solemn communication of the measurement of a scientific instrument.

Not *essentially* different: there are, however, *relative* differences of various kinds. That is, these types of discourse may be seen not as absolutely distinct by virtue of their radically opposed claims to "truth" or "objective validity," but as occupying different positions along a number of relevant continua. Thus, although the value of all objects is to some extent subject-variable, the value of some objects will be *relatively more uniform* than others among the members of some community — as will be, accordingly, the judgments concerning their value exchanged within that community. Similarly, although the conditions under which a particular judgment or report can be appropriated by other people are always to some extent limited, they will be *relatively broader* for some judgments and reports than for others. And, as I shall discuss below, although fraud, exploitation and oppression are possibilities in any verbal interaction, their occurrence will be *relatively better controlled* by certain types of social and institutional constraints than others. Indeed, the familiar distinctions and contrasts among types of discourse that are at issue here — that is, between "merely subjective" and "truly objective" judgments, or between mere value judgments and genuine factual descriptions, or between statements that can and cannot claim truth-value — are no doubt continuously reinforced by the undeniability of just such relative difference which, however, in accord with certain conceptual operations perhaps endemic to human thought, are typically binarized, polarized, absolutized and hierarchized.

We may return here briefly to the Egalitarian Fallacy, that is, the idea that a denial of objective value commits one to the view that all judgments are "equal," "equally good," or "equally valid." As noted above, this is a strict *non sequitur* since, if one finds "validity" in the objectivist, essentialist sense vacuous, one could hardly be committed to accepting it as a parameter by which to measure or compare judgments, whether as better or worse or as "equal." What feeds the fallacy is the objectivist's unshakable conviction that "validity" in *his* objectivist, essentialist sense is the only *possible* measure of the value of utterances.[8] (The Egalitarian Fallacy illustrates the more general rule that, to the dualist, whatever is not dualistic is reductionist or, *if it's not distinguishable by my dualistic description of differences, then it's the same.*) What the present account suggests is not only that there are other parameters by which the value — goodness or badness — of utterances can be measured, but that there are other ways in which all value, including that of utterances, can be conceived.

As we have seen, value judgments may themselves be considered commodities. What may be added here, glancing at the issue of their alleged "equality" under this account, is that some of them are evidently *worth* *more* than others *in the relevant markets*. Thus, the Michelin guides to Italian hotels, restaurants and altar paintings have, we might say, a well-attested reputation for objectivity and reliability, at least among certain classes of travellers. This is not, however, because there is, after all, just a little bit of objective — or universal subjective — validity to which some judgments can properly lay claim. On the contrary, it may be seen as a consequence of precisely those compromising conditions described earlier and summed up in the lesson that there's no such thing as an honest opinion: no judgment, that is, totally unaffected by the particular social, institutional and other conditions of its production and totally immune to — or, we could say, *because it cuts both ways and that is the point*, altogether *unresponsive to* — the assumed interests and desires of its assumed audience. For, if we do not regard them as the regrettable effects of fallen human nature or as noise in the channels of communication or, in the terms of Jürgen Habermas's account, as "distortions" of the ideal conditions "presupposed" by all genuine speech-acts,[9] then we may be better able to see them as the conditions under which all verbal transactions take place and which *give* them — or are, precisely, the *conditions of possibility* for — whatever value they do have for those actually involved in them.

The Economics of Verbal Transactions

That which we call "communication" is a historically conditioned social interaction, in many respects also an economic one and, like other or perhaps all economic transactions, a political one as well. It is historically conditioned in that the effectiveness of any particular interaction depends on the differential consequences of the agents' prior verbal acts and interactions with other members of a particular verbal community. It is an economic interaction — and thus, one could say, transaction — to the extent that its dynamics operate on, out of, and through disparities of resources (or "goods," e.g., material property, information, skills, influence, position, etc.) between the agents and involve risks, gains and/or losses on either or all sides. Communication is also a political interaction, not only in that its dynamics may operate through differences of power between the agents, but also in that the interaction may put those differences at stake, threatening or promising (again, it must cut both ways) either to confirm and maintain them or to subvert or otherwise change them.

Not all the implications of this conception of communication can be
spelled out here.[10] What is significant for our present concerns is that *all*
discourse — descriptive and factual as well as evaluative — operates by
social economics, and that, under *certain* conditions, speakers are constrained (so that it is, we would say, "in their own interest") to serve the
interests of their assumed listener(s) in the ways we commonly characterize as "objectivity" and "reliability."

Thus, certain conditions relevant to the publishing industry, for example, the need for the Michelin guides or *Art News* to secure a minimum
number of regular readers and subscribers plus the actual or potential competition from other guides or other individual evaluators, will make it more
profitable for professional raters and reviewers to produce evaluations appropriable by a relatively large but still relatively specific set of people and,
accordingly, less profitable for them to accept bribes for favorable ratings
or to play out idiosyncratic or inappropriately specialized personal preferences. Hence the familiar disclaimer commonly attached to such works
(here, an obviously somewhat, but not *altogether*, disingenuous one):

> Note that we have no ties to manufacturers or retailers, we
> accept no advertising, and we're not interested in selling
> products. The sole purpose of this book is to help you
> make intelligent purchases at the best prices.[11]

To increase the likelihood that the review or rating of a particular object (e.g. a new film opening in Philadelphia or an altar painting to be seen
in Palermo) will be appropriable by that group of readers, the evaluator
will, of course, typically sample it for himself or herself, operating as a
stand-in for those readers or, we might say, as their metonymic representative, and, to that end, will typically be attentive to the particular contingencies of which the value of objects of that kind appears to be a function
for people of that kind. To do this reliably over a period of time, the evaluator will also be attentive to the shifts and fluctuations of those contingencies: that is, to the current states of the personal economies of those
readers, to what can be discovered or surmised concerning their relevant
needs, interests and resources, to the availability of comparable and competitive objects, and so forth.[12]

As this suggests, competent and effective evaluators — those who know
their business and stay in business (and, of course, there are always many
who don't do either) — operate in some ways very much like market
analysts. But professional market analysis is itself only a highly specialized
and commoditized version of the sorts of informal or intuitive research,
sampling and calculating necessarily performed by *any* evaluator, and if
we are inclined to reserve particular loathing for professional market
analysts as compared to professional critics, it is no doubt because the latter typically operate to serve our interests as consumers whereas the former

typically operate to serve the interests of our marketplace adversaries: those who seek to predict, control, and thereby to profit from, our actions and choices, that is, producers and sellers. But it must be remembered that some of us — or, indeed, all of us, some of the time — are producers and sellers too. This is a point to which I will return below.

Given the general conditions and dynamics described above, professional evaluators will typically seek to secure as large as possible a group of clients. The size of that group will always be *limited*, however, for, given also that one man's meat is the other's poison, the more responsive a judgment is to the needs, resources, desires, tastes, etc. of one client, the less appropriable it will be by another. It is desirable all around, then, that verbal judgments, professional or amateur, be (as they usually, in fact, seem to be) more or less explicitly "tailored" and "targeted" to particular people or sets of people rather than offering or claiming to be appropriable by everybody or, in the terms of classic axiology, "universally valid." By the present account, of course, such claims of universal validity may themselves serve, and take on value as a function of, particular contingencies.

Validity in Science and the Value of "Beauty"

The market conditions that constrain evaluators to produce what we call objective and reliable judgments have their counterpart in social and institutional conditions that characteristically constrain scientists' behavior to comparable ends. Western disciplinary science has been able to pursue so successfully its defining communal mission — which we might characterize here as the generation of verbal/conceptual structures appropriable by the members of some relevant community under as broad as possible a range of conditions[13] — because it has developed institutional mechanisms and practices, including incentives or systems of reward and punishment, that effectively constrain the individual scientist to serve that particular mission in the conduct and reporting of his or her research.[14]

Physicists and other scientists often recall that, in the course of their pursuit, production and testing of alternate models or theories, they were drawn to what turned out to be the "right" one by their sense of its "beauty" or "aesthetic" appeal. Attempts to account for this commonly focus either on what are seen as the formal and hence aesthetic properties of the model or theory itself, for example, its "simplicity" or "elegance," or on what is seen as its correspondence to or conformity with comparable aesthetic features in nature, for example, the latter's "order," "pattern," or "regularity."[15] What makes such explanations somewhat questionable, however — that is, their ignoring of the historical, social and institutional conditions under which scientific constructs are produced and appropriated, and their assumption of a "nature" with independently determinate features — suggests an alternate explanation more pertinent to our present concerns.

No matter how insulated her laboratory or solitary her research, the scientist always operates as a *social* being in two fundamental respects. First, the language or symbolic mode of her conceptualizations — both its lexicon and syntax: that is, the tokens, chains, routes and networks of her conceptual moves — has necessarily been acquired and shaped, like any other language, through her social interactions in a particular verbal community, here the community of scientists in that discipline or field. Second, in the very process of exploring and assessing the "rightness" or "adequacy" of alternate models, she too, like professional and other evaluators, characteristically operates as a metonymic representative of the community for whom her product is designed and whose possible appropriation of it is part of the motive and reward of her own activity. In this respect, she also operates as does any other producer of consumer goods, including, significantly enough here, the *artist*, who also "prefigures" the economies of his own audiences in the very process of artistic creation.[16]

The process of testing the adequacy of a scientific model or theory is, therefore, never only — and sometimes not at all — a measuring of its fit with what we call "the data," "the evidence" or "the facts," all of which are themselves the products of comparable conceptual and evaluative activities already appropriated to one degree or another by the relevant community; it is also a testing, sampling and, in effect, *tasting* in advance of the ways in which the product will taste to other members of that community — which is to say also a calculating in advance of how it will "figure" for them in relation to their personal economies, including (though not necessarily confined to) those aspects of those economies that we call "intellectual" or "cognitive." Thus, what is commonly called "elegance" in a theory or model is often a matter of how sparing it is in its introduction of novel conceptual structures (novel, that is, relative to conceptualizations current in the community), in which case its "beauty" would indeed be a matter of its "economy" for its consumers: in effect, minimum cognitive processing and hence expenditure would be required for its effective appropriation, application or "consumption." The sense of "beauty" or aesthetic appeal that draws the scientist in one direction rather than another may indeed, then, be a proleptic glimpse of its "fit," "fittingness" or "rightness": not, however, in the sense of its correspondence with or conformity to an independently determinate reality but, rather, in the sense of its suitability for eventual communal appropriation.[17]

I have not specified any of the numerous and quite diverse ways in which a scientific construct could figure for the members of some relevant community. Consideration of such matters would be excessively digressive here, but one further point relating to the social economics of validity should be emphasized. Insofar as the development of a theory, model or hypothesis has been directed toward the solution of some relatively specific set of technological and/or conceptual problems, its structure will have been produced and shaped in accord with the scientist's sense — perhaps largely intuitive — of its fitness or potential utility to that end, and its appropriability and hence social value will be largely a matter of the extent to which that surmised or intuited utility is actually realized. Or, it might be said, its validity will be tested by "how well it works" and consist, in effect, in its working well. Pragmatist conceptions of validity, however, are not much improvement over static essentialist or positivist ones if they obliterate the historically and otherwise complex processes that would be involved in the *multiple and inevitably diverse* appropriation of any verbal/conceptual construct (or, to appropriate Jacques Derrida's useful term and concept here, its "dissemination").

Pragmatist reconceptualizations of scientific validity, then, must give due recognition to the fact that theories and models that work very badly or not at all — or no longer work — in the implementation of specific projects or the solution of specific problems may nevertheless "work" and acquire social value otherwise. They may, for example, come to figure as especially fertile metaphoric structures, evoking the production and elaboration of other verbal and conceptual structures in relation to a broad variety of interests and projects under quite diverse historical and intellectual conditions. One may think here of Marxist economics, psychoanalytic theory, and various ancient and modern cosmological models, including more or less "mystical," "metaphysical," and "primitive" ones — all of these, we might note, also classic examples of "nonfalsifiability" and/or nonscientificity in positivist philosophies of science.

The Other Side of the Coin

To remark, as we have been doing here, the ways in which the productions of verbal agents have value without truth-value is not to imply that value is always high or positive, or positive for everyone. Indeed, what follows from the present analysis is that the value of any utterance — aesthetic judgment, factual statement, mathematical theorem, or any other type — may be quite minimal or negative, at least for someone and perhaps for a great many people. As has been stressed here, value always cuts both, or all, ways. An aesthetic judgment, for example, however earnestly offered, may — under readily imaginable social conditions — be excruciatingly uninteresting and worthless to some listener(s); or, conversely, though a factual report may be highly informative to its audience, it may — under readily imaginable political conditions — have been extorted from an unwilling speaker at considerable risk or cost to himself.

Such possibilities do not require us to posit any deficiencies of truth-value or breakdowns in the conditions that "normally" obtain in verbal transactions or are "presupposed" by them. On the contrary, if anything *is* thus presupposed it is precisely such negative possibilities. Or, to put this somewhat differently, the possibility of cost or loss as well as of benefit or gain is a condition of any transaction in the linguistic market where, as in any other market, agents have diverse interests and perspectives, and what is gain for one may be, or involve, loss for the other.[18]

We engage in verbal transactions because we learn that it is sometimes the only and often the best — most effective, least expensive — way to do certain things or gain certain goods. As speakers, it is often the best way to affect the beliefs and behavior of other people in ways that serve our interests, desires or goals; as listeners, it is often the best way to learn things that may be useful for us to know and perhaps otherwise unknowable, including things about the people who speak to us.[19] And such transactions *may* be quite profitable for both parties. For listeners do — not always, but often enough — respond to utterances in ways that serve their speakers' interests: sometimes because a listener is independently motivated to do so but also because she will have learned that, in so doing, she makes it at least minimally worthwhile for speakers to speak and thereby, possibly, to say something of interest to her. Similarly, speakers do — again, not always but often enough — tell listeners things they find interesting: typically because it is only through a listener's knowing or believing those things that the latter *can* serve the speaker's interests, but also because all speakers learn that, in so doing, they make it at least minimally worthwhile for people to listen to them and thereby to be affected in the ways they desire. It must be emphasized here — though the telegraphic and most other models of communication miss and obscure this crucial aspect of the reciprocality of verbal transactions — that listeners, like speakers, are verbal *agents*, and that their characteristic and even optimal re/actions are not confined to the relatively passive and altogether internal or mental ones suggested by such terms as "receiving," "interpreting," "decoding," and "understanding," but embrace the entire spectrum of responsive human actions, including acts that are quite energetic, overt, "material," and, what is most significant here, *consequential for the speaker.*

Verbal transactions are also risky, however, and in some ways structurally adversarial.[20] For, given the dynamics and constraints of reciprocality just described, it will tend to be in the *speaker's* interests to provide only as much "information" as is required to affect the listener's behavior in the ways he himself desires and *no* "information" that it may be to his general disadvantage that she know or believe[21]; at the same time, it will tend to be in the *listener's* interest to learn *whatever* it may be useful or interesting for her to know, whether or not her knowing it happens also to be required or desired by the speaker. Thus, to describe what is presupposed by all communication is to describe the conditions not only for mutually effective interactions but also *and simultaneously* for mutual mis-"understanding," deceit and exploitation; and although the more extravagant reaches of these latter possibilities are no doubt commonly limited by their ultimately negative consequences for those who hazard them too often or indiscriminately, the converse possibilities remain radically excluded; specifically, the kinds of equivalences, symmetries, duplications and gratuitous mutualities that are commonly posited as normally achieved in verbal transactions or as defining communication.

Indeed, by the account outlined here, there is *no* "communication" in the sense either of a *making common* of something (for example, "knowledge") that was previously the possession of only one party or in the sense of a *transferral or transmission of the same* (information, feelings, beliefs, etc.) from one to the other. What there is, rather, is a *differentially consequential interaction*: that is, an interaction in which each party acts in relation to the other differently — in different, asymmetric ways and in accord with different specific motives — and also with different consequences for each. It is inevitable that there will be disparities between what is "transmitted" and what is "received" in any exchange simply by virtue of the different states and circumstances of the "sender" and "receiver," including what will always be the differences — sometimes quite significant ones — produced by their inevitably different life-histories as verbal creatures. In addition, the structure of interests that motivates and governs all verbal interactions makes it inevitable that there will also be differences — sometimes very great ones — between the particular goods offered for purchase and those that the customer/thief actually makes off with, and also between the price apparently asked for those goods and what the customer/gull ends up paying. *Caveat emptor, caveat vendor.*

It appears, then, that the same economic dynamics that make it worthwhile or potentially profitable for both parties to enter into a verbal transaction in the first place operate simultaneously to generate conditions of risk for each. It also appears that the various normative or regulative mechanisms (ethical imperatives, discourse rules, social conventions, etc.) invoked by speech-act theorists and others to account for the fact that speakers *are* ever honest, and that listeners *do* ever understand their "intentions" and behave accordingly, must be seen as descriptions of a system of constraints that emerges not in opposition to but *by virtue of* the interests (or, which seems to be the same, "self-interests") of the agents involved. To be sure, as already indicated, the motivating interests of the speaker or listener may consist largely of an independently motivated concern — independent, that is, of the particular transaction in question — for the other's welfare or for some more general social welfare.[22] Also, both parties may very well have interests in common, which is to say coincident interests and/or goals, that could be better or only implemented by their reciprocal and, in effect, cooperative exchanges. It must be emphasized, however, that any of these possibilities, which perhaps occur quite frequently, nevertheless occur *within* the general structure of motives that energize and sustain verbal interactions, not outside of or in contrast to their economic dynamics.

Habermas, Communication, and the Escape from Economy

The preceding point requires emphasis in view of the current but du-
bious attractiveness of accounts of communication that produce exclusions
and draw contrasts of that kind. Thus, Habermas regards genuine communication as occurring only when and insofar as the participants' actions
are "oriented" toward an "agreement" that presupposes the mutual recognition by both parties of "corresponding validity claims of comprehensi-
bility, truth, truthfulness [in the sense of 'sincerity'] , and rightness [in the
sense of 'moral justness']" and, moreover, that "terminates in the intersubjective mutuality of [their] reciprocal understanding, shared knowledge,
mutual trust, and accord with one another."[23]

"Genuine communication" so defined must, according to Habermas,
be strictly distinguished from what he refers to as "strategic" or "instrumental" actions, which he defines as those "oriented to the actor's success"
and which he glosses as "modes of action that correspond to the utilitarian model of purposive-rational action."[24] In terms of the analysis outlined
here, it is clear that, in defining genuine communication as something altogether uncontaminated by strategic or instrumental action, Habermas has
secured a category that is quite sublime (and, as such, necessary, it appears,
to ground his views of the alternate possibilities of human society) but also
quite empty: for, having thus disqualified and bracketed out what is, in
effect, the entire motivational structure of verbal transactions, he is left
with an altogether bootstrap operation or magic reciprocality, in which
the only thing that generates, sustains and controls the actions of speakers
and listeners is the gratuitous mutuality of their presuppositions.

It is significant in this connection that Habermas does not recognize
that *listeners* — as such, and not only in their alternate role as speakers
— perform any *acts* relevant to the dynamics of communication: or, rather,
he conceives of their relevant actions as consisting only of such altogether
passive, covert and internal ones as "understanding" and "presupposing."
What is thereby omitted is, of course, the whole range — one might say
arsenal or warehouse — of acts, including quite overt and physically effi-
cient or materially substantial ones, by which a listener can serve a speaker's interests in *all* that might be meant by her "response" to the speaker.
It should be noted, in addition, that a listener's or reader's responses, including here what might be meant by her "interpretation" or "understanding," always extend beyond the moment of hearing or reading itself, a unit
of time that could, in any case, be only arbitrarily specified. Indeed, it may
be questioned whether the boundaries of a "speech act" can be, as Habermas and many other communications theorists evidently assume, readily
or sharply demarcated from the speaker's and listener's other — prior, on-
going and subsequent — activities.

In connection with the more or less utopian theories of communication mentioned above, a final point may be emphasized here. The linguis-

tic market can no more be a "free" one than any other market, for verbal agents do not characteristically enter it from positions of equal advantage or conduct their transactions on an equal footing. On the contrary, not only can and will that market, like any other, be rigged by those with the power and interest to do so, but, no less significantly, it always interacts with *other* economies, including social and political ones. Individual verbal transactions are always constrained, therefore, by the nature of the social and political relationships that *otherwise* obtain between the parties involved, including their nonsymmetrical obligations to and claims upon one another by virtue of their nonequivalent roles in those relationships, *as well as* by their inevitably unequal resources and nonsymmetrical power relations *within* the transaction itself. (The latter inequalities and nonsymmetries are inevitable because they are a function of *all* the differences among us.) To imagine speech-situations in which all such differences were eradicated or equalized and thus "free" of all so-called "distortions" of communication is to imagine a superlunary universe — and even there, it seems, the conditions of perfection will always call forth someone, an archangel perhaps, who will introduce difference into the company.[25]

The image of a type of communication that excludes all strategy, instrumentality, (self-) interest, and, above all, the profit motive, reflects what appears to be a more general recurrent impulse to dream an escape from economy, to imagine some special type, realm or mode of value that is beyond economic accounting, to create by invocation some place apart from the marketplace — a kingdom, garden or island, perhaps, or a plane of consciousness, form of social relationship, or stage of human development — where the dynamics of economy are, or once were, or some day will be, altogether suspended, abolished or reversed. Here no winds blow ill and there need be no tallies of cost and benefit; there are no exchanges but only gifts; all debts are paid by unrepayable acts of forgiveness; all conflicts of interest are resolved, harmonized or subsumed by a comprehensive communal good, and exemplary acts of self-sacrifice are continuously performed and commemorated. Given what seems to be the inexorability of economic accounting in and throughout every aspect of human — and not only human — existence, from the base of the base to the tip of the superstructure, and given also that its operations implicate each of us in loss, cost, debt, death and other continuous or ultimate reckonings, it is understandable that the dream of an escape from economy should be so sweet and the longing for it so pervasive and recurrent. Since it does appear to be inescapable, however, the better, that is, more effective, more profitable, alternative would seem to be not to seek to go beyond economy but to do the best we can going *through* — in the midst of and perhaps also by means of — it: "the best," that is, all things considered, at least as far as we know those things, or think we know them.

Notes

1. An earlier version of this essay was presented at a symposium on "Representation and Value: Literature, Philosophy and Science," February 21, 1986 at the Georgia Institute of Technology, and at the May, 1986 meeting of the International Association for Philosophy and Literature, Seattle, Washington. Acknowledgment is gratefully made to the Rockefeller Foundation and the National Endowment for the Humanities for support for its preparation.

2. See "Contingencies of Value," *Critical Inquiry* 10.1 (September, 1983), 1-35, from which several paragraphs below are excerpted and paraphrased. The account is further elaborated in *Contingencies of Value: Post-Axiological Perspectives in Critical Theory* (forthcoming, Harvard University Press), which incorporates the article and the present essay as well.

3. Among the most recent of those — of course quite diversely produced, articulated and circulated — demonstrations (and critiques of those attempted rehabilitations) are Jacques Derrida, *Of Grammatology*, trans. Gayatri C. Spivak (Baltimore, 1974) and *Margins of Philosophy*, trans. Alan Bass (Chicago, 1982); Nelson Goodman, *Ways of Worldmaking* (Indianapolis, 1978); Richard Rorty, *Philosophy and the Mirror of Nature* (Princeton, 1979) and *The Consequences of Pragmatism* (Minneapolis, 1982); Gonzalo Munévar, *Radical Knowledge: A Philosophical Inquiry into the Nature and Limits of Science* (Indianapolis, 1981); Barry Barnes, *T.S. Kuhn and Social Science* (New York, 1982); and David Bloor, *Wittgenstein: A Social Theory of Knowledge* (New York, 1983).

4. For an interesting approach to such an account, see Humberto R. Maturana and Francisco J. Varela, *Autopoiesis and Cognition* (Dordrecht, Holland and Boston: Reidel, 1980).

5. Here and below, to *appropriate* an utterance (a value judgment or any other type) means to adopt, apply or employ someone else's utterance for one's own purposes. It is understood, of course, that the utterance may have been produced for just such appropriation or, in the terms of the market model developed below, just such "consumption."

6. Having particular *effects* rather than performing particular functions is a more suitable unpacking in many cases.

7. As a current rating service puts it:

   > CONSUMER GUIDE knows what a challenge it is to pick the 'best buy' that meets your requirements...So we call in the experts to do the comparison shopping for you. (*Consumer Buying Guide* [Skokie, Ill.: Signet, 1987] , p. 4)

8. The force of J. L. Austin's insight that there are other measures, e.g., "felicity," has been all but lost in the objectivist appropriation of his work in so-called "speech act theory." It may be noted as well that Austin appreciated, though he did not pursue his own emphasis of it, the radical contingency of "truth":

> It is essential to realize that 'true' and 'false'...do not stand for anything simple at all; but only for a general dimension of being a right or proper thing to say as opposed to a wrong thing, in these circumstances, to this audience, for these purposes and with these intentions. (*How to Do Things with Words* [New York, 1962], p. 144)

9. Jürgen Habermas, "What is Universal Pragmatics?" in *Communication and the Evolution of Society*, trans. Thomas McCarthy (Beacon Press: Boston and London, 1979).

10. See my *On the Margins of Discourse: The Relation of Literature to Language* (Chicago, 1978), pp. 77-106, for an earlier version, and *Contingencies of Value* for further elaboration. Other accounts along these lines includes Erving Goffman, *Strategic Interaction* (Oxford, 1970) and *Relations in Public* (New York, 1971), and Morse Peckham, *Explanation and Power: The Control of Human Behavior* (New York, 1979). Pierre Bourdieu develops a somewhat different but compatible sociological analysis of "the linguistic marketplace" in "The Economics of Linguistic Exchange," *Social Science Information* 16 (1977), 645-88.

11. *Consumer Buying Guide*, p. 4.

12. Thus readers of the work cited above are assured:

    > Our experts are also careful to match the products to the changing needs of consumers, including, for instance, downsized appliances for small households. (p. 4)

13. The mission of disciplinary science is also the production of appropriable *technical skills* and the two may not always be separable, but, in connection with questions of verbal communication and the value of "propositions," our focus here is on its verbal/conceptual products: reports, statements, writings, theories, measurements, models, etc.

14. For recent discussions of the structure and operation of social and institutional constraints in disciplinary science see David Bloor, "Essay Review: Two Paradigms for Scientific Knowledge?", *Science Studies* 1 (1971) 105-15; Pierre Bourdieu, "The Specificity of the Scientific Field and the Social Conditions of the Progress of Reason," *Social Science Information*, 14 (1975), 19-47; Barry Barnes, *T.S. Kuhn and Social Science*, esp. pp. 64-93; and H. M. Collins, *Changing Order: Replication and Induction in Scientific Practice* (London and Beverly Hills, Cal., 1985), esp. pp. 129-68.

15. For a recent attempt to analyze the good-true-beautiful relation in modern theoretical physics, see Paul Davies, *Superforce: The Search for a Grand Unified Theory of Nature* (New York, 1984), pp. 50-69.

16. As I indicate in "Contingencies of Value," pp. 24-25, the process of artistic composition may be seen as a paradigm of evaluative — and thus simultaneously "creative" and "critical" — activity. The relevant passage can be abbreviated and paraphrased as follows:

    > A significant aspect of that process is the artist's (here, author's) pre-figuring or pre-enacting of the *reader's* experience of the

work. That is, in selecting some word, adjusting some turn of phrase, rejecting one rhyme or example in favor of another one, the author is all the while testing the local and global effectiveness of each decision by, in effect, impersonating in advance his possible or presumptive audiences. Every literary work — and, more generally, artwork — is thus the product of a complex evaluative feedback loop that embraces not only the ever-shifting economy of the artist's own interests and resources as they evolve during and in reaction to the process of composition, but also all the shifting economies of his assumed and imagined audiences, including audiences who do not yet exist and are in many respects altogether unimaginable, but whose emergent interests, variable conditions of encounter, and rival sources of gratification the author will nevertheless intuitively surmise and to which, among other things, his own sense of the *fittingness* and *fitness* of each decision will be responsive.

17. Many elements of the present account occur in the analysis by Paul Davies cited above (cf. n. 15). He points out, for example, that the "rightness" of certain highly abstract features of a theory cannot be a matter of their validation "by concrete experience," that "beauty in physics is a value judgment involving professional intuitions," and that with regard to theories, "better" means not truer (he does not, in fact, use the term) but more "useful," "more economical," "smoother," "more suggestive," etc. (*Superforce*, pp. 66-69). Davies nevertheless moves repeatedly towards gratuitously objectifying formulations (e.g., "Nature *is* beautiful" and "Nevertheless the aesthetic quality *is there* sure enough" [68, 69]) that obscure the significance of the relationship, here emphasized, between the scientist's intuitive sense of the "beauty" of a theory and its suitability for appropriation by the members of a relevant community.

18. *May* be, not *must* be: this is certainly not to suggest that every verbal transaction or other form of social interaction is a zero-sum game.

19. "Speakers," here, are those who produce verbal forms in any mode or medium; "listeners" are those who respond to (*N.B.*, not simply "receive") such forms.

20. The adversarial quality described here coexists with whatever mutual benevolence otherwise and simultaneously characterizes the relation between the parties: it does not contaminate the latter, but neither does the latter transcend it.

21. The term and concept "information" and also its traditional conceptual syntax ("getting," "having," "giving," "transmitting" it, etc.) are among those by which traditional discourse segments, arrests and hypostasizes the complex processes through which our behavior is modified by our interactions with our environments. In an account more rigorous than that offered here, the entire problematic terminology of "information" would be replaced by a description of the specific dynamics of such interactions.

22. The present account does not exclude what are called moral or ethical (inter)actions though it would, in any elaboration, necessarily reconceptualize their dynamics.

23. Habermas, "What is Universal Pragmatics?" p. 3.

24. *Ibid.*, p. 41.

25. Some of the inequalities and nonsymmetries indicated here are no doubt often negotiated or adjusted under conditions of partnership, paternalism or mutual good will, and a case could certainly be made out for the desirability of more extensive negotiations and adjustments of that kind and/or for more extensive good will generally. It is unclear, however, how — or, indeed, by what kinds of "strategic actions" — any more radical social engineering along these lines would be pursued, and unclear also how (since equalization does not have equal consequences for everyone) the costs and benefits would fall out. Even more fundamentally, however, especially in view of the supposed political implications of Habermas's program for the reconstruction of the presuppositions of all speech-acts, one must wonder what those implications could actually be for a *sublunary* universe. For, of course, the closer one moved to the ideal speech-situation of Habermas's fantasy, the less motive there would be for any verbal transactions to occur and the more redundant all speech would become.

Mary Louise Pratt, "Ideology and Speech-Act Theory," *Poetics Today* 7.1 (1986), 59-72, offers a spirited critique of the "idealized" and "utopian" conceptions of verbal transactions in speech-act theory. Interestingly, however, the sole exception Pratt makes to her censure of models of communication as cooperative exchange is the Habermas version, redeemed for her by the fact that it has been expressly designed to function "as the basis for a social critique" (p. 70). She acknowledges that Habermas's account "has a number of features in common with [Paul] Grice's ideal" (p. 70), but does not acknowledge that they are the very features which she has herself already excoriated as politically naive, out of touch with reality, and decisively contradicted by what goes on in "almost any press conference, board meeting, classroom or family room in the country" (p. 68). The real issue, perhaps, is the political effectiveness, inspirational and otherwise, of the production and invocation of "counterfactual" (Habermas's term for his own) images of communication.

2

ART AND THE SOCIOLOGICAL EGO: VALUE FROM A PSYCHOANALYTIC POINT OF VIEW*

Charles Levin

Symbolization, Substance, Aesthetic

> *We are witnessing a more and more powerful historical deployment of a general writing of which the system of speech, of consciousness, of meaning, of presence, and of truth, etc., would only be an effect and should be analyzed as such.* — Jacques Derrida[1]

The discursive situation of the term "value" has usually been somewhat precarious, especially in the *economic* and *ethical* domains, which have defined, for the most part, the fields of conscious social struggle throughout human history. My concern in this paper is with a third domain: the *aesthetic*, which I shall approach as if it were a kind of primitive substance of social process. As will be seen from the conclusion, no new answers are proposed, but throughout the discussion I have tried to adumbrate a new sense of the place where we might look for them.

The specificity of the problem of value in the present age may very well be linked to the fact that the aesthetic domain, though largely unconscious, has begun to take on a kind of quasi-discursive existence, like the economic and the ethical. There has been an enormous increase in our intellectual awareness of the aesthetic levels of social processes, an in-

---

* For Anne Telford

crease with which we lack any reflective means to cope, apart from psychoanalysis. But psychoanalysis is furnished to deal with such questions primarily on an individual basis. Whether the aesthetic domain is comparable to the economic and ethical domains in that it can be generalized into an area of social contestation and collective "working through" is a question which shall be left on one side (although it is an important one for contemporary movements in the arts). In the present contribution, only the difficulties and uncertainties of the aesthetic enterprise will be examined. Freud defined three kinds of internal barriers to the psychoanalytic process itself: the ego, superego, and id resistances. If the problems of economic and ethical value may loosely be compared to the ego and superego resistances, which are the easiest to uncover, then the problem of the aesthetic domain corresponds to what Freud described as the "resistances of the id," which are more difficult to get out in the open.

In my use of the word "aesthetic," I am referring to something which is still only remotely related, in common understanding, to aesthetic judgment in the technical sense. To date, we have equipped ourselves with rather delusory verbal models of metaphor. In consequence, we have only the vaguest notion of how the intense bodily sensations and wild imaginings of prelinguistic infants, which inaugurate the whole (psychic) process of metaphorizing organic life, connect up with the cultural forms, attitudes, preferences, and habits of adults.[2] It is my view that the explanation of aesthetic judgments will remain largely a question of arbitrary taste, and that attributions of aesthetic value will continue to be intelligible only in sociological (ethical and economic) terms, so long as the field of aesthetics remains dominated by philosophies of consciousness and linguistic theories of meaning.

My main effort in this paper has been to adumbrate the category of the *aesthetic* through an examination of inherent tensions in the psychoanalytic theory of *symbolization*. The aim is to explore alternatives to both the reductionistic tendencies of "representational" theories and the obverse strategy of "interpreting upward" characteristic of linguistic and social thought. In order to round out the discussion, I have yoked terms for symbolization and aesthetics to the philosophical problem of *"substance."* Since psychoanalysis is notorious for having made the concept of the subject difficult, and since the failure of traditional notions of substance remains a goad to modern philosophy, this triangle of terms (the aesthetic, symbolization, and substance) brings the problem of value into line with the presenting symptoms of contemporary thought.

As described later in this paper, the dominant practices in contemporary thought are conducted by the *sociological ego*. The "sociological ego" is not simply an aspect of the rise of social science in response to the social upheavals of the nineteenth century. It has other strands of development, including the philosophical discovery (always resisted, but nevertheless irreversible) that the noumenal beings populating the history of human thought are fundamentally "irrational." For the sociological ego, subjects and objects are unintelligible, indeterminate, and probably illusory as well (in modern parlance — specular, ideological, fantasmatic, metaphysical, etc.).

Locke described substances as "nothing but several combinations."[3] The "Doctrine of Signs," for which he was the first to propose the name "Semiotic," encouraged recognition of the arbitrariness of value. If Marx revealed the ideological contingency of economic value forms, Nietzsche exposed the derivative character of even the species values (e.g., use value) which Marx had reserved as the metabolic substances of the historical process. These philosophical developments were consolidated at the formal level when positivism abandoned the "metaphysics of subject and object," in order to replace them with a problematic of language[4] which has reigned ever since.

Most of the important innovations of twentieth-century thought (pragmatist, linguistic, logical, cybernetic, structuralist, deconstructionist) have been attempts to displace the burden of universality away from categories of things and substances, and onto categories of relationality. From this kind of perspective, it is relatively easy to show how subjects and objects and substances in general are constructed as purely relational beings held together by networks of signification. The whole project of modern thought revolves around this epistemological shifting of emphasis: if the subject is unknowable and the object is indeterminate, perhaps the relations between them can be settled. The proper concern of modern thought is therefore no longer the *nature* of phenomena, but the determination of the *systems* governing their combination and recombination. This is why so much of modern (and postmodern) thought depends on the possibilities of formalization latent in language. Texts and systems of logic furnish an ideal model of determinate relations; they seem to be blocked out into discrete (but purely formal and insubstantial) units whose links are governed by precise rules of combination and substitution. (It is essentially this promise of a new science of language that draws the long tradition of rationalism into the orbit of modern thought.)

One of the most eloquent expressions of the ethos of relationality was Lacan's account of the subject as the resultant of interactions between "signifiers."[5] As Coward and Ellis put it, Lacan's approach "suggests a notion of the subject produced in relation to social relations by the fixing of its signifying chain to produce certain signifieds."[6] Although (like Bion during the same period), Lacan eventually turned to mathematical and geometric metaphors of relationality, his initial impulse to extend the categories of formalist linguistics to the unconscious affords a rare insight into the aims of contemporary intellectual activity. Unfortunately, as Lacan's own work demonstrates, even a relatively straightforward psychoanalytic account of a social relationship tends to frustrate the wish of the sociological ego to render psycho-social process as a system-governed phenomenon.

If a subject is "divided" into at least two experiential dimensions, i.e., a conscious and an unconscious, then a relation between two subjects will have at least eight + n shifting dimensions, since each has at least four "positions" to start from. Subject A will have a conscious relation to subject B, but also a conscious relation to B's unconscious, and vice versa. A will also have an unconscious perception of B, with which he or she will have a relation, both conscious and unconscious, since A will have an unconscious perception of A, as well as B. And the unconscious A will have a relation with the unconscious B, and vice versa [Figure 1].

Figure 1

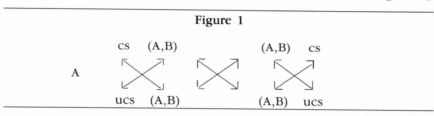

Even a schematic representation of "subjectivity" such as this raises more questions than can be resolved on the combinatorial plane of formal relations between signifiers (or Ideas, or sense impressions). As I shall argue in the latter sections of this paper, the contemporary epistemological drive to propose models of the relations between things is as metaphysical in its inspiration as the traditional concept of substance, with its naive expectation that we can know the things themselves.

The downfall of the traditional concept of substance was that it was conceived in terms of gravity, as a kind of ground, or something to stand on, as Locke[7] pointed out at the very beginning of the sociological era. The substance of a thing was supposed to be the thing that supported it, and prevented it from failling into an empty hole of nothing. This notion of "standing under" and "upholding" (as Locke put it) led a kind of double metaphysical existence. Substance, essence, spirit, were all anti-gravity devices, forms of propulsion and resistance which defined a thing at once as what moved it and what rested on. The substance of a thing was thus etymologically and emotionally something other than it: a contradiction in terms, a category mistake, a paradox.[8]

Perhaps even more important than the fact that the concept of substance violates the identity rule and the law of the excluded middle is the fact that logic itself has abandoned the attempt to determine the universal connections between terms standing for substantive beings, and chosen instead to explore the substantive being of connectives themselves. If substance enjoyed at best a series of half-lives in the syllogism, it met with virtual extinction in the logical deconstruction of language itself, in the evolution from empiricism and early modern rationalism to logical positivism, analytic philosophy, and beyond.

In conjunction with these developments, the sociological ego has succeeded in titrating most of the compound constructions of the metaphysical tradition into contingent economic and ethical value forms. Since Newton, the progressive relativization of the gravity metaphor has desubstantiated a whole symbolic relation to the world, and transposed it into systems of signs, coordinates, and algorithms. The mainstay of traditional being has thus gradually achieved a kind of weightless indeterminacy. In the "bourgeois" world, as Marx and Engels declared, "All that is solid melts into air."[9]

In this century, Martin Heidegger proposed a chilling diagnosis of modernity. He allegorized more than two thousand years of Western thought as a "forgetting of being," and made therapeutic recommendations to recultivate an imaginary, maternal, pre-Socratic soil. For Heidegger, art was a sort of "way back into the ground" of forsaken "Being." Unfortunately, if only from an eco-techno-logical point of view, the ground and gravity metaphors of life have become anachronistic, the subject of exhaustive parody. Aside from biology and physics, there remain only reasons (ethics), or forces and causes (economics). By "thinking Being" as a kind of resting place, or substance, Heidegger merely prolonged ontology in the form of a defunct epistemology of foundations.

Art is certainly bound up with substances — with feces and with noumena; and consequently has suffered the same fate as the subject and the object in the eyes of the sociological ego. But if art is linked to metaphysical categories, this does not mean that it is an epistemologically naive attempt to establish or express the ontological "basis" of existence. The aesthetic substances evoked in art have no *a priori* being; they are nothing more than *emergent properties* of symbolization. Moreover, the symbolic is itself an emergent property. Symbolization emerges out of the "act" — in the sense that it is a process (mysterious, but no doubt biologically accommodated) that surfaces in an infant, and which, *a posteriori*, defines bodily events as actions. Hence, the aesthetic is an emergent property of an emergent property: it cannot be a foundation of anything [Figure 2].

Art is a form of the aesthetic, and as such, it is the kind of thing that exists after the fact, though not because it is an "artificial" by product or after-image of something "more" real that came before it. Screen memories may be "accidents," but they are as real as their supposed referents, and Freud first considered that they were as likely to conceal subsequent as antecedent events.[10] Like screen memories, art objects embody states of symbolic process, and thus maintain experiential links to the mechanisms which generate, out of the body, an antecedent (or subsequent) dimension of facts, grounds, causes, reasons, meanings, and correspondences. The *post hoc* character of the aesthetic does not make art "arbitrary" in relation to nature. If art didn't exist (which in Heidegger's ontological sense, it never does), we would probably have to create it.

FIGURE 2

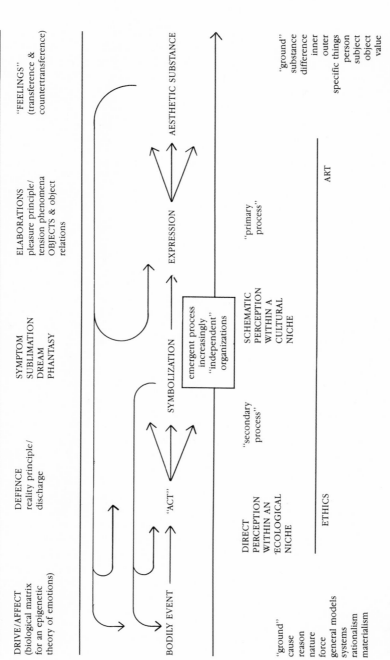

[Aesthetic substances are not even survival values, they merely devolve from symbolic elaborations, while the latter retrospectively inform organismic experience. It is in this sense that we can still make use of the terminology of art as reflection, imitation, expression, representation, or simulation. Our attempts to examine what we do — projective testing, for example — generally assume a disjunction between "literal" (functional) and "schematic" (cultural) perception.[11] As precarious as this distinction may be, there is probably not much point in trying to "deconstruct" it. To observe our own collective behaviour and its consequences is to realize that nature is perfectly capable of objectifying and substantiating "unreal" beings.[12] The problem we have interpreting ourselves is not that our representations are "false," "ontotheological," etc. (or alternatively that everything is representation, including the represented); it is simply that "images" and "transferences" are always prey to the "good" Gestalt principles of form and closure (the traditional sense of the Greek *symbolon*). We insist on trying to make sense out of meaning, by associating it with order and structure, and denying it to "nature," animals — and even infants. Confronted with the embarrassment of the idea that meaning might be objective and universal (or else arbitrary and idiosyncratic), we respond with the claim that it is merely a "public and conventional"[13] artifact: still human (as opposed to "natural"), we reassure ourselves, but no longer implicated in the metaphysics of subjects, objects, and substances.]

The distinction between the aesthetic domain[14] and art as conventionally understood is an important one to try to maintain, although it may never be settled. If the organism has significance because it is somehow "charged up" into a symbolization process (which can be related back), aesthetic substance is a kind of "run" on the symbolized body. Substance in this sense is indeed essential and universal — but only because it is impossible to prevent it by sustaining symbolic controls on bodily events indefinitely. There is no question here of substances objectively and impersonally preexisting or underlying or causing. The difference between "art" and aesthetic substance lies in the fact that art is a more or less formal invitation[15] to the symbolizing body, whereas substance implies the dedifferentiation[16] of formal distinctions in favour of unstructured differences — a suspension of phallic-linguistic-Gestalt defences which permits co-perception of both figure and ground. The art object is an acknowledgment and mnemonic of the perplexities of organismic experience, but not the activity or process itself. It can always be ignored or rationalized away.

It is important to emphasize that symbolization is not something built up like a superstructure on top of something more factual such as instinct, language, experience, force, or matter. It is an emergent property of the body. Symbolization can be fed forward, as well as backward, not only creating Gestalts, but unravelling into what we call pure sensation. The more one relaxes the feedback links, the further one strays from the supporting scene (e.g., the 'cause,' 'ground,' or 'reason') of activity, the more one is lost — or thrown forward — in(to) the indeterminacies of substance. Economics and ethics relate symbolizations to knowledge about the grounds of actions, which may in themselves be deemed to exist in a setting materially prior to (or spiritually higher than) the act. But the aesthetic draws symbolization out into its "emergencies," where even acts begin to look volatile and insubstantial, and the pre-action of grounds and reasons is almost wholly lost in the progressive aesthetic specification of peculiarities and informal differences. In the macroscope of the sociological ego, the subject and the object may lack solidity relative to the unmoving precision of relational models. But in the microscope of the aesthetic, relations themselves lose intelligibility in the obscure encounter between the subject, the other, and their bodily substances.

How Freud Saved the Imagination

> *It was only a logical contradiction — which is not saying much.* — Freud[17]

Although he avoided the term "Will to Power," Freud believed, like Nietzsche, that the symbolic processes of psychic and social life are epiphenomenal by products of the interaction of natural cosmic principles, "somewhat on the analogy of the resultant of a parallelogram of forces."[10] Nevertheless, he was able to open the way to an understanding of the prelogical role of symbolization in human culture: the "imagination."

There has been much confusion between the naturalism of Freud's instinctual metapsychology and the implicit existentialism of his symbolic conception of psychic process — but this has profoundly enriched psychoanalytic thought. As we shall see, Freud tended to cast symbol and instinct in each other's image, giving rise to a theoretic tension which is still being worked through. Like Nietzsche, he did his greatest work on the fringes of the University, where the great biological debate between physicalist reductionism and organicist vitalism raged at the end of the nineteenth century. He lionized the mechanists who came to dominate medicine (e.g., his teacher, Brücke), but never gave up allegiance to the Romantic culture which he inherited (e.g., Goethe).

The psychoanalytic issues to be discussed here revolve around the older problems which Nietzsche and Freud saw banished from the University. But the relevance of these issues today depends on the constructions of the mechanists and reductionists (including those of Freud himself), as well as the vitalists. The persistence of the concept of "imagination" poses the following question: is it possible to sustain a sense of "process" in the "psychic apparatus" such that neither symbol nor experience is reduced to a mere reflection of a natural system of causes, whether mechanistic or organicist? And is it reasonable to have a conception of social life in which the symbol is not merely a token of experience, nor experience simply the effect of an external symbolic system or agency, such as language and myth? I shall argue that "imagination" is the common name for a dimension of psychic life where symbol and experience combine, in a passion of value, to express the enigma of having a relation to an object at all. I shall call this the aesthetic dimension, and assume that it is the central value for the human infant,[19] and not a secondary or tertiary derivative of hunger, as Freud seemed to believe. As Bion once put it: "There cannot possibly be fewer than two minds if passion is present."[20] But if we are to have any respect for this "seething cauldron" of value, we must first make a short historical review of the psychoanalytic theory of the symbol, which affords a more naturalistic interpretation of the traditional metaphysical categories with which the concept of the aesthetic remains burdened today.

The classic psychoanalytic statement on symbolism was Ernest Jones's 1916 essay, "The Theory of Symbolism," which echoed Freud's own discussion of the topic in the same year.[21] Jones sought to establish a technical definition of what he called "true symbolism" — the symbolism appropriate to the psychoanalytic domain of the unconscious — by distinguishing it in principle from all other forms of "indirect representation," such as metaphor and allegory (Jones 90).

The main argument turns on the standard clinical distinction between regression and sublimation. For Jones, a symbol is always an expression of a repressed complex, in the sense that symbols (unlike sublimations) are not modifications or developments of the primitive ideas characteristic of the primary process, but direct expressions of them, telegraphs of the contents of original complexes. According to Jones, "The basal feature in all forms of symbolism is identification" (138). By this he means that the symbol is the resultant of primary fusions devoid of perceptual discrimination: not an internalized link to an object, but the "perceptual identity," or hallucinated satisfaction, which Freud ascribed to the hungry narcissistic baby untutored by the frustrations of reality.[22] The 'truest' symbol for Jones would be a kind of ultimate regression toward "the most completely repressed mental processes known" (115) — a "return of the repressed" expressing the "symbolic equation" of the instinctual aim and the idea identified with the aim (135). As Jones explains, "only what is repressed is symbolized; only what is repressed needs to be symbolized" (116). In contrast with the products of sublimation, symbols are deeply rooted in the primary process and linked "to the most primitive ideas and interests imaginable": the body, the immediate family, birth, love, and death (102). They are necessarily concrete, and the "order of development" — or progress — of human representation is always from the particular to the general, from the tangible to the abstract (113).

The distinct character of the true symbol in classical theory is illustrated by the special role accorded symbolism in Freud's account of the dreamwork. Unlike condensation and displacement, true symbolism does not encourage dynamic interpretation; it is not, as both Freud and Jones emphasize, amenable to the technique of free association which, if at all forth-coming in the case of the symbol, can only lead away from the symbol's 'real' meaning. The symbol appears in the dream as a more or less direct representation of the archaic unconscious, so that there is, in Freud's view, "a constant relation... between [the symbol] and its translation."[23]

In contrast with the rest of the dream-work, symbols are purported to have an essential, "deeper" level of meaning that remains relatively con-stant in human time. The interpretation of symbolic material therefore has little to do with how individual experience is constituted, but with the means by which the latter may be broken down into specific causes (in-stinctual drives) and general effects (mental contents) (Jones, 125). This con-forms to the sharp division, in classical theory, between the "primitive, infantile mind" and the "adult, conscious mind" (104). On the other hand, Jones points out that even if the "magical thinking" of symbolism "be-tokens a relative incapacity for either apprehension or presentation" (137), it still involves a dynamic process, in which the symbol "has to be recreat-ed afresh out of individual material" (98). Thus, the infantile mind gener-ates the new 'Zeppelin' symbol of the phallus out of the contingent perceptions of the adult, conscious mind (104). But this dynamic, implicitly historical view clashes with the main perspective of the theory: that the meaning of the true symbol is universal, not only in the trivial sense that it transcends specific cultures, but in its profound disregard for individuality.

The theory of the symbol as a "constant translation" or representation of the unconscious suggests a static model of repression and entails an im-age of the 'archaic' mind as a quasiphylogenetic, Lamarckian entity. Yet, in practice, psychoanalysis has always understood the symbol in the light of what could be found out about the dynamics of symptom-formation. Here, the 'meaning' of the symbol is sought in the expression or embodi-ment of a psychic process, and the emphasis is on the constituents of the process, rather than its origin or result. As Jones himself argued, the sym-bol must, like the symptom, always be a compromise-formation, the resul-tant of cathexis and countercathexis, "in which both the repressed and the repressing tendencies are fused"(115). The affect attached to the sym-bol derives from an unconscious identification between the symbol ele-ment and the instinctual object of the affect(116). Yet, in these characteristic formulations, it is difficult to tell the symbol apart from the ordinary, on-togenetically relative measures of displacement and condensation which underlie both the manifest dream and the construction of symptoms. The "symbolic equation," however primitive or regressive in character, is still a kind of dynamic substitution, contingent on the experience that the psychesoma has of the world it is in [Figure 3].

The problem in Jones's account is nicely illustrated in Hanna Segal's often cited example of a "symbolic equation." Her psychotic patient had given up playing the violin with the explanation: "Do you expect me to masturbate in public?"[24] But, as in most of Freud's and Jones's examples,

---

Figure 3

Symptom	Symbol

defense   defense

$\downarrow$ symptom(b) $\downarrow$ symbol(b)
$\uparrow$ → (compromise formation) $\uparrow$ → (compromise form)

affect/object(a)   affect/object(a)

---

there is no question here of a "direct translation" without benefit of association and elaboration. The "equations" of penis and violin, performance and masturbation, are obviously specific and opaque to "translation." Moreover, they have the quality of manifest content, masking the symbolic elaboration of a persecutory object (the public = the analyst?) which, in spite of its paranoid construction, observes the subject with a point of view which is quite independent of the subject's "primary process," if only in the sense that it frustrates the pleasure principle by blocking "discharge." As I shall argue later on, it is misleading to interpret the rigidity of this kind of material as "narcissistic," if by that is meant an alleged incapacity to differentiate the "external" world; for the problem seems to be an inability to "fuse" with the object — an abortion of symbolic progression, rather than a regression to "symbolic equation."

The imprecision of the notion of symbolic regression raises the question of its counterpart, sublimation. If symbol, symptom, dream, and defence are all related through a common psychodynamic process, as illustrated in Figure 3, can sublimation escape this metapsychological homology through some final transformation of "instinctual nature" which liberates desire from overdetermination?

Jones's argument in favour of this distinction between symbol and sublimation is the following: if the symbol is constituted essentially through the formation of a psychic equivalence between A (the repressed idea or affect) and B (an item such as a 'snake'), then "further progress can only take place by... a loosening of the ideational links between A and B, and a renunciation of the need of complex A for direct gratification." Sublimation would therefore require a "refinement and modification of the affects investing A, which permits of their becoming attached to non-inhibited, conscious, and socially useful or acceptable ideas and interests"(140-41). But if one asks how this "refinement and modification" actually comes about in psychodynamic terms, the answer always boils down to a "symbolic equation."

According to classical metapsychology, sublimation is a form of psychic discharge, and in this respect it is indistinguishable from the mechanisms of symbolization, symptoms, and dreams. The only difference lies in the terminological distinction between *direct* (symbolic) and *indirect* (sublime) gratification of the instinct. But even the direct unconscious equivalence of the symbol or symptom involves an indirect expression of the repressed complex A, insofar as it is a compromise formation, and the psychical "representative" of the instinct. In other words, from the psychodynamic point of view, the difference between the *sublimation* of A and the *symbol* of A is only a matter of degree. Moreover, the actual mechanism for the sublimation or "indirect gratification" of complex A would have to be some kind of *displacement* of the affect invested in A. But the distinction between this (sublimation) and the attachment of the affect A to the symbol B (symbolic equation) is obscure, since even the most "primitive" symbol requires some deflection of the drive through displacement onto a substitute.[25] The psychodynamic process of sublimation must therefore look something like this [Figure 4]:

Figure 4

Sublimation

defence
$\downarrow$
$\uparrow$ $\rightarrow$　　　　　affect/object(b)...(c)...(d)...

affect/object(a)

In other words, it has the same experientially-contingent and elaborative structure as the mechanisms of symptom-formation and symbolization, as depicted in Figure 3. The suggestion that sublimation still differs from symbols and symptoms and dreams in virtue of its "underlying psychical processes"[26] has never really disposed of the contradiction, since the underlying processes always turn out to be symbolic substitutions.

The inconsistency of the theory of true symbolism is particularly evident in Freud's handling of the Dora case, which was in large measure a construction based on his own (rather than Dora's) free associations to the material she presented.[27] In retrospect, Freud realized that he had overlooked a great deal of what had been going on between himself and Dora (transference), but he did not seem to appreciate the extent to which his own symbolic process (his counter-transference, masked by the assumption that symbols can be decoded without the dreamer's elaboration) had interfered with his perception of Dora's situation, and obstructed her emotional progress.

Nevertheless, the classical theory of symbolism was a significant achievement. If nothing else, it helped to preserve the link between meaning and the body, even at the cost of logical contradiction, at a time when the sociological ego was moving rapidly in the direction of formalism and "upward interpretation." Freud, Jones, and psychoanalysis in general, were trying to maintain the carnal connections by getting the symbol to stand in direct relation to privileged parts of the body (notably the phallus) through the instinctual drive. Unfortunately, the relation they proposed between the instinct and the symbol was a rigid one because metapsychology demanded that instinctual governance be inherently self-referential: the body had to be closed in upon itself and oblivious to difference, i.e., to the object. True symbolism stood for this simple expression of egg-like identity in order to sustain the theory of infantile auto-erotism and primary narcissism.

But the pioneers of psychoanalysis also wanted to show that psychological life could be a development out of this closed system. Jones saw all psychic and civilizational developments as recognitions of difference, and he enshrined this view of progress in the notion of sublimation. As we have seen, however, sublimation is metapsychologically indistinguishable from the formation of symbols. The difference which sublimation is supposed to bring about is already contained in the construction of the "true symbol," because even the true symbol functions as a substitution of the drive — as well as an "equation" or "constant translation" of it. It is, in fact, impossible to think the discharges of the drive without invoking some symbolic displacement onto an object independent of the aim of discharge itself. Thus, the theory of the true symbol serves as an imaginary bridge between a metapsychology of instincts which excludes or marginalizes the object and a depth psychology which interprets nothing else but the vicissitudes of the object in symbolic process.

Freud's metapsychological neglect of the object is analogous to Nietzsche's doctrine of the Will to Power. According to Nietzsche, "Thinking is merely the relation of [the] drives to each other." The world "looked at from inside" is nothing else but the will, and the will "can affect only the will." He described this elemental world as a "pre-form of life" in which "everything still lies contained in a powerful unity before it undergoes ramifications and developments... a kind of instinctive life in which all organic functions are still synthetically intertwined along with self-regulation, assimilation, nourishment, excretion, and metabolism."[20]

The psychoanalytic term for this inchoate state of the Will to Power is "primary narcissism." There are no objects. The world in which there are objects other than the self is a delayed "effect" (to use Nietzsche's term) of the play of drives. One gets into this world through the "symbolic equation," which though identical in content to the objectless "pre-form of life," nevertheless *expresses* it, and thus displaces it. The hungry baby, for example, "hallucinates" gratification of the instinct; and when the hallucination fails, the instinct evolves — eventually into perception. Objects arise, therefore, as derivative phenomena.

The problem with this theory is that it presupposes the difference and the object whose discovery it explains. The symbolic equation requires an experience of something different to be equated, just as the hungry baby's hallucination requires the memory of a gratifying object. One cannot reduce everything to the instinctual drive without reducing everything to symbolization as well. Freud seems to have been quite sensitive to this ambiguity, since he occasionally defined the instinct itself as if it were only a symbolic substitute — "the psychical representative of organic forces."[29]

The Aesthetic Dimension

> [*According to Jones, Rank and Sachs*] *symbolism is a regressive phenomenon... Here it seems to me that a valuable link has been made between symbolism and ecstasy... Some form of artistic ecstasy may be an essential phase in adaptation to reality, since it may mark the creative moment in which new and vital identifications are established.*[30]

The uneasy alliance of mechanical instinctual determinism and organicist expressionism in the classical theory of the symbol provoked many developments in psychoanalytic thought, among them a certain recourse to structural linguistics, as represented by the work of Jacques Lacan and Jacques Derrida, and alternatively, a renewed emphasis on the role of fantasy in psychic life, inspired mainly by Melanie Klein. The structural linguistic approach, which tends to emphasize the arbitrariness of the symbolic relation, would argue that the signifier can never come finally to rest on a determinate referent — a "transcendental signified" — because if it did it would be, in Jones's own terms, a "symbolic equation," or in other words, a psychotic delusion.

It is interesting to note that the structuralist view, particularly in its more radical, deconstructionist form, is the obverse of the classical approach to symbolism. Jones describes the symbolic equation as a "barrier to progress," and defines the development of civilization as "a never-ending series of substitutions, a ceaseless replacement of one idea, interest, capacity or tendency by another" (182). What counts as a barrier for Jones is equally a "metaphysical blindspot" for the structuralists. For both Lacan and Derrida, as for Jones, what is at stake (and at play) in the relation of symbol and instinctual drive (or subhuman force) is essentially a process of "infinite substitution." The structuralist approach suggests, in fact, that there can be no experience of the object except as the effect of the play of signifiers, or in other words, the part object, particularly the phallus.[31] As in Freud and Jones, the symbol is rooted in the quasi-self-referentiality of the instinct. And in the final analysis, the process of endless displacement and substitution which constitutes psychic activity signifies nothing other than the condition of "castration" — or what Derrida calls "dissemination" — which accounts for the separation of signifier and signified, symbol and instinct. For if symbolization and sublimation are opposed, it is not in a strictly evolutionary sense, as Freud and Jones believed, but only to the extent that sublimation, or "desire,"[32] is "always already"

on the move, a breathless *différance* which is forever one displacement
ahead of the instinct and the body.[33]

The Kleinian view differs from this in that it doubts that the psychic
process can begin with a two-term relation, such as mouth-breast, "symbolic equation," or signifier-signified. For Klein, the drive already expresses
an affective relationship with the "external world." This suggests an important shift in orientation, which Klein described in the following manner:

> The hypothesis that a stage extending over several months
> precedes object-relations implies that — except for the libi-
> do attached to the infant's own body — impulses, phan-
> tasies, anxieties, and defences either are not present in him,
> or are not related to an object, that is to say, they would
> operate *in vacuo*. The analysis of very young children has
> taught me that there is no instinctual urge, no anxiety sit-
> uation, no mental process which does not involve objects,
> external or internal; in other words, object-relations are
> the centre of emotional life. Furthermore, love and hatred,
> phantasies, anxieties, and defences are also operative from
> the beginning and are *ab initio* indivisibly linked with
> object-relations.[34]

Klein was interested in psychosis, severely disturbed and even autistic
children, and here she observed the virtual absence of the capacity to symbolize. Her attention shifted to the inhibition of thought and experience
themselves, and she found that symbolization is not only "the foundation
of all phantasy and sublimation but, more than that, it is the basis of the
subject's relation to the outside world and to reality in general."[35] Rather
than being a "barrier to progress" or a metaphysical illusion, the symbolic
process emerges in Klein's work as the generative form of experience.

According to the classical psychoanalytic model, separation from the
object is the condition of viable psychic process. Symbolic expressions
(inevitably expressions or displacements of anxiety about the uncertainty
of the relation to the object) tend to be viewed as signs of malfunction.
The emphasis is on the reality principle, i.e., on mature renunciations (or
what Lacan calls the submission of the subject to the "Symbolic Order").
Pleasure is conceived primarily as a matter of discharge whose success depends on the judicious channeling of the instinct, ultimately by intellect
and social convention. In order not to disturb the equilibrium of this position, classical theory evolved a supplementary hypothesis — that there
is something called a "regression in the service of the ego"[36] — in order
to explain the fact of aesthetic experience as a non-pathological event.

A good reading of Klein makes this model seem too simple. The issue
is not just coming to recognize the separateness of the object — a rudimentary form of which must be assumed to exist from the beginning anyway

— but the unconscious substance of the interrelation with the object world itself: the "internal world." The psyche is not merely an apparatus for discharge, but a passion for the object. What matters is how this passion survives. In order for psychological process to continue, for the imagination to flourish, there must be some measure of possession of the object which does not entail its destruction. This is the essence of the problem of symbolization in Klein. Her work can be interpreted in such a way that the most significant factor is not, as in Freud, whether the reality principle can provide strong enough intellectual guidance for the pleasure principle (to insure its gratification), but rather whether the pleasure principle can sustain enough integrity, given the contingencies of development and the realities of aggression, eventually to introduce some intelligence into reality.

In the classical model, it was the primary process which had definite goals (what Freud called the "aim" of the instinct);[37] the secondary process displaced these goals onto the realistic object world for pragmatic reasons (survival). In the object model, primary process itself seeks the object through the symbol, which is incorporated, projected, invaded, destroyed, fled, mourned, reconstituted, and so on. According to this view, the function of the reality principle is not to reveal the object for the first time (this has already been achieved at the primary process level of symbolization and desire) but to break the spell of the object. The aesthetic substance of the object is experienced by the reality ego as a threat to pragmatic adaptation, an omnipotent projection of the "imaginary" subject, which "in reality" can never have what it wants.

The difference between the two models lies in the interpretation of omnipotent states (magical thinking, symbolic equation). For Freud, omnipotence is an expression of the imperious aim of the instinct (gratification), compared to which the object is secondary, an eventual site for substitutions. For Klein, omnipotence is a "primary" (by no means benign) aesthetic relation to the object itself. This can be interpreted to mean that the devolution of the pleasure principle into the reality principle involves not the rise of the object by means of aim-inhibition, but a kind of pragmatic reduction of aesthetic involvement with the object in favour, precisely, of the aim of the instinct, which is after all real gratification. This view may be seen as complementary to Freud's, a possibility which suggests that the polarity of valences that psychoanalysis has set up (instinct-aim-omnipotence-primary process-symbol *versus* perception-object-reality-secondary process-sublimation) is only an approximation, and sometimes misleading.

The two metapsychological series in fact correspond to Klein's paranoid-schizoid and depressive positions respectively. According to Klein's foremost expositor, Hanna Segal, the symbol emerges in the depressive position:

> The pain of mourning... and the reparative drives devel-
> oped to restore the loved internal and external objects
> [depressive position], are the basis of creativity and subli-
> mation. The infant's... concern for his object modifies his
> instinctual aims and brings about an inhibition of instinc-
> tual drives... Repression takes over from splitting [paranoid-
> schizoid position]...
>   At this point the genesis of symbol formation can be
> seen.[38]

Drawing on Klein, Segal has here modified Freud to the extent that she
has cleared up the artificial classical opposition between symbol and sublimation — but the change is not as clear as it is sometimes made out to
be. Klein established the basis upon which the symbolic function could
be understood generally as the representational and expressive dimension
of developing object relations. Consequently, the symbol no longer needed to be interpreted merely as regression to a primary narcissism qualitatively distinct from symbolizations in the broader, non-psychoanalytic
sense. But this conceptual advance was achieved at the cost of severing
the symbol from primary process and stripping away much of its bawdy
instinctual (erotic and aggressive) content. Under Klein's influence, symbolic process tends to be seen as a reparative defence against the destructive energies of the paranoid-schizoid position.

   This is an ethical interpolation. Segal's distinction between symbolization on the one hand, and psychosomatic manoeuvres such as splitting
on the other, has much clinical, but little metapsychological significance.
In order to get at the aesthetic level of symbolization, the functional hierarchy of the psyche needs to be relativized. If one takes the Kleinian development as the starting point for thinking through the problem of
symbolization, one has to disregard the ethical barrier of the depressive
constellation and retrieve the fragmented, fusional, experiential potentialities of the paranoid-schizoid world. Bion's attempt to recast the Kleinian
"positions" as complementary tendencies in the genesis of thinking was
a step in this direction.[39] The idea that the paranoid and depressive organizations of experience are dialectically related implies the need to deconstruct the underlying opposition between the pleasure principle and the
reality principle as well.[40] If the pleasure principle is to be truly a principle of pleasure, rather than a simple reactive avoidance of the pain imposed
by the reality principle, it must be integrated with Kleinian and post-
Kleinian developments in our understanding of the dynamics of symbolization.

   The argument being developed here is that symbolization is not a *constituent* of psychological process — a signifier or a component instinct
in a system of such elements; it is rather the whole libidinal constitution
of mental life itself: a kind of *"jouissance,"* a passion that links the subject

and the object together in the virtuality of a three-term relationship. There is no psychic process — not even primary process — without the symbol, and no symbolization free of the potential to unravel into the epistemological embarrassment of the aesthetic; and so there is no hope of resolving the enigma of the subject and the object by defining them as *effects* of a relational paradigm (whether through analytic logic or playful signifiers or component instincts) which can be dissolved back into a hypothetically determinate system, such as language or culture or natural force.

Freud wanted to derive the whole object world out of the inbuilt aim of the instinct: hunger would eventually produce the reality principle, and replace hallucinatory gratification (symbolic equations) with perception and reality testing. But infants have been known to imitate facial gestures less than an hour after birth;[41] they probably perceive otherness, in some rudimentary way, before they register hunger. What makes hunger so unbearable for children is that it seems like persecution — which requires an object. There is no rage without symbolic elaboration. The implication of Melanie Klein's work is that symbolization is simply the only means that the human organism has of "having a personality." But if the symbolic inevitably overflows into substances (e.g., the *psychic* experience of hunger), then the aesthetic dimension is probably not, in its essence, the end result, or "highest achievement" of a general process of refinement and sublimation, as the Eurocentric thought of the nineneeth century maintained. The aesthetic, in other words, would not be a product delivered after practical matters have been settled and interests satisfied, but the very material of any kind of life involving "persons" living together, for better or worse, in a "culture."

Nature is not a "scene" where other things, such as values, persons, and cultures take place — it *is* what happens. The psychic reality is that there is no escape from this predicament: values are ineluctable. It is within this context of conceiving the value of a relationship through our capacity to symbolize it that we arrive at basal conceptions of good and bad — what Klein calls splitting. In themselves, however, these conceptions are at first neither ethically nor practically rational, but simply forms of symbolization, the ecstasy and torture of aesthetic flights of symbolized bodily events.

Few dimensions of life make philosophy and sociology more nervous than the aesthetic, because aesthetic states are incorrigible projections of substance. They are threatening, not because they signify a pre-scientific "ground of being" or an "unmoved mover," but because they challenge the coherence of formal systems of relations. Substance is intrinsic to the relation of the subject and the object; it endows biological beings with linked internal worlds, i.e., spheres of virtual experience that cannot be deduced from knowledge of signs and their networks.

Klein's view of the symbol as a 'third term' can be likened to Lacan's thought because the process of symbolization can never embody the "whole" relationship, the whole object, or the whole self, unless one turns the depressive position into a religious absolute, as Klein herself had a tendency to do. When the symbol is circumscribed for structural analysis, it inevitably appears as the mediation of a duality (signifier and signified), the mark of a separation. Like Lacan's phallus (the signifier of signifiers), the symbol becomes the psychic equivalent of the part object, an object of defensive manipulation and control. If the constant displacement of third terms forms the relationship-in-experience, it cannot complete them, and so in a sense Lacan was right to link all symbolization to the theme of castration.

But this interpretation does not, as it claims, reveal the unconscious "structure" of the symbolic process; it adapts the symbol to the quasi-logical requirements of the ego: it is itself a compromise formation. The motif of presence and absence (the phallus, the *fort-da*) is based on the Gestalt model of perception, where the signifier is always a 'figure' against an occluded 'ground.' The sign-phallus is really the "principle of good form": it develops early as a defence (i.e., a symbolization), and defuses the object-experience in order to establish an articulable binary structure. But the unconscious is not "structured like a language"; and the aesthetic imagination cannot be reduced to an opposition between difference and undifferentiation, figure and ground, order versus chaos. What we call creativity is never merely anabolic or negentropic. It is not the "opposite" of disorder, but includes the latter processually. So, Lacan's Jonesian way of relating the Symbolic to the body through the phallus, as the instinctual endpoint of the re-gression and re-petition of signs, is really a kind of secondary revision.

The aesthetic dimension is teeming with unintegrated differences and unrealized objects. We are wary of its fragmentary quality because we imagine substance as a unitary and cohesive thing or force. We think of differences in terms of abstract discriminations (diacritical marks), rather than as psychosomatic intensities. We imagine that unintegration implies dissociation of the senses, that sensory coordination is an acquired ego function. This is why we find it so difficult to accept that an infant can perceive. Our concept of the "whole" is based on the routinization of "higher order" integrations which recombine highly autonomized and specialized perceptual and cognitive functions. From this perspective, it seems implausible that cross-modal experience could be immediate, that substance could be particular, that objects and differences could exist without structure, or that meaning might evolve in the absence of a "ground" upon which it can "stand (or be stood) for."

It is true that the aesthetic dimension is careless — a relaxation of Oedipal-linguistic controls on the symbolic process. But this does not mean that it is a world without objects, a "body without organs,"[42] or a pure expression of the Will to Power. Nor does it entail a naive "equation" to be abandoned in maturity, or a lost totality forever castrated in exchange for "language," or a uniform state of maximum entropy against which creativity and order must perpetually struggle.

Winnicott's reflections on the transitional object touch on the problem of conceptualization which the aesthetic dimension raises.[43] The transitional object (e.g., a teddy bear) involves an experience both of the 'me' and the 'not me'; it is an omnipotent creation that is nevertheless separate from the self, a dimension of the child's environment. It cannot be parsed into discrete, articulated elements (or washed) without losing its meaning. As Marion Milner has shown, the symbol emerges in the 'intermediate' area of "illusion" that subsists as the bodily link between the ambivalent subject and ambiguous object.[44] In terms of sign-logic, this is paradoxical: the psyche cannot exist simply as 'non-object,' nor the object as 'non-subject.' Neither can "refer" to the other. To say that the symbol is a "third term" does not mean that symbolization "mediates"the subject and the object, but rather that the object and the person are, at the level of the imagination, fashioned of "excluded middle": not figure-ground oscillations or *fort-das*, but kinds of "potential space."

Wilfrid Bion's container-contained metaphor highlights the metaphysical issues produced by the logic of the sign.[45] It suggests that the curious ontology of the psyche, the interior integrity — or "internal world" — of the person's objects can be formulated abstractly as the question: how can the container *be* what it contains? This question disgresses from formal juridical and political concepts of the individual or the collective, and shifts the problem of the person onto fundamental aesthetic terrain.[46] Like the paradox of Winnicott's transitional object, the absurdity of the contained container — the symbolically vested person and the enigma of the object — is an effect of discrete, univocal, designator terms. As Winnicott warns, it can sometimes be a mistake to try to resolve such contradictions by recourse to the same kind of "split-off intellectual functioning"[47] that produced them in the first place. To experience being a person — a contained container — as a category mistake is to interpret analytic devices, like logical levels in set theory, as if they were existential imperatives. The ego tends to isolate symbolic fusions as psychotic regressions, and to distinguish them from the 'normal' sign-referent model of communications. This is a useful distinction, but if it is taken too literally, the idea that one is a person (with feelings and thoughts that others can only guess at) becomes, logically, just as psychotic as the claim to be a cockroach or a God. Being a person is like being a child who thinks herself invisible when s/he closes her eyes. Yet the child is right, for when the eyes are shut, one does, in a sense, enter an invisible world.

The orderliness of the ego perspective is not very useful when consideration is given to the way in which thinking itself can become too painful to bear. It may be that the schizoid is not so much wallowing in "fusions" as ill at ease with them, and perhaps reluctant to form symbolic links of any kind.[48] If this view has any merit, then the issue would not be regression to symbolic equations so much as lack of them. The pain of thinking would then appear to be a kind of chronic aesthetic doubt: apprehension about the character of emergent properties and processes, and panic about the "value of the relationship." What does hold together in this way of being tends to be painful and manically sutured, yet also beautiful so long as it can ward off unstructured states in which differences might be experienced and elaborated more freely — or destroyed.

This is a dilemma. Dedifferentiation does not deny differences, but it dissolves the formal structures which control them, and this regressive process is especially threatening to a psyche deprived of "symbolic equations." There is a kind of "ontological" anxiety which is perhaps related in some way to heightened awareness of the unintelligibility of the symbolic being of persons as such. The few links that are established are brittle because they are moral in character and deliberate. Thus, the well-known "symbiotic" desperation, the "object hunger," of schizoid states (so-called "narcissism") would not be merely a question of primitive fusions marked by regressions, symbolic equations, "magical thinking," and so on, but an indication that separation from the object is too literally experienced. At the deepest level, the schizoid may in fact be wary of magical thinking, and refuse to believe that symbolic equations are possible. The internal world becomes a dangerous lie. After all, a container is just a container; and what goes on inside is just the contained: there is no necessary link between them. Everything is just signifier and signified, and relationships are arbitrary (mere cultural conventions); so there does not appear to be much person or object to go round, and there is very little aesthetic substance to be had.

In a discussion of the psychological significance of Paleolithic cave drawings, Arnold Modell has suggested, following Cassirer, that "primitive" art is a form of narcissistic magical thinking, in which the painting on the cave wall, with its spear marks and conformity to the natural contours of the rock, "does not represent a horse, it *is* a horse."[49] This is, of course, the classical *epistemological* judgment of the symbolic. Modell goes on to argue (following Cassirer) that from this fusional state in the primitive mind there emerges by degrees a capacity for "reality testing," so that a "separation begins to take place between the spheres of the objective and subjective, between the world of the I and the world of things..."[50] Such is the reassuring model of step-wise development, from simple to complex, concrete to abstract, chaos to order. But cognitivists like Cassirer and Piaget may be placing too much emphasis on the supposed inability of primitives and infants to perceive the physical separateness of objects. From the point of view of symbolization (as a precondition of psychic process), cognition is not the primary concern. The problem for paleolithic hunters, infants, psychotics, and human beings in general is not how to recognize and distinguish 'objective' reality, but how to exist inside it. Reality-testing in the conventional clinical sense only becomes an issue during psychic breakdown, precisely when the "illusion" will not hold, when there is no intermediate area of experience where 'me' and 'not me' (as Winnicott would say) may flow concurrently. So it is beside the point to smuggle in epistemological assumptions about the factual degree of "separation" that may or may not exist between the 'realm of the I' and 'objective reality' at any time during life or human history.

The psyche is difficult to think about without introducing the principle of the sign into the internal world, as if there were signifiers and signifieds capable of analytic separation into lexicon, syntax, semantics, and pragmatics. The significance of theory lies in the belief that psychosocial existence is based on something definite and logical, and not just an elaboration of vitality affects, sensations, and aesthetic substances. Systematic relational paradigms are indispensable, because the ambivalence of the subject and the ambiguity of the object are incapable of serving as the "foundations" of useful and communicable thought. They demand to be given up, preferably in exchange for degrees of certainty about the structure of their relations. As Bion stated: "It is supposed that a rifle and a penis are similar. But what should be exact is the *relationship* between the particular objects..."[51] The wish to substitute formal relations for substances like "similarity," "otherness" "inside," and so on — the wish to translate bodily metaphors into "signification" — is the drive behind nearly the whole of modern philosophy and the inspiration of the sociological ego.

The reality principle tends to displace the esemplastic power of the infantile body onto something external: if not God, then language or system. Art can be especially reassuring in this respect (even when it is about nothing but death). When we accept the convention that allows art to be "only art," we find it easier to let the omnipotent and aggressive act of symbolization stand, so that it may secretly communicate the illusion that the internal world is real, that it will not fall into pieces. We want to confirm without asserting the vulnerable fantasy that we actually contain and control the nurturing environment that once contained us.

The Attack on Interiority

> The *"blank"* force of dada was very salutary. It told you
> *"don't forget you are not quite so 'blank' as you think
> you are."* — Duchamp[52]

"Modernism" in culture was about the collapse of what E.H. Gombrich called the "schema."[53] The schema was essentially a powerful set of conventions, integrated into an expansive and dynamic civilization, that created a forum for a certain kind of creativity to develop into a more or less continuous tradition — a tradition which, even when it deviated from its own rules, or modified the norms, generally referred back to something that we still call "classical" art and literature. Modernism undermined this cultural method by furnishing a more explicit account in material terms of the insecurity of the classical subject and the indeterminacy of the object. Modernism was very much about the unintelligibility of experience as it was actually felt to occur.

The more recent intellectual response to this insecurity has been christened "post-modernism," a movement which converges at critical points with the sociological ego, and particularly with what has been described as the "structural allegory" (Fekete, 1984). As theory, it is primarily an attempt to erect a conceptual model sufficiently labile to achieve mastery over the enigmas pondered by modernism, and it has done this chiefly through an effort to purify the concepts of relationality. But postmodernism is also an austere apprehension of aesthetic reality — a kind of "anti-aesthetic" — and as such it has, as a cultural movement, yielded uncommonly fertile models of thought. The problem of postmodernism has to do now with the question whether (and more remotely, how) to establish a new 'schema' within which a tradition of creativity can develop in relatively confident circumstances.

There is a link between the all-inclusive relationality of the epistemo-sociological paradigm and the abstract ethos of (post-) modern art, but it is subtler than a mere homology. Through the contradictory gesture of presentation, the contemporary artwork parodies the idea of the system: the subject is concentrated into a theoretical point on the projected grid of the object's attempted embodiment of absence, where the subject may then move about at will. But, in contrast to paradigmatic sociology and epistemology (which always strive for ideological relevance and historical determinacy), this aesthetic erasure of the symbolic is a dramatization of the human scandal of substance, a kind of collective blush of cultural embarrassment. Minimalism, Conceptualism, Earthworks, and Happenings implicitly refer themselves to psychosomatic economies of scale. They are projected body egos, cortical *homunculi*.[54]

The intellectuality of these artforms does not consist in the attempts to represent or signify a concept, but in the work of discovering precise methods of displaying the negative of experience. Whether or not the latter is possible, they ask the question: What is the nonhuman, as conceived through the imagined nonhuman? The postmodern aesthetic stretches the relationality of systems like canvas across every conceivable material until suppressed particularities begin to erupt in the thin, ungeneralizable hyperbole of the artwork. Sticky identifications break out everywhere. Ultimately, the paradigmatic goal of institutionalizing indeterminacy as a controlled effect (the technique of deconstruction) is foiled by the aesthetic gesture itself. The nearer art comes to realizing the dream of a pure, non-referential language, devoid of the otherness of substance and free of the difference of subject and object, the more the annoying incoherence and irrelevance of substance, subject, and object emerge. The idealized synchronic presentations of postmodern art obviate every sublimating response of the cognitive ego; formal relationality is made to congeal into a blank thing that evokes nothing but the incog(n)ito of the symbolic relation itself.

The broad transition from the modernist discovery of experience to the paradigmatic climate of postmodern thought has been documented by Rosalind Krauss in a major study whose title, *Passages in Modern Sculpture*, is the precise metaphor of a unifying theme in modern cultural practice.[55] The "passages" are retrospective glances at experience, views that pass through experience by tracing their own governing idea: the passages themselves. More than any other art form, the convention of sculpture is to "present" an object to a subject, to establish a relation between these unknowns held sufficiently constant, in physical terms, to invite a kind of intrinsic elaboration. Multi-dimensional presentation typifies the modernist problematic, and for this reason, by questioning its own formal conventions, twentieth century sculptural "syntax" provides a succinct and eloquent insight into the grammar of contemporary thought.

The problem that Krauss addresses in *Passages* is the aesthetic recovery of embodied experience. Her argument begins with an exemplary contrast between the dynamic ambivalence of Auguste Rodin's figures and the internally balanced rationality of neoclassical sculptural anatomy. Krauss argues that the modernist impulse is epitomized in Rodin's capacity to seize the opacity of bodily surfaces. "It is this communication between the surface and the anatomical depths that Rodin aborts," explains Krauss, for "we are left with gestures that are unsupported by appeals to... prior experience within ourselves" (Krauss 27). Rodin forged a new perceptual situation, argues Krauss, and "this condition might be called a belief in the manifest intelligibility of *surfaces*... It would mean accepting effects themselves as self-explanatory" (26). The significance of this development, for Krauss, is that the subject-object quandary of modernist culture has induced sculptural practice to challenge the rational models of perception. The aesthetic object, in its ex-centric guises, including collage, construction, mobile, ready-made, and *objet trouvé*, begins to subvert the gravitational centre of intelligibility — the hallucination of an ordered experience radiating from a fixed core of reason — and to deny any cognitive explication of the world through transparent emanations of the object from its imagined depths.

In Krauss's approving view, modern sculpture cuts down the forest of illusions to reveal the *literality of decentered space*. The tactility of Rodin's epochal break with neoclassical idealism sharpens into a kind of optical Occam's Razor that divests the object of all narrative projection and renders it as an encapsulation of its own immediacy, an objective correlative of the privileged moment of encounter with its surface. "Conception arises with experience rather than prior to or apart from it," and "meaning itself surfaces into the world simultaneously with the object" (51). Aesthetic being, in Krauss's marvellous phrase, exists in "the real time of experience, open-ended and specifically incomplete" (114). The "mute opacity," "wholeness," and "self-sufficiency" of the sculptural surface links Rodin's work with Brancusi's seamless forms, Duchamp's objects, and even Jasper Johns's Ballantine Ale Cans (32,106,259). The general trend is "to defeat the idea of a center or focus toward which forms point or build," i.e., futurism, constructivism, organicism, expressionism (250). This leads to the "rejection of an ideal space that exists prior to experience, waiting to be filled, and of a psychological model in which a self exists replete with its meanings prior to contact with its world" (259).

By challenging the idea that the experience of sculpture can retrieve a system of meaning that transcends objects and functions independently of aesthetic relations, Krauss adumbrates that dimension of thought which leads to consideration of the aesthetic substances of the infantile body. With psychoanalysis, she doubts the perspicuity and the rationality of the psyche. Yet Krauss interprets the idea of interiority *per se* as a rationalist myth, and identifies it with consciousness and "transparency" (267). The internal world is portrayed as a "rigid, internal armature," while object-relations are assimilated to a positive, essentially sociological exteriority. Though Krauss recognizes the arational opacity of the object, she insists on the "manifest intelligibility" of surfaces. In her analysis of Rodin's "abortion of anatomical rationality," for example, Krauss does not not discern the immanence of unconscious body imagery, and thus reduces the indeterminacy and non-identity of aesthetic encounter to an ideal point of factual interface between the externalized audience and the manifest sculpture. Experience becomes the disembodiment and exteriorization of the self in a Cartesian (Husserlian) ego, which is "the same entity both for myself and for the person to whom I am speaking" (28):

> We are not a set of private meanings that we can choose or not choose to make public to others. We are the sum of our visible gestures. We are as available to others as to ourselves. Our gestures are themselves formed by the public world, by its conventions, its language, the repertory of its emotions, from which we learn our own (270).

Krauss's intersubjective behaviourism obscures the existential dimension of everything but signs and their graphable cross-connections. Symbolic process is renounced in favour of positive faith that the immediacy of 'observable' relations, the transparency of writing, and the 'manifest intelligibility' of sign and gesture will reveal everything. All uncertainty is dissolved in an ideal discourse of "real space" (53ff), "real time" (62,114), "real" movement (113), "real ambience" (55), "factual reality" (57), "literal space" (51, 114), "the facts of an object's exterior" (266), the "externality of meaning" (266), the "space of reality" (131), and most importantly, a causal, combinatory, "intelligible" model of sign relations governed by the "conventions of public space" (266).

François Rude (1784-1855): *La Marseillaise,* 1833-36.
Arch of Triumph, Paris (Photo, Giraudon)

The doubleness of Krauss's argument emerges in the ambiguity of the sculptural examples themselves. The conventional, public, synchronic, externalizing structure of Rude's *La Marseillaise* on the Arc de Triomphe is interpreted as a model of interiority, on the grounds that interiority is always supposed to signify a "rational core," or Idea preceding real experience. It thus becomes a misleading point of reference throughout the text (11). In contrast, Rodin's tortuous, almost entirely interiorized, bodies are claimed to have a "locus of meaning" that is "external and public" (29). According to Krauss's narrative, this "lodging of meaning on the surface" is said to be epitomized in Rodin's *Balzac,* which is described as "a representation of the subject's will, " the expression of a genius "concentrated into the contracted features of his face" (30-31). The oppositional structure of Krauss's interiority vs. exteriority, Idea vs. experience frame of interpretation also influences her account (for example) of Johns's *Target* as a "flat" representation of pure decentred externality (259-260). Yet this work has an amazing *depth* of contrasting textures. Moreover, its theme is precisely the inner centre of the target, the bull's eye, and the latter's violent relation to the outer boundaries, the sensuous mouths and nostrils of the eye-

Auguste Rodin, *Balzac*

less faces poised behind the target, unable to "see" outward. Few objects comment so brutally on the rationalization of interior spaces.

The basis of Krauss's reading of contemporary sculpture is the view that Duchamp's irreverent eccentricity was a sober study of "impersonal processes" that ensured that the "connection between object and author be wholly arbitrary" (108). By overlooking the mythic, narrative dimension of Duchamp's work (*Fountain*, a central example in *Passages*, is surely an icon of the anality of art and its public exchange), Krauss is able to present it as a formal study in the true forms of experience, an objective exploration of the "conventional source of meaning" (76) in 'literal' space and time. Somehow, the idea of the minimalist object becomes more real and less metaphorical than other objects. The "objective" techniques of "arbitrary," "random," "automated," and "serial" sculptural composition are interpreted as cognitive demystifications, almost as if they were neutral products of the growth of knowledge. The result is a dilution of the implications of Krauss's insight that perception is already symbolization, that "meaning... occurs *within* experience" (27).

The irony of postmodern thought arises from its penchant for desacralization of the object in the name of pure exteriority. Devaluations chase after idealizations. The object reemerges from analysis without substance:

Jasper Johns, *Target with Four Faces*,
Museum of Modern Art, New York.
Gift of Mr. and Mrs. Robert C. Scull

it is nothing but a cross-section of the same network of objective relations
which are alleged to "produce," "position," and "interpellate" the "subject." This neutralized object is the mirror of the sociological ego — a kind
of abstract negation of the Cartesian "I". As experience is diluted into the
literality of decentered space, it can no longer well up inside a body; it
must instead be projected infinitely onto a relational screen. Nowhere is
this view more explicit than in the "anti-aesthetic" account of art. Rosalind
Krauss says of Michael Heizer's enormous earth sculpture in the Arizona
Desert ("Double Negative") that "the only means of experiencing this work
is to be in it, to inhabit it the way we think of ourselves as inhabiting the
space of our bodies" (280). But rather than discovering an internal dimension that escapes the grasp of the ego, we "only stand in one slotted space
and look across to the other." If the work is the body, then the 'I' (for Krauss
identical for subject and object) can exist only as an external, perceptual,
sociological relation to the body.

The experience of both the self and the object becomes a summation
of cogitos, a collection of cognitive relations between parts, each viewed
laboriously through a different 'passage,' and finally brought together in

Robert Morris, *Labyrinth*
Institute of Contemporary Art
University of Pennsylvania
(Photo: Will Brown)

a kind of cogivertigo: in Krauss's book, a labyrinth photographed from on high (285). This "decentering" of the 'I' does not complicate the experience of the interior, but rather eliminates it. No longer perfect, the internal world explodes into the diagram of the relational model. As Krauss explains, "Double Negative" "depicts the intervention of the outer world into the body's internal being, taking up residence there and forming its motivations and meanings" (280). This formula of simultaneous ingression and externalization expresses the essential strategy of the sociological ego.

The Sociological Ego and the Scenic View of Art

> *Art as we know it is bound to disappear shortly... We are witnessing the death throes of the classical art impulse and more than likely the birth of a totally new understanding of the social use of sign systems.* — Jack Burnham[56]

In a text entitled *Art, An Enemy of the People*, the reader will find the following statement: "Art is an historically situated set of social processes and not a basic human orientation."[57] The view that art is "not a basic human orientation" is now well entrenched in schools of Marxist, pragmatist, analytic, behaviourist, semiotic, and neostructuralist thought. It is based on two general kinds of argument. The first is a theory about the conventional nature of meaning, usually drawn from structural linguistics or analytic philosophy. The second is an interpretation of Darwin, Marx, Nietzsche, Freud, or Pavlov designed to assert the "super-structural," "epiphenomenal," or "conditioned" nature of meaning.

The deceleration of art actually has its roots in one of the most promising themes of twentieth-century aesthetics: the reintegration of art and life. Apart from Brecht, Dewey was perhaps the most influential exponent of this idea. Dewey wanted to link aesthetics to 'real' — as opposed to 'ideal' — experience. Unfortunately, his notion of real experience was much too benign to accommodate the realities of symbolic and social processes. The aesthetic was, for Dewey, simply a good, wholesome, and rational thing — a "clarified and intensified development of traits that belong to every normally complete experience."[58]

Although the pragmatist concern with social adaptation continues to inform aesthetic theory, particularly through semiotic and sociological investigations of social and ideological norms, Dewey's practical, middle-American vision of art is now considered idealist. Professional philosophers have replaced it with a more formal approach that is devoted chiefly to discovering a logically indefectible definition of art. The result is that the relationship between art and aesthetic theory has developed in such a way that actual works are now considered as "cases" that aesthetics has to "account for." It is assumed that art is a "class" of "things" possessing "properties" by virtue of which these things have or may become "members" of the "class of art objects." Most of the aesthetic qualities of artworks are eliminated in this way — particularly if they have an overtly psychological or dynamic aspect (like concepts related to "expression"), since it is difficult to ascribe psychological or dynamic properties to a thing in the same way that an object may be described as 'red' or 'triangular.' It follows from this that what distinguishes works of art from other ideological constructs, such as tables of law, is essentially honorific or ascriptive, and from this has emerged a theory of the "artworld" and, in particular, an "institutional" theory of art.[59] The basic tenets of the institutional theory are, according to George Dickie, that a work of art must be an artifact, and that it must have had the status of art conferred on it to be an authorized member of the artworld.

It has been objected that the notion of ascribed status implies competent judges, who must in turn possess a body of knowledge about art, on which members of the artworld could be expected to be more or less expert; in other words, there must be something more to know about art than mere institutional facts.[60] Unfortunately, this criticism is ineffectual, since the point of the institutional theory is to deny that there is anything to know beyond the correct rules and conventions of aesthetic behaviour; indeed, on its account, the only universal criterion would seem to be social authority, which may or may not feel the need to establish an institution of art in the first place. The theory logically assumes no more familiarity with an entity called 'art' on the part of those invested with the ceremonial power to confer art-status than lovers assume of magistrates concerning 'marriage.'

One of the advantages of this approach is that it appears to "let a hundred flowers bloom." Timothy Binkley has argued that "the concept 'work of art'...marks an indexical function in the artworld. To be a piece of art, an item need only be indexed as an artworld by an artist."[61] In contrast to Danto and Dickie, Binkley emphasizes the artist's, rather than the cataloguer's, act of indexing. But the institutional theory would be merely inconsistent (its worst nightmare) if it permitted the ascriptive status of 'artist' to inhere in individuals unindexed by the artwork (children, chimpanzees, cranks, amateurs, and, for a very long time, women).

Another apparent advantage of this kind of aesthetic theory is that it rejects the classical metaphysical theories of "aesthetic attitude" and "aesthetic experience." Dickie's objection to the notion that there is a special aesthetic attitude is that every description of its content (disinterestedness, "psychical distance") can be reduced to the features of ordinary perception. As he points out, all the examples of perceiving something by way of the aesthetic attitude are just examples of paying attention to something, and all the examples of failing to adopt an aesthetic attitude while perceiving a work of art are merely examples of being distracted by something else. This is an effective criticism, so far as it goes, but it only makes sense if one assumes that when we engage with a work of art we know exactly what it is to which we are "paying attention" (or that there is a viable rule that will settle the question). The argument depends on the classical view that both perception and the percept are discrete, unproblematical data. Thus, in objecting to the aesthetic attitude theory, Dickie is actually subscribing to the essence of the theory: the prescription that the aesthetic object be isolated and somehow "perceived" in its purity.

Something like this kind of perceptual decontextualization may be a phase of experience that works of art try to invite in order to enable the play of fantasy. But Dickie agrees with the aesthetic attitude theorists that fantastic symbolic elaboration — described by Eliseo Vivas as "loose, uncontrolled, relaxed day-dreaming, woolgathering rambles, free from contextual control" — constitutes a failure to "attend" to the work of art.[62] The champions of the aesthetic attitude view the intervention of the imagination (or lack of "control") as not adopting an aesthetic attitude, while Dickie calls this having an attitude to something other than the aesthetic object. At bottom, the adversaries have the same attitude: that having an

aesthetic experience is a matter of "paying attention," or of properly directed "perception." Thus, the institutional theory of art is doubly restrictive.
It not only requires that works of art be authorized, but that their boundaries be fixed as parameters for our controlled consumption.

The argument from convention is the sociological ego's first line of
defence, but it rarely appears without a second, the argument from functions, or cause and effect. As our examination of the institutional theory
of art suggests, the view that meaning, behaviour, and value are arbitrary,
because relative to *conventions* of meaning, behaviour and value, is singu-
larly uninformative. However, if the conventions, rules, regularities, and
redundancies of meaning, behaviour, and value can be shown to depend
on some other dimension of the world which is not, in itself, a meaning,
behaviour, or value, then it appears that some kind of knowledge is in the
offing. This is where the functionalist, or infrastructure/superstructure argument, comes in. The characteristic stance of the infrastructure/su-
perstructure model is that functions always have a significance that is, in
the last analysis, more real and more essential. A function is natural in the
sense that it is an impersonal, causal force. Whatever happens to subserve
the function is, on the other hand, a kind of secondary phenomenon: an
effect which is, in consequence, something less real, something metaphorical, or even "merely symbolic."

There are endless variations of this paradigm in the anthropological
disciplines. It does not matter whether the infrastructure represents a fundamental order (deep structure) or a primal chaos (amorphous energy or
force). In either case, the basic assumptions are the same. Reality is two-
tiered: there is always some sort of natural or supraordinate force (or ac-
tivating principle), and some sort of cultural product, effect, or resultant
of forces.[63] The force, or causal structure, is usually thought to be organized in the form of an *economy*, whether of production, adaptation,
interest, libido, or signs. In Marx, and all of liberal thought, the economy
develops; in Freud, and counter-structuralist thought, it fuses and defuses;
in deconstruction, and formalist thought, it differs and defers (sometimes
according to laws of restriction, sometimes according to laws of expansion); and in pragmatism, behaviourism, and social scientific thought generally, it either evolves or conditions or both. In short, the economic
infrastructure is a "material" force that throws up structures of social and
cultural illusion (notably persons and the forms of their relationships, works
of art and aesthetic experiences). Everything that might have to do with
object-relations in the psychoanalytic sense (the nontransparency (or substance) of subjects, objects, and the relations between them) is explained
away as the resultant of forces, or to put this in behavioural terms, as a
"secondary drive" (something learned) or a "dependent variable" (something which could always be substituted or displaced by something else).

The assumption that object-relations are secondary by-products of
primary drives such as hunger or auto-erotism is so deeply rooted in (post-)

modern intellectual culture that even those disciplines that concern themselves with the symbolic process have tended to limit understanding of object relations to the parameters of social constraint and convention. Since language has come to be considered as a system of rules (under the influence of logical positivism, analytic philosophy, and structuralism), it is generally thought that the relations between the infrastructural forces and the superstructural products are mediated by language-like structures: fields of signs, conventions, institutional norms, and regularities.[64] Thus, the individual is held to be "socialized" by language; indeed, the very existence of the 'person' is said to be produced as a linguistic effect — and so language comes to be conceived as a kind of proxy for whatever causal force is acting on society (e.g., Coward & Ellis).

The problem here is not just that the dominant paradigm proliferates exclusively linguistic models of psyche and society; the language models are themselves inadequate representations of what language does (in their neglect of the symbolic annealment of semantic domains). Moreover, the privilege accorded to formal language carries with it the implicit assumption that object relations (the symbolic dimension in which a 'person' exists) have no purchase on the human organism until well into the second year of life, or even the Oedipal period, when language capacity begins to fill out. Infancy is viewed, at best, as a kind of "sensory-motor development" that lays down the schematic basis for the acquisition of linguistic rules and conventions of behaviour, which in turn prime the effect of meaning in the subject. The sociological ego generally discounts the intensity of symbolic interaction, particularly the infant flux of wonderment, violence, and devotion, in which the individual's psychic existence is saturated with the semantic, and social relations consist almost entirely of aesthetic elaborations.

The somewhat schematic disposition of the sociological ego arises also from its characteristic separation of process and product — the very dichotomy that necessitates the hypothesis of a systematic order of cultural effects. When a function is conceived as the logical ontological primary cause, it tends to be a very general kind of thing (e.g., the will to power, differance, desire, production, interest, utility), and such concepts are difficult to link in any specific way to the conventions and structures which they are supposed to be supplying with fuel. In this respect, the base-superstructure argument is rather like the Freud-Jones theory of true symbolism: there are many symbols, but "the number of ideas thus symbolized is very limited indeed" (Jones, 102). Even a theory with a very sophisticated concept of function to supplement its emphasis on conventions cannot, by this means alone, account for the choice of one meaning over another. It may be that, from the point of view of an abstract meta-science, a particular conventional effect is under the remote control of a function; but how the function produces that particular effect is not clear. Either the theory has to find out more about the way the alleged "superstructure" actually works, or else it must resort to yet another relational concept.

This is where the concept of "contingency" has begun to play a role. In general, the term 'contingency' suggests "chance," and this has seemed to provide an answer: a function produces a particular effect by chance. But this formulation is not quite satisfactory, since it leaves the regularized meaning-effect unexplained. By degrees, however, the idea of contingency has evolved from the sense of 'chance' to the connotation of 'cause.' In fact, postmodern theory, inadvertently developing a strategy of conditioning theory, has completely altered the penumbra of the word. Now, when we say that a piece or a type of behaviour is 'contingent' on something else being at 'play,' we seem to be suggesting *why* it happens, while at the same time we leave the impression that something else might very well happen instead. Thus, we have found a way to be determinists and relativists at the same time.

On such an account, the aesthetic can be defined as a *functional* effect, a *contingency*, without being considered a *necessary* effect, since it can always be substituted by another and different effect. One only has to think in terms of shifting fields of presence and absence — or what Foucault calls "discourse." As Barbara Smith explains, there are, in the last analysis, only "verbal artifacts (not necessarily 'works of literature' or even 'texts') and other objects and events (not necessarily 'works of art' or even artifacts) [which] perform... various functions." Moreover, there is not necessarily any specific correlation between these artifacts, objects, and events, and any particular underlying functions, since "the totality of such functions is always distributed over the totality of texts, artifacts, objects and events" in any given culture.[65] Like Dickie's recourse to institutional norms, the emphasis on functionality provides a useful foil to certain kinds of aesthetic theory, such as the theory that the world is a text, or the theory that aesthetic value is, in Smith's felicitous aspersion, "the continuous appreciation of the timeless virtues of a fixed object."[66] Its drawback, however, is that it makes the aesthetic dimension contingent in roughly the way that the world is contingent on the big bang.

Conclusion

And thus, as in all other cases where we use Words without having clear and distinct Ideas, *we talk like Children; who, being questioned, what such a thing is, which they know not, readily give this satisfactory answer, That it is* something; *which in truth signifies no more, when so used, either by Children or Men, but that they know not what... The* Idea *then we have, to which we give the general name Substance, being nothing...* — John Locke[67]

> *Transference... is a universal phenomenon of the human mind... and in fact dominates the whole of each person's relations to the environment.* — Freud[68]

The foregoing reflections surely bring us to the timeless issue of relativism, and to the question of what sorts of things it is useful or possible to be relativistic about. There are certainly good reasons to be relative about particular things, and since particular things, notably particular persons and particular works of art, very often become the most important aspects of our lives, it seems to follow that the capacity to relativize, that is, to contextualize and thereby to identify, is indispensable. We normally expect that an aesthetic experience will be relative to a variety of circumstances. The more we understand the patterns and habits of thought we are likely to bring to the artworld, the richer the aesthetic experience will presumably be. But it would be tedious to rehearse the entire range of factors that may, consciously or unconsciously, influence our experience of art (or anything else). The determination of such details awaits, in every case, the particular, relative experience that we have. In fact, it would seem that the whole point of relativism ought to be that we do not know in advance what to be relativistic about. If we did, we would have to give up relativism, and become determinists. But we cannot predict what properties and relations our encounters with objects will press upon us. We cannot entirely control the symbolic process, or the materials we invest it in.[69] It is in this sense that contingency itself is a significant value, vitally important to art. The interesting question, therefore, is not whether the aesthetic is contingent on something else, as is usually argued, but whether contingency itself is aesthetic and, hence, substantial, as I have attempted to argue in this paper.

There seem, on the other hand, to be some issues about which it would be rather difficult to be consistently relativist without being dogmatic. As Kant originally pointed out, in reply to the empiricists, one cannot be a total relativist about sensory experience. Whether or not we accept the hypothesis of a "manifold of perception," and regardless of whether we are atomists or holists, we know that the world around us is saturated with complex detail, much of it potentially within the range of ordinary sensory perception. Yet we are normally not overwhelmed by this wealth of stimuli. In fact, the evidence is now clear that even neonates have highly organized experiences — no "blooming, buzzing confusion" — and evince a quite remarkable capacity (relative to the traditional assumptions of behavioral and Piagetian psychology) to coordinate the sensory modalities and to select and recognize salient features of the environment, including the mother's eyes, the human voice, the distal properties of objects, three-dimensional space, and a host of other qualities universally considered significant by human adults, but usually felt to depend on conditioning, learning, or the formation of mental schemas and concepts (Locke's "signs").[70]

But even if we were to discount this kind of evidence entirely, the thesis of total cognitive realism would commit us to radically counterintuitive premises. If cognition is initially vacuous, then, in order to answer for the actual degree of consistency in human affairs, the relativists would have to refute themselves by presupposing an extraordinary degree of objective redundancy and immediately obvious structure in the randomly perceived world of objects and events. There would be no other way of explaining how regularities of cognitive structure could be achieved by environmental conditioning alone. But the amount of environmental homogeneity and immediacy required to condition an initially disorganized cognitive apparatus successfully would almost certainly be too great to allow for the amount of epistemological difference we actually tolerate.

It seems much more likely that a goodly but limited dose of inborn structure combines with a certain amount of redundancy in the environment to go quite a long way, while leaving substantial room for intelligent variations in point of view, both about the nature of our organism and its activities, and about events in the physical world. But this rules out *metaphysical* relativism as a viable conceptual stance for thinking about experience. In order to differentiate contingencies, an organism must be organized enough to perceive them; if coherence is entirely conditioned by the environment, then the environment must be much less chaotic, which means that contingency and randomness would bulk far less large in human experience than they do.

It would appear that the dilemmas of relativism will have to be posed in a different way if they are to have any relevance to the discussion of value. The value debate continues to revolve around the schoolmen's distinctions — inherent existents on one side, and contingents on the other. But skepticism about one of these polarities does not entail certainty about the other. As I have tried to show, the problem of persons and substances is incomprehensible when it is mapped onto the ontological hierarchy of essences and accidents. The issue for the discussion of value today is not the epistemological unity or disjunction of fact and value, but the psychic relation between persons (which includes their projections and objectifications). The problems of indeterminacy, contingency, and relativity are not as cognitive as they appear to the sociological ego. They have more to do with "primitive" states of the psychesoma.

Psychoanalysis taught that the position and meaning of the 'I' cannot be fixed; and epistemology that there is no final way of determining the object. *Aesthetics reveals that the relationship between them cannot be formalized either.* The aesthetic undermines paradigms; it is the bane of all attempts at systematic rationalization. The aesthetic attitude is infantile, and value is an infant transference phenomenon. Infants will believe in the reality of the subject and object without knowing the slightest thing about them. But this is not a question of faith: the infant believes because that is the only way to have a thought. The subject has not the foggiest idea who he or she is. But s/he knows that s/he *is* someone, and that the "object" is a revelation. That is the precondition, not only of value, or of the invaluable, but of worthlessness and destruction as well.

People provoke feelings in each other. Someone else's success or happiness or discovery of pleasure or, alternatively, defeat, loss, and pain, make another biological human organism feel excitement, envy, hope, bereavement, and so on. The combinations are endless, varying according to the way and the degree to which the "I" is included in the other's symbolic process, as a radiating aesthetic. Transference and countertransference, weighed down by history like Marx's "brain of the living,"[71] but brimming over in new constellations of present intensity, unfamiliar and full of promise, are the mechanisms of the entire value dimension of existence as we aspire to know it.

A theory of value must be a theory that admits the aesthetic irreducibility of the internal world. There is no other way round. The sociological ego is rooted in the discovery of determinacy and control in the value sphere: history, collective structures and representations, logical systems, pragmatic rationalities, and technological imperatives; but it will probably not get very much further by holding the aesthetic dimension constant, so as to cancel it out of the equation. The "aesthetic attitude" is like our unconscious relation to another person. It is a symbolic equation — magical thinking. This does not entail the assumption that the work of art has the 'properties' of a person. Nor does it commit us to some incredible philosophical error in which we abandon all the most rudimentary distinctions between self and other, animate and inanimate, cause and effect, language and thing. We create or discover the aesthetic object in order to invite ourselves to explore transferences consciously, even deliberately and ritualistically. The experiment will be as foolhardy as we can bear, and we thereby realize our own implausibility, arrogance, violence, vision, passion, and love.

Notes

1. Jacques Derrida, *Marges de la philosophie* (Paris: Editions de Minuit, 1972), p. 392.

2. The missing piece in the psychological puzzle of value is the gap in our understanding of the link between gross bodily events or vitality affects (hunger, thirst, falling, collapsing, exploding, increasing, decreasing, holding together, disintegrating, suddenness, gradualness, stability, precariousness, rising, descending, going in, coming out, being inside, being outside, etc.), and the metaphorization of the self, the object, and the "world" upon which culture is based.

   For discussions and bibliographies on preverbal meaning, see Margaret Bullowa, ed., *Before Speech: The Beginnings of Interpersonal Communication*

(Cambridge: Cambridge University Press, 1979). Interestingly enough, treatments of the problem of metaphor most subversive of the language approach have come from linguists and linguistic philosophers. See Donald Davidson, "What Metaphors Mean," in *Inquiries into Truth and Interpretation* (Oxford: Clarendon Press, 1984), pp. 245-64; and George Lakoff and Mark Johnson, *Metaphors We Live By* (Chicago: University of Chicago Press, 1980).

3. John Locke, *An Essay Concerning Human Understanding*, ed. Peter H. Nidditch (Oxford: Clarendon Press, 1975), p. 298. The subject of "Semiotic" is discussed on p. 720.

4. Milton K. Munitz, *Contemporary Analytic Philosophy* (New York: MacMillan, 1981), pp. 3-31.

5. For example, Jacques Lacan, *The Four Fundamental Concepts of Psychoanalysis*, trans. Alan Sheridan (Harmondsworth: Pelican, 1977), p. 20; *Ecrits*, trans. Alan Sheridan (New York: Norton, 1977), p. 316.

6. Rosalind Coward and John Ellis, *Language and Materialism: Developments in Semiology and the Theory of the Subject* (London: Routledge and Kegan Paul, 1977), p. 93.

7. Locke, *Essay*, p. 296.

8. Cf. Kenneth Burke, *A Grammar of Motives* (Berkeley: University of California Press, 1969), pp. 21-58. The concept of "scene" used in this essay is borrowed from Burke's dramatistic "pentad."

9. Karl Marx and Friedrich Engels, "Manifesto of the Communist Party," in *Basic Writings on Politics and Philosophy*, ed. Lewis S. Feuer (New York: Doubleday, 1959), p. 10.

10. Sigmund Freud (1899), "Screen Memories," in *The Standard Edition of the Complete Psychological Works of Sigmund Freud, 3* (London: Hogarth Press, 1953-74). Further references to Freud will be to the *Standard Edition* (*S.E.*), title, volume, and page.

11. J.J. Gibson, *The Perception of the Visual World* (Boston: Houghton Mifflin, 1950), pp. 210-13.

12. For a provocative account of the "unreality" (or *a*reality) of human objectifications, see Jean Baudrillard, *For a Critique of the Political Economy of the Sign* (St. Louis: Telos Press, 1981), or any of his subsequent works. Baudrillard has reworked the Marx-Lukacs tradition of reification theory (commodity fetishism) with structuralist socio-linguistic categories and Nietzschean ethics to produce a stark Archimidean point of culturalist reflection.

13. Stanley Fish, *Is There a Text in this Class? The Authority of Interpretive Communities* (Cambridge, Mass.: Harvard University Press, 1980), p. 336. See also Richard Rorty, *The Consequences of Pragmatism* (Minneapolis: University of Minnesota Press, 1982).

14. Like Herbert Marcuse, I use the term "aesthetic dimension" to suggest a convergence of the "sensuous" and the "unconscious." Cf. *Eros and Civilization: A Philosophical Inquiry into Freud* (Boston: Beacon, 1955), Chapter 9; and *The Aesthetic Dimension* (Boston: Beacon, 1978).

15. Adrian Stokes, *The Image in Form: Selected Writings of Adrian Stokes*, ed. Richard Wollheim (New York: Harper & Row, 1972), pp. 101ff.

16. Anton Ehrenzweig, *The Hidden Order of Art* (Berkeley: University of California Press, 1967).

17. Freud (1918), "From the History of an Infantile Neurosis," *17*, 79.

18. Freud (1899), "Screen Memories," *3*, 307.

19. Cf. Daniel Stern, *The Interpersonal World of the Infant: A View from Psychoanalysis and Developmental Psychology* (New York: Basic Books, 1985), pp. 37-68.

20. Wilfrid R. Bion, *Elements of Psychoanalysis*, in *Seven Servants* (New York: Jason Aronson, 1977), p. 13.

21. Ernest Jones, "The Theory of Symbolism," in *Papers on Psycho-Analysis* (London: Hogarth, 1948), pp. 87-144. Freud (1915-16), "Introductory Lectures on Psycho-Analysis," *15*, 149-69. Further references to the Jones article will be indicated in the text.

22. Freud (1900), *The Interpretation of Dreams*, *5*, 565f.

23. Freud (1915-16), "Introductory Lectures," *15*, 183.

24. Hanna Segal, "Notes on Symbol Formation," *International Journal of Psycho-Analysis*, *38* (1957), 391.

25. One proposed solution to this problem is the concept of drive "neutralization," which at best is a descriptive term designating the effect of progressive symbolic displacement. Another is the concept of a "conflict-free" sphere of the ego. This term is misleading, since anything can be drawn into conflict. If the term means "psychic functions which are not produced as drive derivatives" (such as colour, form, depth, sound, and texture perception, vocalization, primary attachment, etc.) then it has no bearing on the problem of sublimation.

26. Freud (1910), "Leonardo Da Vinci and a Memory of his Childhood," *11*, 88.

27. Freud (1905), "Fragment of an Analysis of a Case of Hysteria," 7, e.g., 94-111. On Dora's transference, see 112-22.

28. Friedrich Nietzsche, *Beyond Good and Evil: Prelude to a Philosophy of the Future*, trans. Walter Kaufmann (New York: Viking, 1966), #36, pp. 47-48.

29. "We regard instinct as being the concept on the frontier-line between the somatic and the mental, and see in it the psychical representative of organic forces." Freud (1911), *The Case of Schreber*, *12*, 74. On the variations in Freud's definition of 'Trieb,' see Strachey's "Editor's Note" to "Instincts and their Vicissitudes," in Freud (1915), *14*, 111-16.

30. Marion Milner, "The Role of Illusion in Symbol Formation," in *New Directions in Psycho-Analysis*, ed. Melanie Klein, et al. (London: Tavistock, 1955), p. 84.

31. Jacques Lacan, *Ecrits*, 285; 315-16; cf. Jacques Derrida, *La carte postale: de Socrate à Freud et au delà* (Paris: Flammarion, 1980), pp. 441-524.

32. On the interpretation of Lacanian "desire" as an analogue of Freud's concept of sublimation, see my "The Epicenity of the Text: Lacanian Psychoanalysis and Feminist Metatheory," *Borderlines*, 7 (Spring, 1987).

33. Derrida, *La carte postale*, pp. 270-437.

34. Melanie Klein, *Envy and Gratitude & Other Works: 1946-1963* (New York: Delta, 1975), pp. 52-53.

35. Melanie Klein, *Love, Guilt and Reparation & Other Works: 1921-45* (New York: Delta, 1975), p. 221.

36. Ernst Kris, *Psychoanalytic Explorations in Art* (New York: International Universities Press, 1952), p. 177.

37. Freud (1915), "Instincts," *14*, 122.

38. Hanna Segal, *Introduction to the Work of Melanie Klein*, enlarged edition (London: Hogarth Press, 1973), p. 75.

39. Bion, *Elements*, Chapter 9. See also Ehrenzweig's exploration of aesthetic and creative regressions and perceptual dedifferentiation in *Hidden Order*.

40. Cf. Derrida, *La carte postale*, pp. 270-437.

41. Andrew N. Meltzoff and M.K. Moore, "Cognitive Foundations and Social Functions of Imitation and Intermodal Representation in Infancy," in *Neonate Cognition*, ed. Jacques Mehler and Robin Fox (London: Lawrence Eirbaum, 1985), pp. 139-56.

42. Gilles Deleuze and Felix Guattari, *Anti-Oedipus: Capitalism and Schizophrenia*, trans. Robert Hurley, et al. (New York: Viking, 1977).

43. D.W. Winnicott, *Playing and Reality* (Harmondsworth: Pelican, 1971).

44. Milner, "The Role of Illusion."

45. W.R. Bion, *Attention and Interpretation* (London: Tavistock, 1970).

46. The politics of formal and juridical concepts of the person ('individual') in 'Western' cultures have misled many cultural anthropologists to doubt the existence of the 'person' in 'non-Western' cultures, where these politics may be less in evidence, or simply different. The fact that such philosophical, juridical, and political concepts do not reflect the life of the person in Western cultures either is usually overlooked. See, for example, many of the essays in Schweder & LeVine (1984).

47. Winnicott, *Playing*, p. xii.

48. W.R. Bion, *Second Thoughts: Selected Papers on Psycho-Analysis* (New York: Jason Aronson, 1968), Chapters 5 and 8.

49. Arnold Modell, *Object Love and Reality* (New York: International Universities Press, 1968), p. 19.

50. Modell, p. 19; quoted from Ernst Cassirer, *The Philosophy of Symbolic Forms: Volume 2: Mythical Thought*, trans. Ralph Mannheim (New Haven: Yale University Press, 1955), p. 157.

51. Bion, *Attention and Interpretation*, p. 5.

52. Marcel Duchamp, "Painting... at the service of the mind," in *Theories of Modern Art*, ed. Herschel B. Chipp (Berkeley: University of California Press, 1968), p. 394.

53. E.H. Gombrich, *Art and Illusion: A Study in the Psychology of Pictorial Representation* (Princeton: Princeton University Press, 1969), p. 90: "[Pictorial representation] is an end product on a long road through schema and correction. It is not a faithful record of a visual experience but the faithful construction of a relational model."

54. Freud (1923), *The Ego and the Id. 19*, 26.

55. Rosalind Krauss, *Passages in Modern Sculpture* (Cambridge: M.I.T. Press, 1977).

56. Jack Burnham, *The Structure of Art* (New York: Braziller, 1971), pp. 179, 180.

57. Roger L. Taylor, *Art, An Enemy of the People* (Sussex: Harvester Press, 1978), p. 89.

58. John Dewey, *Art as Experience* (New York: Putnam, 1934), p. 46.

59. Arthur C. Danto, "The Artworld," in *Philosophy Looks at the Arts*, ed. Joseph Margolis (Philadelphia: Temple University Press, 1978), pp. 132-44; and George Dickie, *Art and the Aesthetic* (Ithaca: Cornell University Press, 1974).

60. Richard Wollheim, *Art and its Objects*, 2nd ed. (Cambridge: Cambridge University Press, 1980), p. 160-65.

61. Timothy Binkley, "Piece: Contra Aesthetics," in Margolis, p. 37.

62. Eliseo Vivas, "Contextualism Reconsidered," *Journal of Aesthetics and Art Criticism, 18* (1959): 231; quoted in George Dickie, "All Aesthetic Attitude Theories Fail: The Myth of the Aesthetic Attitude," in *Aesthetics: A Critical Anthology*, eds. George Dickie and Richard J. Sclafani (New York: St. Martin's Press, 1977), p. 806.

63. For further reflections on this problem, see my "Carnal Knowledge of Aesthetic States: The Infantile Body, the Sign, and the Postmortemist Condition," *The Canadian Journal of Political and Social Theory, 11*, 1-2 (1987), 90-110.

64. Barbara Herrnstein Smith, "Exchanging Words: On the Economics and Ethics of Verbal Transactions," in *On the Margins of Dicourse: The Relations of Literature to Language* (Chicago: Chicago University Press, 1978), pp. 79-154.

65. Barbara Herrnstein Smith, "Contingencies of Value," in *Canons*, ed. Robert von Hallberg (Chicago: University of Chicago Press, 1984), p. 35. [Originally published in *Critical Inquiry* (Sept., 1983), *10*, 1, 35.]

66. Smith, "Contingencies of Value," p. 30.

67. John Locke, *Essay*, p. 296.

68. Freud (1925), "An Autobiographical Study," *20*, 42.

69. See Marion Milner, *On Not Being Able to Paint* (London: Heinemann, 1957). [First published in 1950 under the pseudonym 'Joanna Field.']

70. For an overview, see T.G.R. Bower, *Development in Infancy*, 2nd. ed. (San Francisco: W.H. Freeman, 1982). Theoretical issues in developmental psychology are also given excellent treatment in George Butterworth, ed., *Infancy*

and Epistemology: An Evaluation of Piaget's Theory (New York: St. Martin's Press, 1982), particularly in the articles by Russel, Costall, Gibson, Meltzoff, Butterworth, and Lock and Brown.

71. Karl Marx, "The Eighteenth Brumaire of Louis Napoleon Bonaparte," in Feuer, p. 320.

3

VAMPIRE VALUE, INFINITIVE ART, AND LITERARY THEORY: A TOPOGRAPHIC MEDITATION

John Fekete

In this paper, I shall broach four major associated topics: a conceptual/historical mapping of some dimensions of value discourse and of pertinent paradigm transformations; the strategic transitional character of the historical commotion of our own time with respect to the social ontology of value; within the horizons of these two, as a case study of particular interest, the conflicted politics of the literary culture with respect to the question of value — in particular, the ambivalence of the emergent reinscription of the latter under the controlling influence of the contingency argument; and finally, but not least in significance, the possibilities, in the postmodern frame of conceptuality, for jointly re-theorizing both aesthetic value and the troublesome issue of aesthetic autonomy at a level of abstraction aligned with the horizons of philosophical anthropology.

For reasons that will become apparent, but particularly because the articulation of a renewed contemporary value discourse is barely emergent, I consider my discussion here a mere prelude to much further work: these are essentially sketchy notes for the agenda of a broad, collaborative research program concerned with probing the parameters, topologies, and social-historical situations of value and valuation. It seems appropriate to offer in advance my consenting sympathies to the reader who would wish for deeper, more comprehensive, more detailed, or politically sharper and more topical reflections; equally, I am hopeful that the sympathetic reader will find here something to value.

•••

1.   Representational models have accustomed us to taking for granted
a picture of value as a derivative or metonymic property, with the result
that we speak routinely of the semantic value of a word, the time value
of a note in music, the quantity of an algebraical term, or the equivalent
that may be substituted for a commodity. Evaluation, accordingly, comes
to be understood as a procedure to provide the comparative measure of
such representations. Value is taken as consubstantial with objects, positions, or relationships, or else contingent on a founding subject; it is
ascribed, assigned, acquired, made, lost, possessed, shared, or exchanged;
in short, it is finite, determinate, and distributed. It is both localized and
warranted by some originary or final authority. In general, it is referred
to (logically speaking) relatively stable and immobile subjects and objects.
     It has become possible in recent years to see the outlines of alternative
conceptions of value that could be developed from the side of contemporary (post-) structural and pragmatist currents of thought. Modern structural models of value, as they rise to prominence, may be poised to effect
a great reversal. On the analogy of genetic indetermination, quantum non-
locality, semiotic play, and cybernetic control, the structural allegory of
value could come to be developed as a move to displace the commodity
conception of value and to advance a picture of value as the regulative
medium of preference, the language whose grammar (the "code" of choosing and its significations) is the discursive form within which the adaptations, transformations, and disciplinings of mankind take place.[1] I say
"could come to be developed," because in practice the structural model
of *value* has been slow to emerge, so widely has the structural reaction
against representationalism taken the form in the past thirty years of a persistent neglect or rejection of value discourse. The rudiments of such a
model are available, however, and will be employed (with some risk) in
the characterizations below.
     On this account, value neither represents nor derives from either the
energetics of personal economies, needs, desires, interests, and the like
or the public system of objectifications and institutions. Value is regulatory of such dynamics and stabilizations, on the cybernetic formula: evaluative systems measure and govern them. In consequence, value is not to
be reduced to an innocent preference between entities separated at a distance. It follows further that the social form of the organization of value
is likewise not to be regarded as ultimately representational: it is not to
be conceptualized in terms of value as property, or the conflict of stable
values, or the hegemony or unequal distribution of values — as though
values were fixed, localized, and delimited by particular agencies, rather
than functions of the force field of value, of the network of strategic evaluations, of the circulation process of a collective system of value relations
and practices.
     Distinct from all specific contents of phenomenal existence, value can
thus be modelled as the medium through which human life is oriented,

mediated, conflicted, adjudicated, sedimented, prolonged, enriched, improved, degraded, threatened, and seduced: in short, processed and substantialized through all of its various options and alternatives, which are themselves value formations. If the last judgment has always been a value judgment, so is the first, the second, and the third; but it is the force field of value that judges, so to speak. In the structural allegory, the medium is the message and the massage, as the brilliant, underrated Marshall McLuhan was the first to say. It effects changes in the scale, pace, or pattern of human affairs.[2] The point is that subject terms and object terms are deconstructed and drawn into the circulating medium of value; or, more precisely, subject and object terms are radiated outward as effects — but, by the same token, precisely *producing*, value-driven effects, and not static representations — from the medium of circulating value where their relationships are constructed, deconstructed, and disseminated, on what we might call a circular, not linear, scale.

The traditional discussion of value has pivoted on two centralized questions: the grounding of values, and their validity. The structural discussion of value, in contrast, properly pivots on the question of politics, on the formation, consolidation, operation, and deconstruction of the strategic and tactical moves of valuation (although in practice, as I shall suggest below, the political is frequently collapsed into the sociological). The classical representational discourse on the "something other" that could be understood as the objective foundation, source, or cause of values in fact divided between two contending currents: positivism and rationalism. The issue over which theoretical battles were fought — still pertinent if differently inscribed — was whether values were derived or constructed, that is, derived from elements of empirical existence (for example, traceable to pleasant or unpleasant feelings), or transempirically constructed by universal reason, in either its synchronist (Kantian) or diachronist (Hegelian) variants.

The classical discourse also divided over the objectivity and scope of the validity of values, as to whether the validity of values was universal and independent of value realization in practice, as the rationalist construction proposed, or whether the validity of values was limited in scope to those individuals, groups, and contexts that considered them valid, and therefore synonymous with *de facto* value judgments, as positivism preferred. The principle that values are always attached to valuations was not the point of contention; the continuity of values (from one context to another, in space or in time) was.[3] In this respect, the continuist positions were challenged by historicist positivism, in an earlier version of the conflict currently replayed in the structural allegory.

The structural model — of which the economic discourse on value is arguably an early form, although its customary variants have been largely representational in character — can be expected to displace these questions from both the positivism of phenomenal experience and the transcendentalism of rationalism. The answer to the positivism, pragmatism, or indeed rationalism of traditional individualist psychology or ontology is readily social-structural: *viz.*, the validity of socially instituted orientational value *categories* must precede value *judgments* if valuations are to be at all possible. But the derivation problem is not thereby resolved, only shifted toward a different configuration. A representational version is possible in this context; it would urge the derivation of value and validity from social structure.

The next move for an alternative conceptualisation, therefore, is to take a pragmatist turn, with the effect of referring value structures through the procedures and processes of the structuration of value orientation to the indefinite totality of the practices of valuation. At this level, every existing entity — objects, relations, actions, institutions, responses, feelings, concepts, functions — can enter into value relations in respect to generalizable choices made, under the guidance of value orientational categories, in concrete situations. Such choices are articulated in some relation to dynamic and interactive systems of both subject and object representations, i.e., both personal configurations of desires, needs, and resources and the regulated social medium of objectified customs and norms. Value, then, is a medium of orientation, a primary, underivable, and universal category of social praxis.[4]

We arrive here at an anthropological or social-ontological level that calls for elaboration. To echo Ágnes Heller, the configuration of value orientational categories that arises co-extensively with the demolition of instincts serves as the primary navigational system for the regulation of the associated life of the human creature.[5] It circulates through the networks of social objectifications that create the heterogeneous spheres of possibility within which the movement of primary categories of the individual's self-production and self-representation, such as "needs" or "desires," is effected. Since even the biological heritage is socially communicated, the formation of historical human characteristics is inconceivable without the circulation of value through the systems of objectification (for example, language, customs, institutions of work and communication) and through the differentiated systems of subjective representations, which together substitute for "instincts" in order to guide, as a kind of "second nature," the options and imperatives in the world of human life, in the reproduction of self, society, species.

But we can say more. Significantly, because in their variable alignments and specific contents and interpretations, according to context, these objectifications and subjectifications can be recreated and reconstituted without limit, and because human nature from the standpoint of behaviour does not unfold from within but can be built in (relative to the possibilities of subjectivization offered by the relations of objectifications), the obverse of value as a *regulative* category of orientation also obtains: orientation is itself a category of value *creation*. This is perhaps Nietzsche's most profound intuition: that in the most comprehensive sense, beyond the valuation of existence itself, "existence is this valuing itself!"[6] Or rather, to be precise, such is the case with *social* existence, conceived without regression to any unitary founding principle (such as the will to power).

The indefinite entirety (or *magma*)[7] of valuing practices that is the world of social praxis is a *magma* of value creation. The body of history, then — including the concatenations of contexts and practices, sedimented and reinforced investments, which account for its continuities — is the perpetual creation and recreation, repetition, differentiation, regulation, dissemination, and circulation of value through all the variegated forms of interaction between objectifications and subjectivizations that emerge and get instituted, sustained, transformed, and re-instituted in the limitless play of polyvalent orientational practices.

It should go without saying that the *magma* of value which, to be sure, allows structuration, regulation, and perspectival interpretation, and which, indeed, is not otherwise concretely available to human experience, is nevertheless not reducible to these except on the basis of a realist *post hoc ergo propter hoc* type of error. Value as a *topos* of social praxis is creative and constitutive *a priori*, and regulative *a posteriori*. One way to characterize the alienation of the modern period would be to point to its moral-behavioural topographic bias: a forgetting of value, i.e., a forgetting of value creation in favour of regulation, a forgetting of the internal relations that articulate the medium of value as a dynamic field of creation and regulation.

In other words, from the standpoint of what one might now describe (with apologies) as a meta-structural pragmatism, value as a creative/regulative medium is a primary and general category of human co-existence. Everything in society bears the imprint of the articulation of options and relationality, fundamental to the constitution and regulation of the social meanings, significations, and functional relations that make and sustain the social world (within which we need to include both private and public arrangements and their transactions). Not everything in society, of course, bears the imprint of acts of *rational* evaluation, of the schematised alignment of the sphere of desires and needs with the spheres of heterogenous objectifications. Nevertheless, in its social-ontological dual form as a constitutive/regulative mediation, the order of value is structurally imbricated with the bio-psychological order of libidinal energization, the cognitive-affective order of predication, and the "real-rational" order of functional instrumentality.

We can say, with reference to this expanded circuit, that it is value that mediates the partial emergence (and consolidation) of man's social second nature from biology. Indeed, on an upbeat narrative construction, the emergence (still largely in the unguaranteed future) of man's third nature from the second — that is, the emergence of relative auto-institution or *auton-*

omy out of relative *automatism* (of both society and personality) — also depends on the circuit of value. By autonomy, I mean here, in part, the emergence of representations of self and society as value-creative (rather than, for example, norm-conformative). The sticky problem of human "agency," for example, can be reconceived within these horizons, as not so much a given as a goal: a problem of how to develop self-producing instrumental representations of the self as self-producer. Art, or the aesthetic dimension, has arguably a particularly important role to play in this regard, as I will emphasize below.

The argument is a probing of history through the concept of value as a category of social metabolism. Its speculative suggestion, put schematically, is that the social circulation of value has been more or less attached and more or less held (in ways that vary historically) by two orders of social objectifications that mediate between the *social* and the subjectivized *personal* orders of value. The first order of objectifications — language, custom, and work (to follow here broadly the analysis of the Budapest School) — can thus be said to group and attach value relations that construct and regulate the *second nature*, so to speak, of humankind, and mediate its differential subjectivization as it is built into individual behaviour. The realm of economic value belongs to this domain. The second order of objectifications, which arises out of the first — for example, philosophy, science, ethics, art — groups and attaches value relations that permit both social and personal distance from the first order objectifications and their boundaries and that therefore institute the horizons of self-conscious value autonomy.

It would be a mistake to conclude from the self-evident fact that the order of value cannot, in effect, be articulated in the absence of functional and symbolic relations that value as a medium of the ways of human living is therefore reducible to such relations, as if it were the representation of some pre-existing functional content or symbolic form. Nor is value a limited independent sphere in *post festum* transaction with the functional and symbolic. These latter are emergent properties of the medium of value, concretizations of the creation and regulation of value wealth. Both the functional and symbolic presuppose a dimension of value, an orientation of desires, needs, and attentions; a capacity of preference, a reference to the irreducible alternativity and creative character of social praxis. If human conventions and practices are examined either as to their valuative elements or their global significance, some operative orientation is always found at both the lower and upper limits — that is, some constitutive value relation that is axiomatic and *a priori*, and situated at a level where it is not derivable from functional and symbolic determinations. This is not to claim that value is some kind of ultimate factor; simply that it is a primary and ineradicable one without which the determinations of the functional and symbolic — their emergence, maintenance, sedimentation, orientation, and transformability — remain unintelligible.[8]

To be sure, posterior valuations are disseminated, sedimented, and elaborated throughout the life of cultures and individuals. Indeed, these posterior valuations make up the experiences and structures of value from which the germinal/genealogical creativity must be reconstructed. If selves and societies constitute value and are constituted by it, in a process *sui generis*, the process is neither totally undetermined nor totally determined — but there is in principle always unlimited mobility, never yet a closure, in relation to the relative intractability of what is always already the historically articulated value wealth of mankind. That the intractable may become independent and despotic is not foreclosed; that it may be volatilised can never be ruled out. This is always a matter of concrete social praxis, and the specific state of the relations that pertain to these options is always a subject for concrete historical/social-ontological interpretation mediated through the concretely available interpretive disciplines.

2.   Three optics on the nature of contemporary ("postmodern") culture may be usefully cited here to contextualize and topicalize these probings into the scene of value, even though they cannot be adequately elucidated below. The first is the characterisation of our times that follows from the work of Michel Foucault: an age dominated by the union of knowledge and power, an age where rationalized micro-normativity, decentered but ineluctable, delivers all aspects of life to a dead power whose circulation is justified in the name of life itself.[9] This is a variant of Durkheim: a picture of hypernormalisation. As an articulation, it also draws on Parsons and structural functionalism, and its ironic popularity as a leftish political perspective to some extent is rooted in the philosophical soil fertilised by the neo-Weberian "iron cage" theorists *par excellence*, the Frankfurt School, in the most pessimistic formulations of their "critical theory" of "total administration." The Foucauldian reversal, unlike the Adornian defence of the particular against the identities of the concept, remains at the level of concept, translating value into discourse and looping the discourse of value into the circuit of power. The former may then be exposed, and by acolytes denounced, as no more than a legitimating mirror of the latter's irreversible functionality.

The second is the picture of our times that follows on a thematisation of the countervailing tendencies. On one hand, it shows the continuing centralization of power in the form of an apparatus of prohibition and an exaggeration of uneven developments around the world, as well as a penetration of certain rational systems, e.g. juridical forms, into everyday life, right down to the quasi-contracturalisation of equity in sexual orgasm. On the other, it shows a relaxation of norms and normative guidance in many areas, and a spreading of disorientation and irrationality through all strata of Western societies.

The third is the periodization of changes in the history of communication on the model of Jean Baudrillard, according to which our age is an era of hyperreal signification, an era of the simulation of simulation, where signification recoils on signification without reference to utility or, for that matter, rational exchange. This becomes then a period of the structural law of value, where sign-values exchange with reference only to the circulating system of signs, in severance from symbolic representation, rational exchange, or utility.[10] Certain aspects of the sign, detached from earlier contexts of symbolic relations, circulate as autonomous and mobile values, capable of entering into a wide range of contexts, and thus endowed with meaning by the active consumer. Signs no longer belong to, mediate, or enter into organic contexts; they float relatively independently of concrete social relations, coded with a genetic programme that can fan out into a near-infinity of variations on its model.

The question of value today is thus posed in a conceptual context marked by such categories as the *hypernormality* of Foucault, the *hyperreality* of Baudrillard, or what we may see as a pervasive *hyperorientation* that follows from the relaxation of normative automatism in a bureaucratic commodity framework. This is an extraordinarily complex and novel topology for which we have no really adequate model, but which likely shares some combination of these features, among others, as tendencies. It may paradoxically be easier today to take some distance from customary compulsions, but also easier to drift — in different ways, styles, and directions — with the particularistic dispositions of the self. More latitude, less self-creating autonomy: perhaps a structurally constrained value contradiction. The everyday circuit of value tends to become a medium of regulative simulation, generative of overdetermined and undersymbolized, simultaneously vacuous and saturated value signs that circulate through pre-coded variations of thought, feelings, and behaviour. Values are broadcast and narrow-cast; the representations comprising variable subject formation tend to oscillate with irregular frequency between social cloning and the theatre of role ritualization, with periodic intervals of uncertainty and schizoid inappropriateness of affect.

It would follow from this account that value relations loosen or lose their symbiotic attachments to objectifications and, correspondingly, to subjectivisations. These investments yield to a sweeping drift, unregulated by either psycho-logic or socio-logic, but only by the general principle of the abstract equivalence and interchangeability of values. This is the equivalence of simulations, the exchange economy of values unanchored to the great classical referents of theology, morality, economy, or polity, of the interplay and circulation of values severed from the traditional solidifying operations of essences, necessities, or objectives, and of the panic search for the lost value horizons that once cemented a more stable world of subjects and objects. Such a system of circulation entails that causes and effects are uncoupled; indeed, the pace and pattern of contiguous association among floating value effects far outstrips the operations of causal or teleological controls. The dominant result seems to be an alogical, unaffective parataxis of recycled value referents, abstracted from originating contexts and circulating *ad libitum* in a rapidly expanding value universe of tactical manipulation, infectious contact.

Baudrillard would call this the ecstasy of panic: "a mode of propagation by contiguity, like contagion, only faster — the ancient principle of metamorphosis, going from one form to another without passing through a system of meaning."[11] In the world of hyperreal sign-values and value-signs, potentialities without end, the medium of value tends to become the frame of a flickering half-life, anemic, parasitic, and thirsty for real bodily fluids. Insubstantial, dematerialized, dead value joins up with insubstantial, disseminated, dead power in a panic passion of resurrection through the fresh blood of desire which, upon commutative transfusion, ever recedes into a bloodless and dis-oriented desire of desire. It is not inappropriate to speak here, at least in tendency, of a culture of vampire value. In intellectual culture, both the nostalgic pursuit of the permanent value referents as regulators and the nihilistic refusals of value discourse altogether may be perhaps characterizable as mimetic replications, incarnations, and effects of the vampirical postmodern displacement of creatively oriented value-life.

Inasmuch as some such historical model of cultural topology is an ineluctable modality of the contemporary scientific mythos,[12] the question of value is not least the question of how to vitalize and invest with significance the new transitional space that is opened beyond the classical subject and object and the corresponding representations of value. The relationship between anthropological and historical horizons is always a matter for concrete, contextualized interpretation, but also a matter for value creation in the social-ontological sense, including the project of creating representations and practices of self, society, and value that can compete successfully with the diminished figurations of life under subjection to vampire value.

3.   A theory of literature and literary evaluation will want to confront the burden of these issues in the light of its own definitions of its history, procedures, and objectives, and, one would want to add, its own sense and choice of its future. The pure arts that emerge late in social history have been the social objectifications that most directly and fully circulate in the symbolic sphere the combined force of radical creative value and radical imaginary — i.e., differentiation, the positing of alternatives, of things that are not, the articulations of *nova*. These are functionaries of the never-yet. In recent years, it has become increasingly clear that the claim of the elite arts to universality of value (and of materials or audiences) must be scaled down, and that the arts must reach new arrangements with both the forms of popular, commercial or mass culture and the practices of critical response, and, in general, with the pluralization of audiences and information processing. It is noteworthy then, as Barbara Herrnstein

Smith has brought to our attention in her admirable agenda-setting article, " Contingencies of Value," that value discussion, especially in the form of literary evaluation, has been exiled from cultural discourse during the past half-century — during a very lively time, in fact, as far as development of non-valuative interpretive models is concerned.

On her account, the positivist tenor of modern institutional literary studies has led to a foregrounding of cognitive and epistemological features of the structure of literature and criticism and a reductive classification of literary evaluation as redundant, irrelevant, vacuous, or damaging. The most prominent statement of such objectivist cognitive preferences was Northrop Frye's polemical attack in *The Anatomy of Criticism* on value judgments. As the position it articulated acquired hegemonic influence, the result was a double exile of value: the inhibition of overt evaluation and evaluative conflict in criticism and neglect of the study of the nature, functions, and dynamics of evaluation in literary theory. What such an antiaxiological position conceals is its attachment to the established literary canon. In other words, the forgetting of value is really the ratification of established evaluative authority, and thus rests on a politics of interpretation, evaluation, and institutionalization that ought itself to be an object of investigation.

The literary politics of a counter-position, therefore, would be partly distributive: they would draw attention to the claims of value made on behalf of non-canonical works and non-canonical audiences. But more broadly, they would be pragmatic and dynamizing: the central emphasis would fall on the radical *contingency* of all value as the product of the dynamics of an economic system, i.e. of dynamic transactions under particular conditions between the interdependent, mutually defining, and mutable economies of the subject-self and the world of object-relations.[13] As a consequence, value would be seen to be, firstly, subject-relative, and differentially subject-variable, according to such factors as the diversity, stability, and conditionability of personal economies in the pertinent respects. Secondly, the continuity of value could be seen not as non-contingency, but rather as a function of a co-incidence of the contingencies that govern preferences and expectations, a co-incidence of personal and social transactional contexts and their dynamics. The counter-position calls, therefore, for an accounting in terms of the social and political mechanisms by which such co-incidences and, consequently, aesthetic value, are produced. This is to point to the domain of the cultural reproduction of value, and to highlight the role of institutions — in this case, primarily the literary academy — in ensuring the continuity of mutually defining canonical works, functions, and audiences.

"Literature" and all its sub-categories can thus be recognized as value-terms that clarify and endorse the performance of certain desired/desirable functions.[14] The reproduction of such value terms can then be approached in detail by accounting for the contextual organization of the contingencies that govern them. The net result is to set an agenda for literary theory: to clarify the concepts of literary value and evaluation in relation to a general theory of value; to explore the dynamics of literary value and evaluation in relation to all other factors in constituting "literature"; and to account for those dynamics in relation to a general understanding of human culture and behaviour.[15] In short, the literary institution is invited to reorganize literary studies as a result of a recognition that literary evaluation is "a complex set of social and cultural activities central to the very nature of literature,"[16] and, indeed, as a result of a recognition that the value of the accounts that would follow would depend on their contingent utility to all those who had an interest in them and would be shaped by those interests.

It follows that I would wish to endorse the broad outlines and the basic principles of such a research program. I would like, however, to raise some *caveats* that might contribute to the elaboration of such a program. I confess my belief that the contingency argument is at its strongest when it takes as its opposition a variety of realist, supernaturalist, essentialist, and transcendentalist assumptions that reduce multiplicity, inhibit change, and foreclose value conflict. On the other hand, it seems to me that it is less compelling in some other respects. Anticipating here my argument in the next section, the question of aesthetic value touches on the possibilities of the human community to such an extent that it would be unwise to risk surrendering it entirely to descriptive behavioural accounts relativised in a sociologistic frame.

Value, as I have argued, cannot be derived from desire, need, or interest, because it is the medium of the concretization and measure of these categories of the individual, and as primary. Moreover, the problem writ large, the cultural reproduction of value, also cannot be accounted for by the institutional formation of desire, for at the level of institutional orientation too, value is already on the scene. Value orientation, as an activity of the total body and personality, individual and societal, perhaps especially in the aesthetic dimension, as Charles Levin argues in this volume, is *a priori* and axiomatic, although its application through actual posterior valuations is contingent.

It is increasingly commonplace in the current climate of literary discussion to oppose claims for the universality and objectivity of interpretation or evaluation by the claim that these are context-bound contingencies, operating under the authority of institutional direction. Let me not be misunderstood here. I agree that the context argument moves us onto the right course, as against both transcendent universality (here differentiated and localized) and interminable interpretive dissemination (here provisionally terminated and stabilized). But, at the same time, it should not be overlooked that, beyond any set of context-derived evaluations that halt interpretive dissemination, there is always a value surplus, an underived structural excess that mediates the adjudication of the *comparative* force of those contextual constraints pertinent to interpretation and those pertinent to other activities. However far contextuality is regressed, it will be found that value cannot be empirically or structurally derived without remainder.

By the gambit of recourse to a sociology of knowledge, literary theorists repeat some of the classic moves in the attempts of Pyrrhonian skepticism simultaneously to refuse both essentialist knowledge claims and also charges of idiosyncratic arbitrariness, that is, the two heresies of non-contingency. Hume, for instance, insisted that epistemological skepticism, which was irrefutable, did not entail psychological skepticism (suspension of judgment) in practical matters.[17] Pragmatic judgments (to which class all literary evaluation tends today to be assigned) were seen as warranted by nature. If, today, we read "nature" as our second nature, the realm of customary norms, and take its authority to be externalized in a literary institution in order to be re-internalized, then, on one side, the options of professional pluralism are reinforced against the universalist dogmatism of objective interpretation, and, on the other side, the dangers of interpretive plurality are tamed in the consolations of a context-bound contingency that delimits randomness. The strategic move is thus deployed on two fronts: to refute universalism and to regulate skepticism. It is a strong move in the framework of a pervasive cold war in the academy over the Western knowledge project — a war between forces positing hypostatized beliefs to support the knowledge project and forces seeming to posit prophylactic anti-beliefs to pre-empt the knowledge project.

Several practical problems remain troublesome, however, for the contingency argument. It is difficult to stipulate the jurisdictional scope and competence of the institutional authorities, themselves hard to delimit. A *given* context in this sense is always too large and too small to fix valuation: too small, in that the range of potential and real contextual transactions is greater than the stipulated interaction actually budgeted for (so that the circulation of value escapes the historicist and positivist entrapment); and too large, in that an institutional context is coextensive with the subjects who are endowed with the collective power to alter the rules that the context would impose (so that, at this level, context slides over from partial *explanans* to *explanandum*,[18] and value escapes the structuralist entrapment). Both of these problems are versions of the problem of *the relevant context*, which is, in our terms, a problem of value. It arises from the dual character of value as both *a priori* and *a posteriori*. A pragmatist move to resolve this tension at the purely formal level of relational logic is no better than the rationalist move to resolve it in transcendentalism or an anti-rationalist move to resolve it in nihilism. It is possible and preferable to say that this tension can be embraced as a substantive tension and lived fruitfully.

The point is that the model of an institutional context through which evaluative acts and the normativity of rules and procedures coincide, that is, the model of a unity of rule, situation, and mode of action, is more than just a critique of a subjectivism or of an objectivism of value. It is a particular model that gives priority to the derivation and regulation of value over the creation of value. Canon formation, the selective tradition that effects the consolidation of value, and the social-political mechanisms that support and sustain the selective tradition, form a network of regulative processes that govern the contingent applications of value in acts of valuation. If value is reduced to the contingencies of evaluation, if it is said in that context that evaluations on their own create value, if value is identified with practised value, then the radical of orientation, its *a priori* creativity, is lost to investigation. If the creativity of literature and the arts is to be highly regarded, particularly as having a relatively independent bearing on the circuit of regulated value — that is, as creating/evoking dynamic value articulations to bring into transaction with what is otherwise in play — then a consideration of literary value solely within the optic of repetition and substitution is problematical.

It would seem, among other considerations, that the interpretive/evaluative model of consumer sovereignty might well be revised or supplemented with due regard for what it is that artists do as producers and texts do as objectifications or objectified practices. There is always a danger when analogies are turned into identities, when difference is subsumed by repetition. Artists are more and other than first readers and evaluators of the texts; texts are more and other than contingencies of reading and evaluation; and professional interpreters and evaluators are more and other than variants of amateur readers and evaluators. None of this is something that the contingency argument can't handle in principle. On the contrary. But these distinctions open up to the farthest reaches of literary theory and pose real challenges to the current state of theoretical attention and orientation. In the simplest sense, the asymmetry between artists (as producers) and readers (as consumers) — an asymmetry as to their conditions of possibility, skills, and responsibilities — makes a difference for a theory of value. In the broadest sense, the circulation of value through the networks that define literature engages writers, texts, and readers in different capacities.

This is not to argue in any simple sense that writers produce value and meaning. A theoretical account of the aesthetic functions developed in literary production would be possible, but would not offer sufficient conditions for valuation. These functions still need to be socially validated and realised, and, as social aesthetic value, may amount to more, or less, and probably always other, than their hypothetical measure prior to the finitudes of practical response. The truth is that aesthetic value and meaning live only in the responsive reception of art;[19] the meaning and value of art is the history of its reception, particularly as the anticipated conditions of the responses to art become formative principles in its composition.

What is nonetheless called for is a recognition that the necessary conditions (the selection of utilities, and the criteria, rules, and procedures of reception) on which (the realisation, the identity, and the very intelligibility and experiencability of) aesthetic values, meanings, and texts are contingent are not the sufficient conditions for the *existence* of value, meaning, and texts. At another level, it is aesthetic value and meaning that give themselves procedures of evaluation and interpretation, because it is only in and by the latter that they exist and endure. These perform not only the task of regulating the utility of art as a function in the world. They also satisfy the aesthetic demand of the world of art that it should be meditated on, interpreted, and valued. Without engaging the problems of (mis)-alignment that these considerations suggest, the current crisis of the elite arts relative to their earlier situations can hardly be given a satisfactory formulation.

The question here, again, is the question of initiative and innovation, the question of value creation. The neglect of the artist's side of things, and of its objectivation within the frame of relations among objectifications, amounts to a structuralist prejudice, first nurtured in the anti-subjectivist cradle of the New Criticism; it amounts to a neglect of value creativity in favour of value regulation. In effect, one difficulty in coming to terms with this question from the currently prominent standpoint of consumer sovereignty alone rests on a difficulty in recognizing the differential regulative force of the literary institution as it bears on different nodal points in the circuit of literary exchange.

Specifically, the regulation of the distribution and reception of literature is arguably far more powerfully instituted than would seem to be the regulation of literary creation.[20] As a general consequence, a theory of literature and literary value cannot be narrowly identified with a theory of evaluation from the perspective of reception; that is, a theory of literature must be more and other than a theory of literary criticism, if it wants to take in the entire circuit of literary value. To take up the question of the relatively less repetitive, less impersonal, less rule-bound aesthetic practices of creative writing exclusively from the side of the relatively more institutionalized contingencies of reader response amounts to abdication from the opportunity to engage with one of the most prominently available instances of the creative will to value and the emergencies of contingency (with respect to value, symbol, personality).

4.   The tendency of the contingency argument — of modern historicizing arguments generally — is not only to take account of the mutability of aesthetic tastes, technologies, and valuations but also, unnecessarily, to abstract from the larger contingencies of art, whose own value norms (not just their more immediately contingent application) are called into question. Aesthetic history has recently tended to be transvalued as a function of other discourses, as cultural history, cultural sociology, the history of

feelings, form tendencies or ideology, and so forth. Two hundred years of post-Enlightenment debates about art have circled around the question of whether art, inescapably a value category, was an independent value-form or a contingent value-function, that is, whether it was discontinuous or continuous with everyday utilities. The two poles of this argument, including their interpretations of art history, have tended to be grouped around demands for the emancipation of art as a created "other world" (objectively or pluralistically recreated and recreatable in reception) versus demands from avant-garde or conservative quarters (Benjamin or Gadamer) for the retraction of aesthetic emancipation and universality in favour of "this-worldly" (everyday) functions.[21]

The study of literary value has been inexorably involved with the autonomy discourse and the question about the possibility of universal validity in a complex, articulated, historical world. (Today, the question of even extensive or fairly stable, never mind universal, validity remains in dispute. It is worth noting that the larger contingency model of value is not *ipso facto* a termination of this dispute, in so far as the admission of co-incidencies of contingency allows for universal validity in principle. How such contingencies then play themselves out in practice and to what foundations they are referred is another matter. Desire, for example, cannot be the basis of universal validity because *the* desire of culture or of mankind, or *the* desired or desirable function, do not and cannot exist, and the variable valorizations of desire are not derived from some intrinsic, canonical signification of desire.)

In the dispute over utility we reach a critical crux of the contingency argument. As with the context-related boundary questions discussed above, so here with the topographic classification of value, *caveats* would seem to be in order. The argument arrives at a crossroads, where either it confronts the substantive problems in its path, even if this means slowing down the rush to theoretical elegance, or else it selects an increasingly formal trajectory. The latter option will greatly expand its logical reach, but at the expense perhaps of correspondingly reducing its grasp. The functional or behavioural model of value summed up in the notion of use value can be stretched — as Barbara Smith, in this volume, does brilliantly and persuasively, through the conception of economy, and a Heraclitean dynamic of transactions between subject-economies relative to the functions performed by entities in relation to them — so as to colonize the entire territory of valuation in the form of a unitary topology, albeit with multiple dimensionality (i.e., utility or profit as the sole *mode* of value, however dispersed through heterogeneous articulations).

It would seem to me useful to ensure here that the formulation of value does not become primarily terminological, encapsulating linguistically the unfalsifiable logical congruence constructed between "utility" (as redefined, away from narrow instrumentality) and "value" *per se*, but losing significance and explanatory power. The victories against transcendentalist notions of value could then become Pyrrhic victories, won at too high a price. Surely other moves are available which, while forfeiting the power of the minimalist closure around the profit/loss calculus of value, instead, and among other things, may be able to come closer to valuing the historical struggles fought to achieve, and the cultural advances objectified in, the differentiation and relative autonomization of such spheres of value as, say, the aesthetic or the religious, not to mention the economic proper. The problematic sides of such differentiation are obviously also of interest, and need not detract from the real cultural attraction of a polymodal model for value theory.

It may be that the problem could come into sharper focus if it were not merely value that appeared as a contingent instrumentality but if the personal economy within which evaluations occurred were itself to be seen — as Jonathan Bordo argues in a different context[22] — as an instrumental representation, that is, the subject as an instrumental representation of *Dasein*. Perhaps then one could inquire more fully into the large "hows" and "whys" of the emergence into the world of different instrumental representations of the self and its "economy" and differentiated modalities of value that have exercised variable attraction for, and power over, such pictures of subjectivity.

A related problem, with particular reference to the value domains of the humanities, is that the strong version of the contingency formalism, by filtering research attention predominantly toward behavioural and institutional parameters, may advance the process of conceding these value domains to the positivist social sciences. The construction of an economic simulation model and the programmatic deployment of economic metaphors for the reinscription of humanistic valuation run the risk of subverting these spheres of value (including the literary culture) to an extent that may be more disabling than can be repaired by the cognitive yield from a program so organized.

The point is really about theory as an intervention, particularly where its ethos of non-normative description commits it, in practice, to adducing masses of data from a base of empirically given valuations and existing, practised structures of desires, needs, and so forth. It is difficult to see when the strong version, on its own — given its imperial reach and its functionalist satisfaction (in principle if not in practice) with the sense that the order of the world is conducted (at least by each subject) for the best, or, more precisely, and in a more pragmatic-technical formula, at least according to the best we can do, as far as we know — will come to theorize, for instance, the pervasiveness of ill-conceived needs, ill-informed desires, disfunctional behaviours, and one-dimensional valuations — in short, a world in disarray, disorder, and disorientation.

It is not my intention here, or anywhere in this article, to try to invalidate the contingency thesis. In fact, I am broadly supportive of its critical cutting-edge, provided that this can be introduced practically into the in-

terventions that are built around it. Particularly within a research program
that would renew the discourse of value from a vantage point in the critical humanities with their civilizing mission, a contingency-oriented analysis should expect to be called on to face up squarely to the dangers in
accepting, at least in its style of analysis and attentiveness, the givenness
of valuations and contingencies, and to account for its approach to the
slippery slope that leads down from there to the perhaps (unwitting) valori-
sation of such givenness, even as this latter is (perhaps unwittingly) endowed with the attraction and power that our culture has long reserved
for fatality: in this case, the constraints on desire, valuation, and behaviour
by the parameters of authorized possibility. Under the pressure of such
dilemmas, I suppose that I want to remember both faces of the concept
of contingency: that is, that the concept refers not only to localized constraints, exercising (provisionally) stabilised authority, but also, and as a
premise of that reference, that its object is a social ontology of alternativity.

To turn more directly now to literary or aesthetic value, I would suggest that there is value in aiming for a model that correlates aesthetic autonomy and functionality. But this would not then be a function continuous
with everyday utilities; aesthetic value would not be regarded as continuous with everyday values. I am not persuaded that the attempt to differentiate aesthetic value from all forms of particular utility, whether serving
lower or higher ends, "is, in effect, to define it out of existence," on the
grounds that "when all such particular utilities, interests and sources of
value have been subtracted, nothing remains."[23] Nor am I convinced that
the only direction of departure from the biases of everyday social utilities
is towards some value-free sources of aesthetic value (as in the Kantian tradition), which could arguably be reducible finally to infra-social, "biological utility and/or survival value."[24] On the contrary, it can be suggested
that aesthetic value is a different order of value from everyday use-value,
and that if it can be described as a utility, it is a different order of utility
from the particular pragmatic functions. I believe that the arts grow out
of everyday life and maintain an active relationship, so that I would wish
not to be misunderstood as proposing a radical discontinuity. On the other
hand, I have to resist the sway of a radical continuity thesis, in order to
create conceptual space for a significant historical role for the relatively
autonomized arts. Put differently, their independent anthropological contribution is premised on their differences from, not only the contents, but
also the modes of normativity, as I shall sketch below.

In other words, I am arguing that aesthetic value is not a consequence
of some *particular* everyday interest, nor even a utility *sui generis* within
the same continuum as the particular everyday sources of interest and value.
Instead, aesthetic value may be intelligible as the name for a significant
reflexivity of value: aesthetic value may be described as a force-field of
value most prominently polarized around a special type of objectification
(art) whose dynamics permit and demand the recoiling of value upon it-

self. Art may therefore be regarded as a site of a reflexive organisation of perceptual, rational, affective, and imaginary elements, all in terms of value. It is saturated with particular values, perspectivally coded and articulated, constructed, deconstructed, and disseminated. This is its quasi-representational, quasi-historical dimension. But it is more, in a sense, related to recent views of art as an advertiser of its own fictionality. Aesthetic value thus also rests on the subordination of symbolic and value saturation to a mode of organization that I would call, on a grammatical analogy, the infinitive mode. This is its quasi-structural, quasi-anthropological dimension.

Heidegger noted that the infinitive was a late form in the order of linguistic development (as we may remark that autonomous art is a late form of the aesthetic dimension). It points by contrast to the earlier verbal forms in the *modus finitus*, a mode of limitation and determination of verbal signification, referring to a class of words that articulate taking a position, inclining, achieving a limit, a *telos* (holding-in-the-end), a fulfillment, a form — in short, a presence. The *modus infinitivus* is the mode of unlimitedness and indeterminateness in the manner in which a verb accomplishes and indicates its significative function and direction; meaning is drawn out and abstracted from all the particular relationships.[25] The infinitive form need not be seen as naming something *essential* that underlies all the inflections of the verb; it can be regarded as a late form that emerges to abstract from the *presence* of inflected forms, to deconstruct their fixation in permanence, to take distance (as a reservoir of possibilities) from particular verbal values.

In this respect, of course, it has a contingent situation within the frame of human practices. I take it that the main rival theories of art, based on other grammatical analogies, and thus representing art, for instance, in the indicative mode (e.g., as realism, mimesis, defamiliarization) or in the subjunctive mode (e.g., as utopian, transcendent, subversive), can be accommodated as prominent inflections that are allowed by the infinitive mode but do not exhaust it. The value language of art can draw all entities into its valorizing orbit, its perspectival codes, only to be surpassed in the infinitive which institutes a strategic orientation toward all particular values: it enables the creation of a transitional space[26] in which subject, object, and their value relations can be conjointly reexplored and in which particular values can be autonomously reinstituted.

I suspect that an entire tradition of value discourse — from Schiller's endorsement of the aesthetic disposition as the restoration of self-determination against one-sided compulsions in feeling or thought, through Eliot's impersonal medium and Richards' synaesthetic equilibrium preserving the free play of all impulses, to Ransom's irrelevancies of aesthetic texture, Wellek's and Warren's structure of norms, and McLuhan's aesthetic suspension of judgment as a navigating device — is pertinent to this problem-area and should be reviewed to identify the epistemological and axiological strategies that differentiate the formulations. Some of these will turn out to be strategically more helpful than others; and most of them are problematical in one respect or another. But all of them, including Coleridge's "willing suspension of disbelief," can be read as partial contributions to an emerging paradigm of aesthetic value (and autonomy) which can be reconceptualised but need not be abandoned.

I would add, however, that the aesthetic reflexivity of value is not a matter of regulating the play of rival particularities and compulsions. Rather, the evaluation of evaluation that art offers to reception, its specific autonomy in regard to particular values, is the creation of an emerging (and thus contingent) orientation that bears an anthropological novelty. As the infinitive mode presses back the limits of perceptual, rational, and imaginary experience, what is created is a model of autonomy, of autonomous orientation to particular utilities and conventions, of a valued distance from the particular practised values, dispositions of valuation, and the automatism of individual particularities and social customs. Speculatively speaking, the concepts of the autonomy of individuals and the auto-institution of society are modelled, among other things, on the autonomy of art; art creates this value orientation as part of a system of second-order objectifications whose function is to mediate the emergence of self and society from the automation of "second nature" to the autonomy of "third nature."

If art is seen as an orientational objectification, pressing back the limits of perceptual, rational, affective, and imaginary experience, and as an order of relations, orienting to autonomy in contrast to the automatism of individual particularities and social customs, then this autonomy can be regarded as not referring primarily to value-utility at the level of individual appropriation, not even to the utility of autonomy as a value content, but referring rather to other systems of social value and establishing an order of relations to these. At this level, the aesthetic can be understood to be engaged with economies of every kind, but to be as much apart from them as it is part of them. This order of autonomous relations can be made intelligible as a universal anthropological horizon of human life: it is a mode of evoking the human as a problem for us. It challenges the instrumental subject of modern culture and, through it, also addresses the whole being. Not every being will respond. Yet it is no more and no less than autonomously posing and responding to the question of the relation between what I have been calling the second and third nature in the construction of the human. Every work of art as a value relation creates *de novo* both its own codes and its own mode of evocation of a generative transitional space into which the codes are displaced.

Aesthetic value is thus arguably a set of orientation relations, an operative value field, that exists *relatively* independently of actual valuations: rather, it plays a role in the choice and organization of the latter, and generally in the organization of human options and behaviours. It is not the sum of interpretations or evaluations, although it allows them to be interpretations and evaluations of art. Curiously, no particular interpretation or evaluation can take hold of aesthetic value, although their plurality confirms the value. It is graspable only by way of interpretation and evaluation, but it is, beyond these, their condition of possibility, a value that lies not in the register of epistemology and psychology, but in the register of social ontology. It is given to understanding in the form of its consequences — not merely the transvaluation or dissemination of its codes, but the transposition of the transitional space that is created.

To be sure, the contexts of response will regulate the larger efficacy; and, to be sure, many responses, much of the time, will be guided by particular interests. As a result of its value saturation and its diverse possibilities for evocation, art has much to offer to satisfy particular utilities. But these do not sum up, in principle, to aesthetic value, even if their sum were knowable. Aesthetic value is a matter of aesthetic competence; but it is not a question here of fitting ideal readers to idealized texts. Aesthetic competence is distributed unevenly from a sociological point of view, but not from a philosophical perspective. Although art cannot guarantee its own reception (sociologically, interpretively, affectively or politically) any more than any objectification, and although the contemporary democratization of response and its contexts poses entirely new sets of questions, nevertheless autonomy is an objective possibility for every individual, and always has been.

I don't mean by autonomy, of course, any transcendence or abstraction from interests, particulars or contingent situations. I mean, rather, a mode of orientation and organisation through their economies. How much the regulative institutions constrain, impede, or enable is always a matter of concrete historical analysis. But art is a human organ of a possibility, and practices it as a value wherever access is not blocked. Aesthetic validity thus has a peculiar kind of universal scope, as an emergent invitation on the scene of value, although its validity is also provisional and local, and tested, falsified, and reconfirmed ever anew in the historical process and according to historical contingencies.

The perspectival orientations with which art saturates its mode of infinitude can be regarded, then, not as expressions of sectoral interests solely, but as paradigmatic offerings from such sectors to the common store of value, as both creations of and struggles for participation in what we take to be the pluralistic universe of aesthetic value autonomy, whose final validation remains a permanently open riddle of history. The tendency of a culture of vampire value to decontextualize, detextualize, and reabsorb aesthetic value into the continuity of everyday circulation is a particular postmodern way of answering and refashioning that riddle, or, in a different idiom, of deconstructing and reinscribing it. Of course, we are all at stake, and it is, finally, our bodies and our lives, and our futures, on which the inscription is being carved. For the moment, I will conclude as profes-

sionally as I began: my wish here has been only to contribute some preliminary considerations toward a research agenda and a discourse on value.

Notes

In conceiving and writing this paper — a short version of which was presented
at the Modern Language Association Meetings, New York, 1983 — I have been most
directly and broadly stimulated and provoked, as far as I am aware, by Barbara
Smith's "Contingencies of Value" (*Critical Inquiry* 10.1, September 1983, 1-35),
and by the work of Cornelius Castoriadis (especially *L'Institution imaginaire de
la société*, Paris: Seuil, 1975); Jean Baudrillard (especially *The Mirror of Production*,
St. Louis: Telos Press, 1975 and *L'Échange symbolique et la mort*, Paris: Gallimard,
1976); and Ágnes Heller (especially *A Mindennapi Élet* [*Everyday Life*], Budapest:
Akadémiai Kiadó, 1970; *Towards a Marxist Theory of Value* in *Kinesis*, 5.1, Fall
1972, Carbondale, 1972; *On Instincts*, Assen: Van Gorcum, 1979; and *A Theory
of Feelings*, Assen: Van Gorcum, 1979). Although I find I have to part from all of
these in some respects, I acknowledge a general indebtedness — particularly to
the work of Heller (and her colleagues in the post-Lukacsian "Budapest School")
from which a great deal has rubbed off over the years.

1. For a related discussion of power — which I take to be engendered by value
   as one form of its organisation — see Arthur Kroker, "Modern Power in Reverse
   Image: The Paradigm Shift of Michel Foucault and Talcott Parsons," in John
   Fekete, ed., *The Structural Allegory: Reconstructive Encounters with the New
   French Thought* (Minneapolis: University of Minnesota Press, 1984).

2. See *Understanding Media: The Extensions of Man* (New York: New American
   Library, 1964), pp. 23-24; also (with Quentin Fiore) *The Medium is the Massage:
   An Inventory of Effects* (New York: Bantam, 1967), p. 26. For a recent
   discussion, see John Fekete, "Massage in the Mass Age: Remembering the
   McLuhan Matrix," *Canadian Journal of Political and Social Theory*, 6.3 (Fall
   1982), 50-67.

3. See Heller, *Towards a Marxist Theory of Value*, for a review of 19th and early
   20th century value discussions.

4. Heller, *Towards a Marxist Theory of Value*, sets up a comparable framework,
   although one that gravitates somewhat more decidedly towards
   objectifications.

5. See Heller, *On Instincts*.

6. Friedrich Nietzsche, *The Will to Power: An Attempted Transvaluation of All
   Values*, trans. Anthony M. Ludovici, II (New York: Russell & Russell, 1964),
   p. 147 (aphorism 675).

7. For a fuller discussion of *magma*, see Castoriadis, *L'Institution imaginaire*.

8. Castoriadis's analysis of the institution of the symbolic, its autonomization,
   and its relation to the imaginary dimension is an important related discussion.

9. See Kroker, "Modern Power."

10. See Baudrillard, esp. *L'Échange symbolique.*

11. "Forget Baudrillard: An Interview with Sylvère Lotringer," *Forget Foucault* (New York: Semiotext[e], 1987), p. 78.

12. See John Fekete, "Descent into the New Maelstrom," in Fekete, ed., *The Structural Allegory.*

13. Smith, p. 11.

14. Smith, pp. 13-14.

15. Smith, p. 10.

16. Smith, p. 6.

17. See the discussion of Hume in Richard H. Popkin, *The High Road to Pyrrhonism*, ed. Richard A. Watson and James E. Force (San Diego: Austin Hill Press, 1980), pp. 103-47.

18. For a very interesting, if somewhat differently oriented (rationalist) discussion of this and related problems, see Martin Hollis, *Models of Man: Philosophical Thoughts on Social Action* (Cambridge: Cambridge University Press, 1977), especially pp. 185-90. See also Martin Hollis and Edward J. Nell, *Rational Economic Man: A Philosophical Critique of Neo-classical Economics* (Cambridge: Cambridge University Press, 1975), especially pp. 163-64.

19. This point is widely established. For quite differently oriented examples, see Stanley Fish, *Is There a Text in This Class? The Authority of Interpretive Communities* (Cambridge: Harvard University Press, 1980); and Sándor Radnóti, "The Effective Power of Art: On Benjamin's Aesthetics," *Telos*, No. 49 (Fall 1981), 61-82.

20. See Ferenc Fehér, "What Is Beyond Art? On the Theories of Post-Modernity," *Thesis Eleven*, Nos. 5-6 (1982), 5-19.

21. See Sándor Radnóti, "The Historization of the Concept of Art: Max Dvorak," and "Savage Reception: Erwin Panofsky," both in typescript.

22. "Fritz Zorn *Mars*: Pathography as Cultural Critique," unpub. ms., delivered as a talk at Trent University, March 23, 1987.

23. Smith, p. 14.

24. Smith, p. 14.

25. See Martin Heidegger, *An Introduction to Metaphysics*, trans. Ralph Manheim (New Haven: Yale University Press, 1959), pp. 54-70.

26. See the interesting, related discussion of the paradoxes of potential space and transitional objects (mediating between "primary narcissism" and object relations), in Donald W. Winnicott, *Playing and Reality* (Harmondsworth: Pelican, 1971). See also the discussion of Frankfurt, Baudrillard, and psychoanalysis in Charles Levin, "Traditional Critical Theory and Transitional Theory," *Canadian Journal of Political and Social Theory*, 8.1 (Winter 1984).

4

AESTHETIC ALIENATION: HEIDEGGER, ADORNO, AND TRUTH AT THE END OF ART

Jay M. Bernstein

Artworks talk like the good fairies in tales: if you want the unconditioned, it will be bestowed upon you, but in a way that is unrecognizable. By contrast, the truth of discursive knowledge, while unveiled, is precisely for that reason unattainable. — T.W. Adorno

Postivism, Truth, and Art

1.   Aesthetic alienation is the name of the *question* of literary and artistic value, as the question of value poses itself to us in our culture.

Yet, in these apparently post-metaphysical times, nothing is easier than to deny that there is *a* question of value, that we are questioned in and through the series of practices of value attribution in which we engage. Have we not forsaken the attempt to ground or metaphysically legislate epistemological and normative issues? Can we not be satisfied by either (i) noting the way in which the social rules governing the practices of aesthetic valuation govern, order, and rationalise those valuations in the same way, and perhaps at the same time, as they control the practices of interpretation? (Does not the interpretive-evaluative community itself do the work that used to be assigned to a metaphysical foundation?); or (ii) naturalistically tracing the many functions that artistic works have in our lives without, however, presupposing that there is some one function unique to works of this sort? or (iii) having recognized that literature (and art) is a motley, not one thing but many interrelated and diversely connected modes of activity, charting the various "grammars" at work in our making and justifying evaluative claims? Is it not time that we stopped looking for philosophical illumination on these questions and settled, instead, for natural histories, sociological analyses, or evolutionary explanations?

What can, or should, unsettle the easy trajectory of these various — pragmatic, naturalistic, sociological, reductionist — programmes is the recognition of the possibility that our practices as a whole may be in a state of disorder, a disorderliness which would be contained and/or explained away were we to adopt any of the suggested programmes for research.[1] Symptoms and signs of such a disorder tend to assert themselves at what ordinarily are taken to be the boundaries or margins of inquiry. For example, one may duly register contradictory functions which artworks have in our culture (e.g., providing imaginary satisfactions to repressed needs, and inscribing those satisfactions in a domain isolated from other forms of social practice), but without an explanation of those functions and contradictions no cognitive gain is achieved in noting or analysing them. Again, it might be quite true that ascriptions of truth, (moral) rightness, and aesthetic merit obey quite different and distinct grammars; and further, that we can discover different evolutionary functions and social interests served by such a differentiation. Still, misogynist and racist texts unsettle our willingness to leave this differentiation unquestioned, as does our experience of finding works 'insightful' or 'illuminating.' Moreover, as we discover more about the social and historical dynamic of scientific activity and progress, we feel less inclined to grant it unchallenged hegemony over questions of truth.[2]

One, rather general, way of stating this point would be to say that naturalising, pragmatist, and associated programmes tend to elide the question of the social and historical totality, and in so doing they keep us from interrogating that place at which our agreements and disagreements may be called into question (or seen to have a point), and a perspective on them attained. Nor is this surprising for, since Kant, *the* antimetaphysical gesture has been denying the propriety of questions concerning totality (the world as a whole).[3] And this denial has an evident rationale, for it makes sense to believe that all references to totality involve an attempt to transcend human finitude, to transcend the conditions within and against the background of which our practices can and do have sense. All this, however, assumes what needs to be demonstrated: that totality and finitude are components of incompatible conceptual frameworks; and that we are fairly clear about what is involved in postmetaphysical inquiry (if that is really what we are about).

In opposition to the reductive tendencies of much current thought, I will attempt in what follows to defend five theses.

1. At the centre of the problem and riddle of art for us today, and this means at the centre of the problem of the value of art today, lie the phenomena of aesthetic alienation. By aesthetic alienation I mean, as a first approximation: (a) that the value framework and horizons of art are not, in contemporary society, inhabitable (or at least are largely uninhabited); (b) that we experience this uninhabitability in terms either of art's loss of its truth function or through the unredeemability of its truth claims; and (c) since the "aesthetic" understanding of art involves conceiving of art objects as non-cognitive, then our aesthetic comportment toward works of art is our alienation from art.

2. *The displacement of art's truth-function is a consequence of art's being displaced, marginalised, autonomised by something that is external to art, by some other social practices. Which practices these are and how they are described determines how, precisely, aesthetic alienation, aesthetics as alienation, is to be theorised and specified.*

3. *Thinking of art in terms of its relations to other forms of social practice requires that we re-institute some conception of the social totality as a necessary component of our discovering the place of art in society.*

4. *Any post-metaphysical philosophy which reflectively foregrounds the question of historicality (historicity) will, either directly or implicitly, theorise the problem of art in terms of aesthetic alienation.*

5. *We can only come to a proper understanding of aesthetic alienation by discerning which history is our history, that is, by adjudicating what the correct philosophical-historical comprehension of the present is. This too, of course, is a question of the totality, the historical totality.*

At this juncture, two interconnected questions arise. First, what grounds are there for *now* returning to the value question, and more, of thinking that question through in terms of truth? And secondly, what are we to count as 'post-metaphysical' reflection on art? Both questions receive an answer from the same direction: in our *culture*, the repression of the value question is bound up with the dominance of positivism; with positivism's general relegation of all value, ethical and artistic, to a non-cognitive limbo, while providing science with hegemony over questions of truth. Now the emergence of a post-positivist philosophy of science must be conceived of as throwing into doubt positivism's strong separation of the cognitive and non-cognitive, while simultaneously laying down the guidelines for post-metaphysical philosophical inquiry. Later I shall be arguing that, anachronistically, Heidegger's conception of historicality can best be comprehended as a generalisation of the leading theorems of Anglo-American post-positivist philosophy of science.

2.   The theoretical etiolation of artistic value was a consequence of a double isolation: first, the diremption of questions of moral value from

questions of truth and falsity — the fact/value distinctions; and secondly, the separation of artistic worth from moral worth — the inscribing of art within the autonomous domain of the "aesthetic." This latter separation received its most perspicuous representation in the Kantian dictum that works of art are purposeful in themselves, while lacking any positive, practical (ethical) end over and above their complexion. Of course, even in Kant, art was defined not only by means of the exclusion of cognition and moral worth, but equally through the *approximation* and *analogy* in aesthetic judgment of judgment in a concept and the requirement of universality. Which is to say, from the beginning there was a strain on our conception of art, assuming for the purposes of argument that 'our' conception of art is roughly delineated by the Kantian exclusions; for what can we make of a domain in which questions of truth, goodness, efficacy, even pleasure (remember our 'interest' in art is 'disinterested') are eliminated at the outset?

We come closer to understanding our present predicament if we *consider* these theoretical exclusions as consequences of a cultural ideology, namely, the ideology of positivism. This ideology presented science, through the operation of its value-neutral methodology, as the model, arbiter, and sovereign over all questions of truth. Now, it is the recent, sustained challenge to the positivist conception of science, following in the wake of Thomas Kuhn's *The Structure of Scientific Revolutions*, which gives moment to the necessity (and possibility) of reconsidering artistic value.

The attack on the positivist conception of science is a version of the general critique of foundational epistemology. But the claim that science as a form of knowledge lacks *a priori* foundations has more far reaching consequences than does that same denial of foundations elsewhere, for scientific knowledge grows, changes, alters. The questions of scientific rationality are historical questions, questions that must take into consideration the actual practices, assumptions and the like of scientific communities, for the "reason" of scientific reason will be, in some sense, 'their' reason. How radically this point should be stated is still an open question, but at the least it seems plausible to claim that what different scientific frameworks provide are different concepts of the object to be investigated; that is, the existence of differential frameworks entails the rejection of the Kantian thesis that what it is for anything to *be* an object can be legislated *a priori*, for all time. History enters into our conception of science not only on the side of the subject, in terms of changing theories, practices, experimental procedures and rationality, but equally it enters on the side of the object, in terms of what it is to be an object in general. With this latter recognition — that not only does science itself have a history, but that history has constitutive functions for both what science is and what its objects are, and moreover that these two histories are components of the same process — then we are no longer talking about history, a series of events within a neutral temporal continuum, but about historicality.

3.   What are the implications of these alterations in our understanding of science for our conception of artistic value? This can be regarded as the question raised by post-aesthetic theories of art. They begin with the view that artworks must be understood in non-aesthetic terms, because the very idea of aesthetics is based upon a series of exclusions that themselves assume a conception of truth in terms of that isolation from normative and 'aesthetic' values which post-positivist philosophy of science has undermined. Further, since science itself has turned out to lack an *a*historical essence, post-aesthetic theories of art attempt to interrogate art historically, asking not what art ahistorically is, but what it has been and has become. To understand art, to answer the question of the value of art, is to understand, to grasp, and to gather a certain history. *Which history, however, is just the question in dispute among competing post-aesthetic theories.*

In what follows, I want to defend my five theses by examining a prominent episode in the history of the post-aesthetic philosophy of art which is not usually associated with the question of alienation. Within this overall programme I shall want to centre two claims: (i) that moving in a direction opposite to that of post-positivist philosophies of science, post-aesthetic theories of art tend to locate the value of art in its cognitive dimension. This should not surprise us for, in denying positivism, we deny the separation of domains, and thus the central plank in science's claim of a hegemony over questions of truth is taken away, opening the possibility that other forms of activity might possess significant cognitive capacities, however different those capacities are from those of science. (ii) However, although the history of art appears to license the claim concerning art's cognitive potential, contemporary experience of art does not; on the contrary, contemporary experience of art, it is argued, is the experience of art's loss of cognitive capacity. It is this loss, no matter how theorised or explained, that I am calling aesthetic alienation.

Great Art, Historicity and Some Old Shoes

4.   In the "Epilogue" to his "The Origin of the Work of Art," Heidegger offers us a significant clue as to what the beginning intention, the original problem, governing his meditation on the work of art might be.[4] People speak of immortal works of art and of artworks possessing eternal value; even if these claims are inflated, claims like them are always in circulation in those places where art is seriously considered. What substance or content do such claims possess? Heidegger regards Hegel's *Aesthetics* as the most comprehensive — because metaphysically informed — reflection on the nature of art that we have, and hence its conclusions as our necessary starting point. Hegel claims that "Art no longer counts for us as the highest manner in which truth obtains existence for itself"; and because this is so, "art is and remains for us, on the side of its highest vocation, some-

thing past" (quoted in *OWA* 80). Art will continue to advance, change, develop, and perhaps even perfect itself; hence art will continue along its historical way. Nothing Hegel says is meant to deny these obvious truths. However, according to Hegel, art is no longer for us the place in which the truth (of who and how we are, and of how 'things' are for us) occurs. The "death of art," the "end of art," denotes not the halting of a historical movement, nor, then, the cessation of an activity and the concerns surrounding it, but a dislodgement, as it were, of those activities and concerns from the (metaphysical-historical) centre to the periphery. That such a fate can befall a mode of human activity is easy to grasp; it is commonly claimed as the fate of religion in the transition to modernity. Of course, once such a dislodgement occurs, then those activities and concerns cannot be quite the 'same' as they were prior to the dislodgement; the sense, meaning, or significance of those activities must change too, and those changes will have repercussions on the activities and concerns themselves.

Two distinct theses are at work here. The first is that any complex social totality will be composed of a variety of interrelated forms of activity: political, moral, scientific, religious, recreational, economic, etc. It is at least historically true that the separation of domains into cognitive, normative, and aesthetic did not traditionally rigidly follow the lines of demarcation between various forms of activity. Indeed, in traditional societies, different forms of activity each might have had their own distinct cognitive capacities and normative authority. However, different forms of activity stood in definite relations of dominance and subordination with respect to one another. So, at different historical junctures, myth, law, scripture, or science might have been dominant — been at the cognitive/normative centre — while other forms of activity stood in definite relations of subordination (and autonomy) with respect to the then dominant centre. Those forms of activity whose cognitive and normative authority were most marginalised by the centre, stood at the cognitive/normative periphery of the society in question. Analogous to changes between scientific frameworks, we can consider one major sense of historical change to be any shift in what the centre of a social totality is.

Now if we conceive of social totalities along the lines of scientific frameworks understood in terms of their historicality, then a change in the meaning (sense, point, significance) of a form of activity that occurs in a dislodgement (or 'lodgement') of a form of activity from centre to periphery (or vice-versa) will involve a change in the 'essence' of that activity. This is to say that the essence of phenomena is not unhistorical; historicity invades the very nature of the modes of activity (and their products) with which we are concerned.

In order, however, for this conclusion to carry — thus far involving only a historical induction over the variety of forms of human activity and their changing relations with respect to one another — a further thesis is required. For Heidegger, like Hegel, what marks the centre, as opposed to the periphery, is "the manner in which truth obtains existence for itself." But this does not mean that both what is and truth remain the same throughout history, while all that changes is our mode of apprehending what is. For one thing, such a realism presupposes some form of subject/object dualism: what is remains the same, but we bring to it various instruments (art, science, religion, philosophy) in accordance with which we make different types of claim as to what is, in truth, there. In order for such an approach to have a chance of being valid, it would have to be the case that things were just 'there' and we could thence just bring our cognitive instruments to them. In both *Being and Time* and the first part of "Origin," Heidegger denies that this is the case.

His weakest argument, directed explicitly against the projection of the propositional structure of subject and predicate onto things, making things substances having properties, claims that such projections are impossible unless the things are already visible. The argument is weak because the fit between things and propositional structure can be explained in either evolutionary or causal terms. Better is Heidegger's quasi-transcendental argument to the effect that our various representational attitudes toward things are derivative from a more primordial form of accessibility. Before a hammer or a pair of shoes is an object — out there — before us, we are familiar with it as something having a place within the circuit of our practical engagements. Hence its functional and purposive properties are an original component of our non-representational comprehension of it. Equipment becomes an object, a mere thing, only defectively: when the shoe rubs or the hammer breaks, only then, when it stops being functional, does it call attention to itself, fall out of place and become a mere thing, something without purpose, to be noticed and viewed (re-presented). The usual practice of treating equipment as things with an extra, added property, *viz.* purposefulness, thus inverts the true order of dependency. Our ontology of the thing, and our representational stance toward things in general, depend on making defective, broken things paradigmatic, and on our standing back from things and viewing them, on our contemplative comportment prior to our practical engagement.

Placing this critique of subject-object dualism together with our previous historical induction — together: things are not available to us independently of our practical involvements with them, and those involvements are always socially and historically specific in nature — entails that truth and the nature of what is (being) are internal correlatives that must be thought together, and that cannot be exempted from the flux of history. It is only in virtue of their movement that we can make sense of the thesis that the essence of phenomena is historical (because "essencing" is itself something historical).

5.   Since the centre of any social totality will provide the normative concept of an object for the social world in question — e.g., things are creat-

ed beings, things are composites of particles having only primary qualities, etc. — then the series of fundamental conceptions of how things are
is the history of truth. As a consequence, Heidegger claims, the history
of the nature of Western art will correspond to the changes in the nature
of truth (*OWA* 81), since within any given social formation what art is will
be governed by the concept of an object of that formation's centre.

Heidegger's consideration of Western art from the perspective of
changes in the nature of truth contains three interrelated lines of interrogation. The first is to understand how art is for us now where the centre
(truth and being) is determined by the essence of technology, for Heidegger believes that it is technology which is at the centre of our social world.
However, this interrogation requires that we first have at our disposal a
historical, non-aesthetic conception of artworks for, aesthetic conceptions
of artworks being non-historical, a change in the essence of art would
necessarily be invisible from within an aesthetic perspective. Secondly,
then, we shall have to purge our comprehension of artworks of those 'aesthetic' categories that have prevailed throughout the history of Western
reflection on art, for those categories — above all: form, matter, and aesthetic experience (of beauty, pleasure, etc) — consider the artwork in terms
of the metaphysics of presence, that is, in terms that make thinking the
essence of art historically impossible. Part of the lure of those categories
is that they also determine or derive from Western thinking about the nature of the thing. So, artworks are things, but things of a special kind: things
that manifest something other (artworks as allegory), or things that are in-
fused with something other (artworks as symbols) (*OWA* 19-20).

Heidegger's meditation on "Thing and Work," the opening section of
"Origin," is negative and destructive in its movement; it is meant to free
consideration of artworks from aesthetic categories, and not, therefore,
to register a true account of the nature of the thing in order to see better
how artworks are things.[5] Indeed, Heidegger will contend (*OWA* 68-69)
that a work's thingly character is no part of it *qua* work; that the question
of a work's thingly character wrongly takes the work first as an object directly there, as a thing, and in so doing hides, so long as this perspective is
maintained, the work's true nature.

(Nonetheless, that we do consider works things, and that they are capable of being dealt with as mere things — weighed, hung, stored, shipped,
etc. — is no idle point to be peremptorily passed over once we have come
theoretically to disqualify their thingly aspects as contributing to their true
nature; for taking them as thingly is not a 'theoretical' error, but is itself
part of the historical fate of artworks, part of their being for us now.)

Taking this destructive argument as given, we can turn to the third part
of Heidegger's interrogation: an account of what overcoming aesthetics
is, and the development of a non-aesthetic theory of art.[6] It is to this limb
of Heidegger's argument that we now turn.

6.   In his account of "Origin," Hans-Georg Gadamer interprets Heidegger's project of overcoming aesthetics in terms of his own programme for overcoming aesthetics in *Truth and Method*. While, to be sure, both Heidegger and Gadamer comprehend the overcoming of aesthetics in terms of restoring to artworks their status as forms of cognition, Gadamer's programme is rather overtly less radical than Heidegger's in that he regards aesthetics as the subjectification of art. This is a product of the age of Enlightenment, where "the autonomous right of sensuous knowledge (was) asserted and with it the relative independence of the judgment of taste from the understanding and its concepts" (*PH* 218). For Heidegger, while this moment is indeed a turning point in the history of knowledge about art, corresponding, generally, to the metaphysical turn in which the individual's states (of thought, will, and feeling) become primary being and hence the "court of judicature over beings" (*N* 83), it does not mark the beginning of aesthetics. Aesthetics, for Heidegger, is *any* consideration of art that comprehends it in terms of the state of feeling aroused by the beautiful; that is, for a theory of art to be aesthetical, it must make sense, sensation, or feeling (in response to the beautiful) primary in our understanding of art. In aesthetic understanding of art, artworks are objects for subjects, where the relation between subject and object is one of feeling (*N* 78).

"Aesthetics begins," says Heidegger, "with the Greeks at that moment when their great art and also the great philosophy that flourished along with it comes to an end" (*N* 80). This statement is ambiguous, for it is unclear from it, or from what follows, whether "great philosophy" includes or excludes Plato and Aristotle (it certainly includes the Pre-Socratics). This ambiguity, however, is systematic, for Plato's and Aristotle's writings on art both belong and do not belong to aesthetics. To the degree to which the vocabulary — above all: form and matter — and the problems that belong to the tradition of aesthetic writing is first set out in their works, then to that degree their writing and argumentation is shaped by aesthetical considerations and must be read accordingly. However, Heidegger also finds in Plato and Aristotle a thinking that is rooted in the experience of a different form of understanding being, one in which being and presence are not identified. Consequently, there also exists in their writing an understanding of art that is not aesthetical. It is well to recall here Heidegger's claim in "Origin" that "Roman thought takes over the Greek words without a corresponding, equally authentic experience of what they say, without the Greek word. The rootlessness of Western thought begins with this translation" (*OWA* 23).

Thus, we should not be surprised when Heidegger finds in Plato, not only our familiar distancing of art and truth, a distancing that will become a separation, but equally, in the *Phaedrus* (250 d), a "felicitous discordance": the radiance of the beautiful liberates us from appearances (from beings, from the oblivion or forgetfulness of being) to allow us a view upon being (*N* 197). We might, however, be surprised when Heidegger suggests an equivalent double reading of Kant on the beautiful (*N* 109-10). So the very text, Kant's *Critique of Judgment*, which institutes the radical autonomy of aesthetics and art in modernity, equally "explodes itself" (*N* 131), providing a non-aesthetical comprehension of art and beauty.

We can understand this eventuality if we record two interconnected theses of Heidegger's. First, the history and tradition of metaphysics is a history of the succeeding construals of what is in general terms modelled on the understanding of particulars simply there before us. So what is in general has been interpreted in terms of our understanding of particular beings. This way of understanding what is, Heidegger terms the metaphysics of presence, and it belies our present recognition of historicality, our recognition that what there is changes. "Being" is just Heidegger's term for the process or history of alterations in what there is. But, secondly, the continual substition of some metaphysic of presence for being, the substitution of beings for being as the key to understanding what there is, is itself, according to Heidegger, the way in which that history of alterations has worked; the comprehension of the being of beings in terms of presence, that is, in terms of beings, operates in accordance with the fatefulness of being itself. It is being, we might say (so long as we do not construe being as some 'thing' or particular being), which in its epochal determinations of what is offers a mode of understanding what is that belies its epochal and historical way of bringing beings into presence; each way of bringing things to unconcealment, of making them available *überhaupt*, corresponds to a mode of being's concealment. Hence, in any fundamental metaphysical thinking, being is licensing its displacement by beings.

As a consequence, we who read metaphysics at the end of metaphysics, we who can no longer ignore the place of history in the essence of phenomena, must read doubly: the texts of the tradition will manifest both the substitution of beings for being, and so the oblivion of being, *and* the presencing of beings by being. If the texts of metaphysics did not explode themselves (for us, deciphering them at the end), then they could not have a place in the history of metaphysics. Fundamental metaphysical gestures are moments of displacement *and* unconcealment; and there could be no history of metaphysics in a strict sense unless that history is understood in terms of the history of being's unconcealment and withdrawal.

Overcoming aesthetics involves noting those moments in the history of aesthetics where thinking on art exceeds aesthetics, just as overcoming metaphysics involves registering those moments in the history of metaphysics where the texts of the tradition explode themselves by exceeding the logic of presence which apparently, and fatefully, governs them. Now the reason for this detour into what many might consider an arcane corner of Heidegger's programme is this: the practice of double reading that Heidegger produces as the way of overcoming metaphysics and aesthetics (aesthetics being the metaphysics of presence in art) is precisely deconstruction as practised by Derrida. Deconstructive readings are double readings that record a text's compliance with the metaphysics of presence and its exceeding that metaphysics. Derrida's terms of art, above all *"différance,"* are places of excess, places in a text where presence must be and cannot be, but whose excess beyond the logic of presence is what allows the text to work. The *necessity* of deconstructive reading — what, if anything, salvages the practice of deconstruction from being the iterated operation of a formalism — is its vantage point: reading from 'here' at the end of the history of metaphysics where texts precisely are double, instantiating and exceeding the logic of presence.

Heidegger's and Derrida's programmes are the same. For present purposes I offer this as a challenge, and as a promissory note for some future occasion. If correct, however, it entails that the 'criticisms' I shall be making of Heidegger necessarily apply with equal force to Derrida.

7.   The practice of double reading does not provide a non-aesthetic theory of art; rather, it is an account of how to read writings on art to reveal their compliance to and deviation from aesthetics. The writings of the tradition exceed aesthetics in the course of their work of instituting and reproducing it. Now, although Heidegger contends that from the very beginning Western thinking on art was bound up with aesthetics, he does mark off what is usually regarded as the era of aesthetics, the period of modernity, as distinctive, as making a radical break with the past; and this break relates directly to the history and value of art itself. Roughly, Heidegger argues that in the age of technology, our epoch, there is no more "great art," this being the key term of his non-aesthetic conception of art. Heidegger attempts to theorise Hegel's idea of the end or death of art in terms of the end of great art so that it is the concept of great art that now requires some elucidation.

Great art will not be great because of its beauty, formal elegance, or aesthetic merit, for these criteria for judging artworks are themselves aesthetical. If the theory of great art is to form the basis for a non-aesthetic conception of art, then the criteria for greatness will of necessity be of a different order from traditional aesthetic criteria. In fact, Heidegger's conception of great art is fairly directly entailed by his epochal conception of history, together with the thesis that within any epoch certain forms of activity will be either central or peripheral. From these two ideas it follows that a non-aesthetic conception of art will seek to demonstrate how works can be epoch-making, possessing an "originating" power in Heidegger's lexicon, and a centre, do the work of centring. Briefly, in his own terms, Heidegger contends:

    (i) Whenever art happens — that is, whenever there is a beginning — a thrust enters history, history either begins or starts over again... History is the transporting of a people into its appointed task as entrance into that people's endowment. (*OWA* 77)

    (ii) Of one great work, Heidegger says: it first gives to things their look and to men their outlook. (*OWA* 43)

(iii) Since the meaning of being, the truth of being is itself epochal (historical), then art is one of the ways in which truth happens. (*OWA* 55)

(iv) Hence, art is history, in the essential sense that it grounds history. (*OWA* 77)[7]

8. At the conclusion of the opening section of "Origin" Heidegger says that "art is truth setting itself to work," and he continues with the leading question of the remainder of the essay: "What is truth itself, that it some-times comes to pass as art?" (*OWA* 39) Now we have already seen how the correspondence theory of truth embedded in the positivist conception of science belies how the growth of knowledge occurs in science; modern science does involve a systematic growth in our knowledge of nature, but that growth cannot be comprehended representationally. Rather, it is scien-tific frameworks — paradigms, research programmes, domains — which at any given time say what any portion of nature is, determine what is scien-tific and what not, guide continuing research, provide criteria for theory choice, etc. What the concept of a scientific framework invokes, then, is a *productive rather than 're-productive' or 're-presentational' conception of truth*. Scientific frameworks provide the measure of nature, rather than being measured against it; the growth of knowledge within a framework is made possible by the framework itself, while the shift from one frame-work to another reveals the parochiality of past knowing and reveals new possibilities for understanding what nature is and what science is. Scien-tific frameworks, in their productive capacity, provide the conditions in general for both 'science' and its objects.[8]

Heidegger's conception of truth in art as bringing into unconcealment is, it seems to me, directly analogous to this productive conception of truth in science, with one exception: what distinguishes great art from region-ally specific acts of truth-production (bringing into unconcealment) — and scientific truth for Heidegger is always regional even if productive (*OWA* 62) — is that it operates for a totality *qua* totality, and not merely for some region or domain within a totality. More, there is such a thing as a totality only in virtue of the work performed by a great work or its equivalent — the act that founds a political state, sacrifice, the thinker's questioning (*OWA* 62). What is meant by totality here is the kind of unity or sense of belonging together that the *different* forms of activity in which a people engage possess for them. So, Heidegger will say, the great art reveals how beings as a whole are: "What is holy and what unholy, what great and what small, what brave and what cowardly, what lofty and what flighty, what master and what slave" (*OWA* 43). This work, I am claiming, 'reveals' a world in a way precisely analogous to the way in which a paradigm or research programme institutes an object domain, providing a concept of an object in general, and hence *unifying* scientific practice by providing guidelines for inquiry, criteria for theory evolution, and so forth. A work of great art can reveal the horizons of a world in just the same way that a scientific framework institutes the horizons of a scientific world.

Because Heidegger's claim that artworks bring into unconcealment in a non-representational way is conceived of as applying to particulars, there is a tendency to read him as making some sort of intuitionist claim. If, however, we consider that what is being brought into unconcealment is a totality, an arrangement of things and their significances with respect to one another, a principle or set of principles of organization against the background of which our actual practices take place, a concept of an object (-world) in general or a complex categorial framework, then the understanding appropriate here can be isolated from all forms of intuitionism.

To be sure, the kind of totality that Heidegger is claiming great art provides is problematic for us, both because, rightly or wrongly — which I shall comment on later — we do not conceive of ourselves as actually inhabiting a totality having this sort of force, and also because it is a normative principle of liberal democracies that the question of what is the good life for man, which includes how each is to make sense of and *unify* the complex of activities in which he or she engages, is a matter for each individual to decide, and is not to be legislated by the state or society at large.[9] Nonetheless, since we take this position to be a historical achievement of liberal states, and Heidegger is restricting great art to (more or less) pre-modern, pre-liberal social formations, then we appear committed to the belief that traditional societies were normative totalities.

9.   If pressured, one might say that even if a work of art could be prominent in reproducing the categorial framework of a social formation, it is surely an exaggeration to say that it might produce a normative totality, and it is this latter claim that Heidegger is making. Some of the exaggeration here can be diminished if we break down Heidegger's thesis into its two constituent parts, an explanatory thesis and a functional thesis. The explanatory thesis occurs in Heidegger's contention that great works happen suddenly, marking the beginning of an epoch. In saying this, Heidegger grants that the beginning made by a great work "prepares itself for the longest time and wholly inconspicuously" (*OWA* 76). Why then speak of a beginning? Because great works are not moments *in* a tradition or a history, but are works that disrupt some previous history and hence set in motion the possibility of another history. This is why Heidegger speaks of great works as "unmediated" (*OWA* 76). The point is not that they spring from nowhere, but rather, they cannot be accounted for in terms of their antecedents (however antecedents are understood). Mediation is something that occurs within a totality, and hence is inapplicable to what brings the totality into unconcealment as a totality. To put this same point otherwise, it is part of what is meant by art being 'creative' that no account of the elements or antecedents of a work is sufficient to explain what it is that

is achieved in it. Of course, works often, if not usually, fall below this level of originality; and not every original work is great art, revealing how things are as a whole. But, if history is epochal, and if epochs are normative totalities, then it is plausible to argue that there are 'places' where the discontinuity between epochs is enunciated. For Heidegger, great art is such a place.

This helps to explain why it is that Heidegger speaks of truth as an event or happening. Again, the point is not to institute an intuitionist view of artistic truth or to legitimate a romantic conception of artistic action, any more than it is Kuhn's point to undermine the rationality of science when he insists upon the revolutionary character of certain developments, or when he characterizes the alteration of understanding that occurs during such developments as a "conversion."[10] Rather, Heidegger uses his terms in order to *contrast* the uneventful activities and works that deal with particulars belonging to a totality with the event of the totality itself. This event occurs through different works throughout an epoch; which is to say, inaugurating an epoch is not a question of temporal priority. When it is a totality itself that is at issue, the distinction between production and reproduction breaks down.

This brings us to the functional thesis. Great art, by definition, brings things into unconcealment, and hence has a (quasi-transcendental) truth function; by definition, great art reveals a totality, and in so doing assigns men a place among things, thereby giving their lives a 'sense.' These functions are the non-aesthetic analogues of the familiar Russian formalist thesis that *the* literary effect is defamiliarization (*ostranenie*), making the world strange, allowing familiar objects to be truly 'seen' rather than recognized — a thesis subsequently reformulated as Brecht's estrangement-effect, where the goal of art is to return the apparently eternal, changeless features of life to history in all its contingency and transience. For Heidegger, the effect of great works is equally one of defamiliarization, only for him the movement is not toward a mere renewed vision of some particular, or against the apparently inevitable toward the flux of history, but rather from the ordinary and particular to the totality itself as that which lets the ordinary and particular have their peculiar shape and meaning. So great art transports men out of the ordinary realm, where to submit to this displacement means: "to transform our accustomed ties to world and earth and henceforth restrain all usual doing and prizing, knowing and looking, in order to stay within the truth that is happening in the work" (*OWA* 66). Letting a work be in this way, letting it have this effect, Heidegger calls "preserving"; where preserving is to be contrasted with connoisseurship or aesthetic understanding that parries a work's "thrust into the extraordinary" (*OWA* 68).

Ostranenie and the estrangement effect work critically; their cognitive claiming is negative in character. This restriction, however, is compatible with the thought that for us art works are peripheral, their significance limited to pointing to or gesturing at the cognitive/normative centre without being able to invade it. Further, in considering the cognitive purport of literature, there is at least some recognition that its thematic concerns (with love, death, power, etc.) address, not our empirical beliefs, but the categories and concepts *through* which we process those beliefs. We tend to read art's truth claims as conceptual or categorial; but because art is peripheral, the significance of these claims is usually read in terms of art rehearsing "possibilities." If art is peripheral, however, then must not those claims function differently when art is at the centre? And will the sense of "possibility" not shift when it is construed historically, as an effect of marginalisation?

Briefly, then, Heidegger's characterization of great art in fact amounts to an extension and reworking of more familiar accounts of art such that these features of works relate to his epochal theory of history in the context of non-modern or traditional societies. Conversely, of course, we might recognize our aesthetic conception of art as a consequence of our repression of historicality in non-normatively totalised social formations.

10.   "Origin" concludes with a question: Are we now in our existence historically at the origin of art? Does art now reveal how things as a whole are? Or is art a thing of the past, something whose value we possess only through remembrance? Heidegger defers here to Hölderlin (*OWA* 78):

> Reluctantly
> that which dwells near its origin departs.
> ("The Journey", verses 18-19)

At the beginning of the modern period, great art began to decline because it could no longer fulfil its essential function of designating the absolute, of beginning history or starting it again. This is not a comment on the quality of the artworks produced at this time, but a recording of their historical place. That decline became the "end of art" at the beginning of the nineteenth century, at the very moment when aesthetics achieved "its greatest possible height, breadth and rigor of form" (*N* 84) in the *Aesthetics* of Hegel.

From a Heideggerian perspective, aesthetic axiology is in a state of disorder because we do not and cannot exist at the origin of art: nonetheless, and however dimly, our response to art is more-than-aesthetical, our sense of the significance of art transcends the aesthetic categories with which we tend to think about and deal with artworks. We are spectators of artworks who, often, behave as if we were preservers, not knowing, of course, that this is exactly what we are doing. In the recuperation of the essence of art we become, through remembrance, preservers of art once removed — preservers of a possibility.

Yet, this thesis cannot be quite adequate as it stands for it says nothing about Heidegger's approach to modern art; and in the one discussion of a modern work of art in "Origin," that of Van Gogh's painting of the peasant woman's shoes, Heidegger appears to be forwarding the claim that, first, the painting reveals the true nature of equipment, *viz.*, its reliability; and secondly, because the painting can perform this cognitive function, we can deduce that the essence or nature of art is to reveal, disclose, bring into unconcealment the being or general essence of particular sorts of things. A modern work of art, then, is deployed to reveal the true nature of art, which, given Heidegger's thesis concerning the end of great art, it ought not to be able to do.

Worse, in "Origin" Heidegger offers the example of a Greek temple to illustrate the nature of great art. The choice is governed by his history of aesthetics, in which Greek art is the first step, the zero point for Western reflection on art. The example of early Greek art is unique because there exists no corresponding "cognitive-conceptual meditation" (*N* 80) on it; it is, as such, pre-aesthetic. Yet, "Origin" is usually read in a manner in which the account of the peasant woman's shoes and that of the temple are construed as paralleling one another. This in untenable. The Greek temple stands at the origin of art, the painting at the end of art: the temple reveals a world, giving to things their look and to men their outlook on themselves, while the painting reveals that the peasant woman knows "without noticing or reflecting" (*OWA* 34); the point of the temple example is to illustrate the worlding powers of a work, while the painting is first introduced in order to help us think ourselves free of the traditional categories of the thing. Indeed, Heidegger's account of the shoes does not require the painting, and an early version of "Origin" did not include a discussion of it.

Given the differences between the temple and the painting, it might seem most appropriate either to consider them as contrasting possibilities within the conceptual economy Heidegger is proposing or to consider the example of the shoes as exhausted with the demonstration of how the equipmental character of equipment requires a mode of accounting that goes outside the terms of the metaphysics of the thing while offering a possibility as to the true nature of art, a possibility that is *finally* revealed in the account of the temple, thus making otiose the original inferences drawn from the painting. Both proposals require that, in one way or another, and for the sake of the general economy of Heidegger's theory, the account of the Van Gogh as revealing, more or less, the essence of art be withdrawn. Neither proposal, however, is acceptable. Heidegger nowhere withdraws his account of the Van Gogh as illustrating the nature of the artwork, as one might expect him to if the example were there solely for a strategic purpose; and worse, near the end of the section "The Work and Truth" (*OWA* 56), he explicitly parallels the way "truth happens" in the temple's standing and in the Van Gogh painting. Neither correctly represents anything; rather, both allow that which is as a whole — world and earth in their counterplay — to attain to unconcealedness.

Here, finally, is the place of our questioning: How can we bring the contrasting and paralleling aspects of Heidegger's accounts of temple and shoes together? More precisely, how are we to regard the happening of truth of an artwork at the end of art? And this question is the question of the value of art, for "whether and how an era is committed to an aesthetics, whether and how it adopts a stance toward art of an aesthetic character, is decisive for the way art shapes the history of that era — or remains irrelevant for it" (*N* 79).

11.   A hint as to how we might approach this question is provided by Heidegger's remark at the beginning of his discussion of the shoes that he intends to disregard the possibility that differences relating to the history of being may be present in the way that equipment *is* (OWA 32). This suggests that the account of the painting, although going beyond traditional categories of the thing and so of aesthetics, does not, in so doing, install our understanding of the work in the history of being. Rather, despite its critical surpassing of the traditional metaphysical categories of thing, equipment, and work, the account of the painting is nonetheless 'metaphysical.'

In order to understand better what this might mean, and in order to comprehend the happening of truth in the Van Gogh, the painting must be put into its place, our place, in the age of technology, for in our epoch art is at the periphery and technology at the centre.

For Heidegger, technology is nothing technical: it is not to be undestood in terms of the domination of means-end reasoning over other forms of reasoning, although this may be one of its consequences; nor is it to be understood in terms of the kinds of instruments and modes of cooperation required by them that come to dominate production in the technological era; nor as a product of a secular hubris harnessed to an unconstrained desire for mastery over nature without and within. To understand technology, to grasp the essence of technology, is to see what gathers these diverse phenomena together as manifestations of the same. To do this is not to regard these phenomena as effects of some central, locatable and identifiable cause. Rather, since the history of being is a history of the essence of truth, of the modes in which things appear as being what they are, it is to grasp these phenomena as coefficients of the technological way of presencing men and things.

"Challenging" is the revealing that rules in modern technology, for in it everything in the world is 'challenged,' transformed, readied, stored, ordered, and secured so as to be at our disposal, to be immediately at hand, indeed, to stand there just so that it may be on call for a further ordering (*QT* 17). Because everything appears as there to be challenged does not entail that it is we who arrange things thus, that the challenge is something we create or bring about. Such an anthropological humanism supposes that the possibilities of bringing things to unconcealment, the modes of world-disclosure, are themselves at our disposal — that men can *decide* what is to be real and what not. This illusion, the utter oblivion of being, the belief that there is only man and not being, is itself clearly a reflective effect of the essence of technology. For Heidegger, only to the extent that man for his part is already challenged can the ordering revealing of the challenge occur.

Heidegger denominates the essence of technology, the challenging claim upon man, *Gestell* — usually and uselessly translated as "enframing." It is *Gestell* which claims man so that what is is always already comprehended, actually or potentially, in terms of the ordering and securing of technological revealing.

12.   In an illustration of how the challenging-forth of technology puts the Rhine river at our disposal, Heidegger asks us to consider the monstrousness that reigns here when we ponder two titles, "The Rhine" as what is dammed up in a power works, and "The Rhine" as it comes to us out of the Hölderlin hymn by that name: "The Rhine" as power and as art. Heidegger goes on to claim that as a river in the landscape we cannot approach the Rhine as it is spoken of in Hölderlin's hymn; it is there, rather, as an object for inspection for the vacation industry.

A nature poem by Hölderlin, the painting of a pair of peasant shoes by Van Gogh: these works claim us, solicit us, to a mode of revealing that we cannot validate, sustain, or even in a sense fully understand. They lure us to another scene of revealing, but one we cannot inhabit. (There is a temptation here to put this thought in more familiar terms: artworks offer us possibilities of understanding phenomena that are not now realised; hence art is fictional because it deals with possibilities rather than realities. Although Heidegger's thesis sounds like this, he is in fact attempting to deny just such a thesis as this because it makes knowing a function of true accounts of what is actual, and relegates art to a consideration of possibilities where the question of truth, in *propre persona*, does not arise.) It is the experience of the gap between the solicitation and the refusal, the lure and its uninhabitability, that I am calling aesthetic alienation. And my claim is: the value of artworks, the value of the value of artworks, lies in aesthetic alienation.

Let us consider again Van Gogh's painting. It solicits and claims us, but how? In the first instance, as revealing the 'truth' of some phenomena, that is, in the manner invoked by Heidegger's phenomenological recounting of the picture.[11] It is not important for Heidegger's analysis that his recounting work for us as an account of the Van Gogh; what is important is that we be able to conceive of a painting or poem that claims us in accordance with the kinds of significances that Heidegger's account displays.

Naively, there are two natural critical responses to such an account. The first is epitomized by Meyer Schapiro's critique of Heidegger on Van Gogh; it treats the account as if it were a defence of one representational characterisation of the painting in opposition to other possible characterisations, and disputes Heidegger's interpretation accordingly.[12] However inadequate and inappropriate such a critique is, it does reveal how thoroughly representational and aesthetic considerations dominate our understanding of art, and how difficult it is to alter the terrain of aesthetic discourse. Schapiro's critique reveals, unintentionally, the artwork's susceptibility before the sway of the centre.

Closer to the bone would be the criticism of Heidegger's account as a naive romanticizing of the peasant world where men, things, and nature engaged one another, and *were* together, differently from how men, instruments, and nature engage and interact with one another now. Significantly, this same charge can be levelled against Heidegger's famous discussion of the hammer in *Being and Time* (Section 15 ff.). In both cases, a claim about the nature of equipment is offered, relocating the item from representational space — as an object before us to be viewed — to a circuit of praxis as its intrinsic place. In both cases, it might be claimed, there is something archaizing about Heidegger's approach. Instead of providing access to a 'true' account of equipment, in both cases Heidegger can be seen as referring us back to an earlier form of understanding and practice. Surely, hydroelectric dams or assembly-line robots are not instruments in the same essentialist sense that Heidegger proclaims for the hammer and the peasant woman's shoes?

When Heidegger says he will offer his analysis of the nature of equipmentality without consideration as to whether that nature might be subject to alteration, *he is explicitly admitting the legitimacy of this criticism of both accounts*. Heidegger's self-critique of the metaphysical posturing of *Being and Time*, and his critique of any ahistorical, revelational theory of art, occurs by means of the displacement that the account of the Van Gogh suffers as a result of being contrasted with the Greek temple. As far as the Greek temple, a Greek tragedy, a medieval cathedral, or perhaps the *Divine Comedy*, are concerned, it is intelligible to us that these works did or might have, in a sense that Heidegger never fully clarifies, given things their look and men their outlook; but this is something that cannot plausibly be claimed for Van Gogh's painting.[13]

Why, then, does Heidegger invoke the painting in terms consanguinous with the cognitive regime of bringing to unconcealment? Because, although the cognitive claim itself of the modern artwork is shown to be defective — the painting is no Greek temple — the claiming itself of the artwork is an invocation of a past possibility of revealing which *is* the claim of the work upon us. To put the same thought otherwise, what we are trying to elicit is the nature of the claim that a modern artwork makes upon us. How does it proclaim itself, authenticating its sway in our lives? One answer has been eliminated: through disclosing a world (past, present, or future). But seen from afar, it does not seem wrong to say that the work enacts a world disclosure it cannot deliver; it lives in its (necessary) failure to attain its ownmost possibility of revealing. Hense the sense of ideality, fictiveness, the imaginary that haunts artworks is not a function of their contents (peasant worlds, ideal futures, et al.), but of their 'form,' of their being artworks; it is the past and future possibilities of art itself that are the source of works' claim upon us. Their failure to reveal, their lack of cognitive power, their exclusion from questions of truth is hence the source of their power.

Artworks thrive on their own essential impossibility, on their failure to be works; and they can do no other, for that is where art is. Hence, through them we come to experience the sense of the periphery *as* a periphery, and thus the meaning of the sway of the centre. The artwork solicits in remembrance *and* anticipation of a power, a potentiality of art. This potentiality, when treated as a present actuality — the presumptive truth-claim of the work — conceals the actual meaning of the work, its work of remembrance and anticipation. When this work is accomplished, the present is brought to presence in its specificity: the impossibility of great art is the historical fate of art under the sway of technology; technological revealing reveals without letting what presences come forth into appearance; its refusal of *poiesis* is the consignment of art to the periphery and hence the alienation of art from its origin.

13.　For Heidegger aesthetic alienation figures our experience of art as a lost (repressed, defused) mode of knowledge; hence, the value of art comes to lie in our experience of it as a mode of self-understanding not presently available to us. However, that unavailability itself signifies and is cognitively meaningful: the experience of aesthetic alienation is one of loss (and not just change), of lack and need (and not just wish and hope). As such, the domain of art remains a central mode of self-understanding.

Having said this, one may still wonder whether this valorization of art is not another version of "affirmative culture," of a deferring or projection of 'social' misery, dislocation, pathology, whatever, into the safe (because marginal) world of art and aesthetics. What, we may ask, is the praxial *force* of the self-understanding achieved through the experience of aesthetic alienation? Above, we noted Heidegger's claim that the essence of technology is *nothing* technical; the essence of technology refers, precisely, to the way being fails to hold sway in modernity. Does this entail that aesthetic alienation is *nothing* praxial; that although our 'praxis' (which is not really, not yet or not any more, praxis) is deformed by its epochal inscription, nothing about that praxis *itself* sustains, reinscribes, gives moment to, for or against, the epochal sway of technology? What is at issue in this question is the way in which Heidegger distances the question of being, the history of being, from the question of *Dasein* (human being); a distance or difference which just is the ontological difference, the difference between being and beings. I should add that the difficulty here is one of which Heidegger was perfectly aware (*OWA* 87).

We can catch a glimpse of the pertinence of this issue if we think together two thoughts of Heidegger's. The first is the claim that precisely because today man thinks he encounters only his own constructs — the historical realisation of Kant's Copernican turn — in truth he nowhere any longer encounters himself, i.e., his essence. The second is the thesis that we, through our doing, cannot bring about the overcoming of *Gestell*, for epochal truth disclosures, while not beyond all human doing, happen neither exclusively in nor decisively through man. Together, Heidegger's two thoughts assert that today our world has become an unworld because, unlike past epochs, we lack a name for being, which is to say, we do not think the possibility of things being present in any way other than through our own constructive activities; we make things present. We are solely concerned with beings and have nothing to say about being. Of course, insofar as beings *are* present to us, then being does presence, but "without really reigning."[14]

If this statement is more or less correct, then it follows that our historical predicament is a unique one. Because for past epochs being did reign, albeit in concealment, social practices were under its sway. Consequently, the works and actions instituting epochal transformations occurred in response to being, in response to something not under men's direct control; and hence men were not, and did not conceive of themselves as, the unique condition for those transformations. We, on the contrary, who live under the dominion of *Gestell*, cannot engage in intentional acts that could yield an overcoming because the sway of *Gestell* fatefully comports us only toward beings and never being. Hence, we can only will not to will, listening to being, so leaving the possibility of transformation possible.

What is troubling in this claim is not the fact of our powerlessness, but its appearance of being *a priori* unsurpassable: everything appears to turn on being, and nothing, bar the active passivity which keeps the thought of being alive, appears to devolve upon us. Now there is a moment in "Origin" which, I want to contend, makes the confident assertion of this difference between being and beings a great deal more problematic.

The very nature of epochality, Heideggerian historicality, entails that all world-disclosures are finite. In his discussion of the concept of "earth" Heidegger contends that in each world-disclosure, in order for that disclosure to be finite, there must occur two kinds of concealment. The first concealment is of what lies beyond that world, hence concealment functions here as the limit of knowledge that is equally its condition. The second concealment relates to truth or error in their ordinary sense; it occurs when one being "simulates" another. If this did not occur, Heidegger says, then "we could not make mistakes or act mistakenly in regard to beings"

(*OWA* 54). Heidegger calls the first sort of concealment refusal, and the second sort dissembling. Truth happens, is an event, because worlds are the product of works; but the unconcealedness that works provide in setting forth a world always and necessarily is accompanied by the double concealment of refusal and dissembling, Untruth — concealment, limit, dissembling — belongs to the essence of truth.

What makes the bifurcation of concealment into refusal and mere dissembling problematic, troubling, is that "we are *never* fully certain whether it is the one or the other" (*OWA* 54; emphasis mine). This "never" marks a place of metaphysical distress, of interchange between being and beings, of the immersion of being in beings which is never fully acknowledged by Heidegger. For him everything happens as if we knew, were in full possession of the scene of being's withdrawal. But always, it now transpires, the beings, the works, that are clues and guides to epochal fates may themselves be dissembling or be being dissembled, hidden, by other works. The very remoteness of being from *Dasein* appears as suddenly parried by the possibility of its dissolving into the ontic altogether. We can never be certain.

Art and Praxis

14.   The clue to our epochal fate provided by the experience of aesthetic alienation is curiously idle in that the centre it brings to presence is known only through its prohibitions; the unknowability of the essence of technology hence paralleling the unknowability of our loss of a name for being. Gillian Rose has commented upon the unknowability of the essence of technology in these terms:

> *Ge-stell* is more revealingly compared with the law which it replaces, *Ge-setz*, "law," or *gesetz*, "posited," of the philosophy of reflection. *Ge-Stell* from *stellen* means, literally, "put," or "placed," just like *ge-setz* from *setzen*, means "fixed" or "posited." If *Gestell* is understood as the dominance of modern technology, this seems as uninformative as the dominance of unknowable law, for all "technology" means here is an unknown law, although the new word, *Gestell*, may sound as if it tells more about the positing in question.[15]

This unknowability we can now see as a consequence of Heidegger's inability to think the ontological difference except negatively, his purification of the ontological from anything ontic. But this consequence derives from a failure of acknowledgement; Heidegger fails to acknowledge the anxiety and risk consequent upon the doubling and duplicity of concealment.

Is the unknown law governing us as unknown as Heidegger says? Let us listen to him for a moment on the operation of this law:

The forester who, in the wood, measures the felled tim-
ber and to all appearances walks the same forest path in
the same way as did his grandfather is today commanded
by profit-making in the lumber industry, whether he
knows it or not. He is made subordinate to the orderabili-
ty of cellulose, which for its part is challenged forth by
the need for paper, which is then delivered to newspapers
and illustrated magazines. The latter, in their turn, set public opinion to swallowing what is printed... (*QT* 18)

This circularity of consumption for the sake of consumption is the sole procedure which distinctively characterizes the history of a world which has become an
unworld.[16]

After hearing this, we should not be surprised to read the following:

The end of philosophy is the place, that place in which
the whole of philosophy's history is gathered in its most
extreme possibility. End as completion meaning this
gathering... With the reversal of metaphysics which was
already accomplished by Karl Marx, the most extreme possibility of philosophy is attained. It has entered its final
stage.[17]

Let us concede, as we must, that the dominion of Capital is not purely
empirical, that a question that is not reducible to the operation of economic laws, say, is posed by Capital; can we nonetheless gain some insight
into the articulation of that question, the question of the interconnection
of history and truth, through just, precisely, art? How might the problem
of aesthetic alienation be affected by its sea-change into the history of
Capital?

Let us begin here with a reconsideration of the Van Gogh example since,
as even his admirers admit, Heidegger's account of the picture is lament-
able. In a recent paper,[18] Fredric Jameson offers a contrasting interpretation, claiming that we ought to recognize as the background and raw
material of Van Gogh's painting "the whole object world of agricultural
misery, of stark rural poverty" where fruit trees are "ancient and exhausted sticks coming out of poor soil." Against this background,

the willed and violent transformation of a drab peasant
object world into the most glorious materialization of pure
colour in oil-paint is to be seen as a Utopian gesture: as
an act of compensation which ends up producing a whole
new Utopian realm of the senses, or at least of that supreme

sense — sight, the visual, the eye — which it now recon-
stitutes for us as a semi-autonomous space in its own
right...

Jameson goes on to present Heidegger's interpretation of the peasant shoes,
claiming that it needs to be completed

by insistence on the renewed materiality of the work, on
the transformation of one form of materiality — the earth
itself and its paths and physical objects — into that other
materiality of oil paint affirmed and foregrounded in its
own right and for its own visual pleasures.

It is noteworthy that, like Heidegger, Jameson abstracts his account of Van
Gogh from the history of painting itself, and further fails to integrate fully
his proper appreciation of Van Gogh's foregrounding of the activity of
painting and the materiality of paint into either his own — or indeed
Heidegger's — account. If we do so, three consequences follow.

First, Van Gogh's concern for some old shoes or a chair was less a willed
transformation of a peasant object world than a continuation of the process
of questioning the relationship between the activity of painting and its
subject matter. More precisely, Van Gogh unmasked the parasitic authority that past art had attempted to claim for itself through its dealing with
august events, persons, and the like.[19] Secondly, then, art's authority, its
value, now has to be recognized as integral to its practice, as a consequence
of the transformations it has wrought upon its subject matter, no matter
how ordinary. Finally, however, because art's authority has become formal, has become a matter of its forms of working, then the foregrounding
of itself, its calling attention to the materiality of the paint and its application to the canvas, functions as a revocation, a cancelling of the (Utopian)
transformation, the bestowal of autonomous dignity, which that very same
painterly act had achieved. Art's autonomous power to transform its now
ordinary (democratised) subject matter, perhaps to wrest it from the domination of commodification and exchange equivalence, was realised at the
precise moment that it came to recognize its real powerlessness with respect
to the object world. Its transformations were henceforth to be consigned
to an autonomous domain whose very distance from the centre, the real
world of commodity production, was the price it was to pay for its authority. What had been (marginally) asserted and recognized in previous painting was now established in the paintings of Van Gogh in a way that made
regression difficult, if not impossible. The moment of Van Gogh then nicely
parallels the place of Flaubert in the history of the novel, where secular
narrative's previous lack of reliance on established plots, *a priori* values,
and given, ahistorical forms, came to self-consciousness through the foregrounding of the transformative power of writing itself.[20]

15.   Art's place at the periphery in the modern age is not, then, just a question of its distance from the centre, the world of capital production, but its consignment to an autonomous realm. That autonomy is required in virtue of, on the one hand, the demand by capitalist economies to be autonomous from non-economic values, and hence the reduction of all use objects to exchange equivalences: and, on the other hand, the formal *a prioris* governing artistic practices themselves, which presumptively require those practices, insofar as they do stay out of the market place of mass art, to recognize the exigencies peculiar to each specific practice. But these exigencies turn out in each case to demand a normative 'conceptualization,' hence a normative truth claim, about their respective object domains.

If this is correct, then we can go somewhat further in specifying, however obliquely, the nature of the displacement of art's cognitive claims.

To say that art is consigned to an autonomous realm is to say that art's own forms have no non-artistic validity. But this is to say that artistic production, insofar as it remains true to its forms, can sustain only artistic — "aesthetic" — significance. So, the explanation for, for example, Gadamer's thesis that the truth-claims of art are unredeemable is that art's forms are autonomous from the discursive forms of non-artistic domains, and since the autonomy of art's forms is a condition for their 'truth' production, then *a fortiori* art's truth claims are unredeemable in terms external to art itself. In Gadamerian terms, say, this is to claim that the differentiation infecting artistic reception equally infects artistic production, and it infects by stripping art's *forms* of their ordinary discursive and teleological significances. The consequence of this is just as Gadamer claims it to be: discursive logic and practical (ethical) judgment are necessarily non-compulsive vis-à-vis judgments concerning artworks. So, although the separation of categorial domains has been *reflectively* discovered to be false in post-positivist philosophy of science, that reflective dissolution clearly has not dissolved art's autonomy because that autonomy refers to the non-ideological conditions of artistic production and consumption, to art's social exclusion, isolation, and marginalisation.

16.   Because art's praxis has become autonomised, consigned to a realm outside the centre(s) of societal production and reproduction, its praxis is a pseudo-praxis, a praxis that transforms without external societal effects. Nonetheless, art's very restriction to an autonomous domain entails that its forms can, although harassed, provide a reminder and a clue as to what non-dominating or normatively constituted praxis might be like. In saying this I am, of course, aligning myself with the central thrust behind Adorno's theory of art, and my understanding of art's truth function at least echoes his as it is encapsulated in the statement at the head of this paper. What, minimally, Adorno is there claiming is that the *only* conception of discursive rationality we have at our disposal is instrumental ra-

tionality, the rationality of Weberian rationalization. Adorno ties this rationality to commodity production, which reduces qualitatively distinct individuals to exchange equivalences. Thus for him art, above all painting and music, figure what it would be like to comprehend individuals without dominating them.

The claim that this is what occurs in art depends upon Adorno's contention that there is a fundamental social truth underlying Kant's account of aesthetic awareness. Works of art do unify their diverse elements by means of their forms; but the operation of these forms is *less than* the unity accomplished through conceptual synthesis. Conceptual synthesis, as identity thinking, represses the non-identical, the sensuous complexity and individuality of any particular item. Art forms, techniques, and modes of ordering, as residues of earlier practices stripped of normative authority and discursive validity, can only insist that the elements and materials upon which they work are susceptible to another sort of integration. Art objects are 'unique,' their uniqueness (non-identity) lying in their non-conceptual form of unification. Art forms, then, synthesise without domination, their work of unification mimicking or analogous to conceptual unification and teleological synthesis without however ever attaining to the level of explicitness of the latter. Because artworks are not conceptual wholes, they are not redeemable through ordinary discursive forms; because their work of unification is an analogue of conceptual unification and teleological (practical/normative) synthesis, they claim for themselves cognitive and ethical attention.

Artworks are indeed impossible objects: if aesthetic praxis were really transformative, then artworks would be "true," that is, art objects would be worldly objects, not purposeless but purposeful; if, on the other hand, they were mere objects or artifacts, they would be just things, or meaningless but purposeful. They are meaningful, they enact a synthesis, but they are not discursively true: they are purposeful but without a practical purpose. Their meaning is a semblance of truth without domination; their purposelessness, an image of use value that cannot be exchanged. Their purposelessness is their form of resistance to exchange — a form that is harassed and subject to defeat. Their non-conceptual form is their form of resistance to identity thinking — a form that is harassed by the will to interpretation. The autonomy of art is the excess, the non-identical, that allows identity thinking to continue unharassed. Art is the remainder, the result of the exclusions that allowed an autonomous economy to centre itself without the encumbrances of the claims of sensuousness or teleology (the submersion of use value by exchange value), and it is equally the periphery forever threatening and threatened by the centre. In this way, the Kantian thought that aesthetic awareness mimics the unifying work of conceptual judgment without however actually bringing the art object under a concept becomes both a conception of artistic practice, of how artistic form is to deal with its raw materials, and a statement about the socio-historical predicament of art, rather than an *a priori* truth about it.

Adorno's theory is less successful in dealing with novels, and this for the simple reason that he fails to take adequate account of the temporal features of existence that narrative forms of ordering address. Although I will not here attempt to rehearse what I have spelled out in detail elsewhere,[21] I wish to point out that the *content* of novels, free heroes/heroines attempting to create a temporal unity of their lives, repeats the work of narration itself. So the novel's pseudo-praxis remembers and anticipates in an individualistic mode a collective narrating and production. The novel points to a possible normative totalization of experience as the truth of narrative praxis itself; in so doing, it equally points to the anti-narrative tendencies of modernity.

If correct, these theses highlight the difficulty of conceiving of works as having a truth function. The Kantian/aesthetic analysis of works of art does present their appearance form; works of art address us only through the non-cognitive analogues of value cognition. We can appreciate this address, its cognitive significance, only by apprehending the historical figure in the theoretical carpet of the Kantian synthesis. Even so, works themselves are figures of a discursive praxis and, being so, they are important before the claims of existing discursive systems. It was due recognition of these two points that led Adorno to insist that, now, only a historically informed philosophical criticism of art was adequate. Art's impotence is historical; but this impotence is called into question by the works themselves. In so doing, they raise the question of truth, how it is produced and inscribed by the economic centre; their particular transformations, figurations, formal syntheses challenge, without force, the reigning cognitive regimes. In so doing, they call for philosophical attention, a philosophical clarification of their praxis. Since, however, philosophy too must obey the discursive regimes of the present, it cannot validate art's claim that alternative forms of praxis are possible; after discursively tracing the current limits of discursive practice, it can only return us to the work of art. Because art's truth function depends upon a questioning of what truth has really become, only philosophical criticism of art can sustain therefore its cognitive significances.

17.   Now there exists an evident analogy between this Adornoesque line of thought and the Heidegger/Derrida practice of double reading (deconstruction). Roughly, for both, Western reason has since its inception been beleaguered and governed by a fault, swerve, repression, forgetfulness: for Adorno this is the repression of mimetic thought or non-dominating thinking, while for Heidegger/Derrida it is the forgetfulness of being, of the difference between being and beings. Analogously, the dialectical interplay between art and philosophy, the production of an aesthetical theory *and* a philosophical supplement to art (in Adorno) recognizes the hegem-

ony of instrumental reason and identity thinking as delimiting the possibilities of its strategic displacement by art, in the same way as deconstructive practice recognizes the hegemony of the metaphysics of presence, the *inevitability* of discursive reason, as the limit to its identification of the excess that underlies it. Finally, for Heidegger, like Adorno, art represents a unique space in modernity where the questioning of the tradition can begin.

Before, however, a negotiation of this strategic dialogue can be begun, we need to comment directly on the question of great art. For this consideration, Adorno's aid can be enlisted.

He defines affirmative works of art as those that claim their qualities are those of a being-in-itself beyond art. Affirmative art belongs to art's past; although not all affirmative art is great art in Heidegger's sense, arguably all great art is affirmative art. About affirmative art Adorno writes:

> In the perspective of the present, the affirmative works of the past are less ideological than they are touching. After all, it is not their fault that the world spirit did not deliver what it had promised. Their transfigurations were too translucent to arouse real resistance. What makes them nevertheless evil is not ideology, but the fact that their perfection monumentalizes force and violence. These repressive connotations are brought out in adjectives like "engrossing" or "compelling," terms we use to describe great art. Art neutralizes force as well as making it worse; its innocence is its guilt. Modern art with all its blemishes and fallibilities is a critique of success, namely the success of traditional art which was always so unblemished and strong. Modernism is oriented critically to the insufficiency of an older art that presented itself as though it were sufficient... (*AT* 229)

Both Adorno and Heidegger see Western history as a decline, as an essential occluding of the impulse inaugurating it. Further, in much the same way as Adorno presents Beckett as revealing the meaning of modern meaninglessness, Heidegger speaks of Hölderlin as showing that "even this doom of the god remaining absent is a way in which world worlds" (*OWA* 45). How then are we to comprehend their different verdicts on the tradition?

I suspect the answer is this: whereas Heidegger sees the effect of technological revealing as debarring us from appropriating great works from the past as world disclosing, as well as, of course, from producing great art, Adorno compels us to read into past art the arrival of the tradition *here*. So the claim that the great art respected self-secluding earth, the unmasterability of nature, is brought into question by the compulsion for mastery in our rationalised, technological society. Great art, in spite of itself, participated in the history that has made it impossible. Modern art, on the contrary, operates on the basis of its exclusion from this dominant history; and it is this that leads Adorno (and Benjamin) to align modern art with the art of ages in decline, the non-great art of the past that was also fatefully excluded from domination.

Because the autonomous art of the present works to undo its own autonomy, while the non-autonomous art of the past is, for us, implicated in the tradition that drove art to the periphery, neither art can therefore be thought of as providing a model for or an anticipation of the art of the future.

18.   For Adorno, this inability of art is of little significance since aesthetic alienation does not figure art's alienation from its true vocation, whatever that might be; rather, art's alienation from truth figures reason's alienation from itself. "Art," he says, "is rationality criticizing itself without being able to overcome itself" (*AT* 81). What is being criticized by autonomous art is identity thinking, where something's being true depends on its being subsumed under some concepts and into some conceptual apparatus. Identity thinking is a mastering of the Other through the regimentation of conceptual thought into frameworks whose goal just is the construing of the non-identical other in the image of the same. Adorno, like Heidegger, sees the present as an ironic and fateful realization of Kant's Copernican turn. For Adorno, that realization occurs through the operation of capital, the domination of use-value by exchange value, and its societal completion. Capital figures identity thinking, what Heidegger and Nietzsche call Platonism, as a force capable of organizing society as a whole.

Artistic practice, at least in its autonomous, modernist guise, is a unique venue for critiquing reason since its history requires it to respect the claims of sensuousness and particularity. So Adorno will claim that the mark of the authenticity of works of art is that their illusion (both: their illusion of truth and their being illusory, fictive, semblances) "shines forth in such a way that it cannot possibly be prevaricated, and yet discursive judgment in unable to spell out its truth" (*AT* 191). And this sounds very much as if such works are making substantial truth claims beyond reason: hinting, perhaps, at some form of intuitionism. Elsewhere, however, Adorno clarifies his thought by saying, "Art works are true in the medium of determinate negation only" (*AT* 187); or, more simply, "Actually, only what does not fit into this world is true" (*AT* 86). What does not fit into this world are particulars who claim us in their particularity. For Adorno, only autonomous art systematically sustains such claims; it reveals what such a claiming is, albeit only in the mode of semblance and illusion.

"The falsehood opposed by art," says Adorno, "is not rationality *per se*, but the rigid juxtaposition of rationality and particularity" (*AT* 144). This is elaborated later: "In the eyes of existing rationality, aesthetic behaviour is irrational because it castigates the particularity of this rationality in its pursuit not of ends but of means. Art keeps alive the memory of a kind of objectivity which lies beyond conceptual frameworks. That is why art is rational, cognitive. Aesthetic behaviour is the ability to see more in things than they are" (*AT* 453). Reason has been deformed by what it has excluded from itself, but aesthetic practice only engages that excluded portion, not the whole; it lacks discursive conceptuality to the same degree to which reason lacks the capacity to engage with sensuous particularity. Art desires non-art, but can only sustain that desire artistically: that is the antinomy which dialectically sustains its practice, its value for us, its claims upon us, and its unhappiness.

For Heidegger, aesthetic alienation is the experience of art's alienation from truth, and hence of the impossibility of great art; for Adorno that same alienation from truth signifies the claim of the non-identical other. For Heidegger the other is always, eventually, *the* Other, being; which is why the history of unredeemed suffering is muted, silenced, within the history of being. In the same way in which great art inherits the guilt of the history of which it is a part, so the thought which thinks that guilt is constituted by its own unavoidable insufficiency, and by its guilt/debt in relation to that which it thinks.[22] Aesthetic alienation figures that guilt/debt through the experience of the non-identical other's claim to be 'true,' the truth of the true from which it has been excluded.

Art is a privileged social space for critique because it alone, among the 'rationally' differentiated specialized spheres of practice (cognitive, ethical, political, aesthetic), 'suffers' that differentiation.[23] Any attempt to mitigate that suffering, e.g., through keeping art aesthetic or prematurely letting art realize its desire for non-art (the false modernism of postmodernism), mutes the question of non-identity and with it the question of truth. Heidegger and Adorno, the oddest of couples, join forces over the recognition that the questions of modernity, history, and truth must be posed together, or the question will disappear altogether. The demand for an emphatic, non-adequation, conception of truth separates their critique from its pragmatist spectral image. It is, of course, truly terribly and terrifyingly ironic, and hateful because this recognition can only be made in the distancing mode of ironic reflection, that the human suffering and misery which is both the sufficient and final cause for these critical engagements, should find its cognitive echo in the marginalized practices of high — bourgeois — art. Equanimity over this fateful disjunction, over history's ironizing of fate into irony, can only be had at the price of unconsciousness.

19.   Discursively, the value of art lies in its questioning of the disciplines of discursive truth in modernity; while, practically, the arts model, albeit not univocally, a normatively constituted, non-dominating praxis. However, because art discharges this role through its truth-claims, therefore, where these claims themselves are repressed, defused, by the discursive regimes

of the present, only a philosophical criticism of artworks will allow them to fulfil their discursive role and only a non-institutionally bound reception will allow them to fulfil their practical function.

Given Adorno's, Heidegger's, and Derrida's skepticism about the opportunities and possibility of emancipating praxis, this claim for art's practical value sounds unduly optimistic. While their skepticism cannot be answered here, it can be mitigated.

The question *"Which* history is *our* history?" assumes an identity between its stressed terms that is itself antinomic, indeed is the antinomy holding our previous antinomies in place. Heidegger and Derrida address this question theoretically in terms of "which," and answer in terms of the metaphysics of presence and its ultimate expression in technology. Someone like Gadamer addresses this question practically, in terms of the agent who is claimed by the tradition: history is inevitably my/our history, the history of this linguistic community — his optimistic solidarity — as it is processed through the life-praxis of its individual members. The Marxist tradition, insistent on linking theory and practice, sought, most visibly in Lukacs, to match history and agent. The failure of this matching has left Marxism with a history without agents, in this not unlike deconstruction.

Yet, there is a hidden imbalance in this resolution, which itself masks a theoretical/contemplative conception of our predicament. The conclusion to the above antinomy reads: which history there is now is no one's history; our history is unavailable; there is no history we can appropriate. But who is this "we"? Writing, thinking, working as *we* (who else?) do, perhaps we forget how formal this "we" is, and forget the gap separating linguistic community, or any naturally (gender or race) marked community, from a substantial community. "We" as yet do not exist, so who is to say that there is no history for us? Who are we to believe them?

Art's deferred praxis, its praxis without effect, poses the question of the truth of truth in modernity. Art's interrogation can go no further than interrogation. In appropriating art we are directed toward another space, place, and time of praxis. The condition for this praxis is a "we," a substantial community for whom the question of history can be raised again. Perhaps, then, the claim of art, its truth-function, is to claim us for one another, to respond to our dispersal as spectators. Perhaps this is what Adorno was thinking when he wrote that "Enshrined in artistic objectification is a collective We. This We is not radically different from the external We of society. It is more like a residue of an actually existing society of the past. The fact that art addresses a collectivity is not a cardinal sin; it is the corollary of the law of form" (*AT* 339). And later: "... the process enacted by every art work — as a model for a kind of praxis wherein a collective subject is constituted — has repercussions on society" (*AT* 543). What might these repercussions be if not a call to solidarity?

Do you hear me?

Do you see that painting? Listen to the words of this poem! Read this story!
Our history, friend, is not yet written.

Notes

1. The thesis that our ethical practices and discourse are in a state of radical disorder has been vigorously pursued by Alisdair MacIntyre in his *After Virtue* (London: Duckworth, 1981).

2. Perhaps it is worthwhile reminding ourselves here that positivism too belongs to the critique of metaphysics.

3. For backing for this claim, see J.M. Bernstein, *The Philosophy of the Novel: Lukacs, Marxism and the Dialectics of Form* (Minneapolis: University of Minnesota Press, 1984), pp. 15-22. Hereafter: *PN*.

4. Parenthetic reference in the text will use the following abbreviations: OWA = "The Origin of the Work of Art" from *Poetry, Language, Thought*, trans. A. Hofstadter (New York: Harper & Row, 1971); N = *Nietzsche*, vol. 1, *The Will to Power as Art*, trans. D.F. Krell (New York: Harper & Row, 1979); QT = *The Question Concerning Technology and Other Essays*, trans. W. Lovitt (New York: Harper & Row, 1977); AT = T.W. Adorno, *Aesthetic Theory*, trans. C. Lenhardt (London: Routledge and Kegan Paul, 1984); PH = Hans Georg Gadamer, *Philosophical Hermeneutics*, trans. David Linge (Berkeley: University of California Press, 1976).

5. This, of course, is the standard reading of the essay; it construes Heidegger as offering an (atemporal) definition of art, and purges the essay of its historical intent — to reflect on the end (death, closure) of art. One consequence of this reading has been altogether to misplace the point of the 'famous' analysis of Van Gogh, to which I shall return below. Two fairly standard readings of "Origin" that misconstrue it in this way are: David Halliburton, *Poetic Thinking* (Chicago: The Chicago University Press, 1981), ch. 2; and Sandra Bartky, "Heidegger's Philosophy of Art" in Th. Sheehan, ed., *Heidegger, The Man and the Thinker* (Chicago: Precedent Publishing, 1981), pp. 257-74.

6. See here Robert Bernasconi's *The Question of Language in Heidegger's History of Being* (Atlantic Highlands, N.J.: Humanities Press, 1984), pp. 30-37. As is clear, I do not think that "Origin" can be grasped independently of Heidegger's other writing on aesthetics from this period, especially his lectures on Nietzsche's philosophy of Art (N). The best short account of this is David Krell, "Art and Truth in Raging Discord" in W.V. Spanos, *Martin Heidegger and the Question of Literature* (Bloomington: Indiana University Press, 1979), pp. 39-52.

7. Of course, Heidegger's new vocabulary for discussing works of art, his concepts of world and earth, are important, but not germane here.

8. Ian Hacking has correctly noted this 'Hegelian' (Hegel without absolute knowledge) conception of science in Lakatos. See his "Imre Lakatos'

Philosophy of Science," *British Journal of the Philosophy of Science* 30 (1979), 381-402.

9. For a radical questioning of this — Kantian — liberal view, see Michael Sandel, *Liberalism and the Limits of Justice* (Cambridge, Eng.: Cambridge University Press, 1982).

10. See Doppelt, p. 75.

11. Remember? "On the leather lie the dampness and richness of the soil. Under the soles slides the loneliness of the field-path as evening falls. In the shoes vibrates the silent call of the earth..." (*OWA* 34).

12. "The Still Life as a Personal Object — A Note on Heidegger and Van Gogh," in M.L. Simmel, ed., *The Reach of Mind* (New York: Springer Publishing Company, 1968), pp. 203-09. For a questioning of Schapiro, see J. Derrida, *La Vérité en Peinture* (Paris: Flammarion, 1978), pp. 291-436.

13. As should now be clear, the question at issue here is the role of art in modern societies and its role in earlier epochs, and that issue raises the question of the truth of art in a non-naturalistic way which, if we can come to appreciate the historical distinction, turns out to be the only way in which that question can be posed. Heidegger's account hence questions our unreflective conceptual framework even if we wish to reject the particularities of his theory.

14. Martin Heidegger, *The End of Philosophy*, trans. Joan Stambaugh (London: Souvenir Press, 1975), p. 104.

15. Gillian Rose, *Dialectic of Nihilism* (Oxford: Basil Blackwell, 1984), p. 83.

16. *The End of Philosophy*, p. 107.

17. *On Time and Being*, trans. Joan Stambaugh (New York: Harper and Row, 1972), p. 57.

18. "Postmodernism, or The Cultural Logic of Capital," *NLR* 146. The following quotes are from pp. 58-59.

19. "It is silly to think that art can augment its dignity by dealing with some august event or other... Van Gogh unmasked such dignity when he painted a chair or some sunflowers in such a fashion that the pictures were ravaged by all the emotions experienced for the first time by the individual of Van Gogh's time, emotions which responded to the historical catastrophe. After this has become obvious, we can turn backward and show with reference to earlier art just how little its authenticity was a function of the greatness, real or imagined, of its subject matter" (*AT* 215). Of course, Adorno's "authenticity" here too quickly collapses the historical problematic of pre-modern art.

20. Again, see my *PN*, ch. 4.

21. *PN*, ch. 4.

22. T. W. Adorno, *Negative Dialectics*, trans. E.B. Ashton (London: Routledge and Kegan Paul, 1973), p. 5.

23. I have argued against the upbeat Weber-Habermas defence of modernity and the separation of spheres in more detail in my "Art Against Enlightenment: Adorno's Critique of Habermas," forthcoming in Andrew Benjamin, ed.,

Modernity and Postmodernism: Adorno and Benjamin (London: Routledge and Kegan Paul). I try to say a great deal more about the connections and disconnections among Heidegger, Derrida and Adorno in my *Beauty Bereaved: Art, Metaphysics and Modernity* (Oxford: Polity Press, forthcoming).

5

INTERPRETATION, INTERMINABILITY, EVALUATION: FROM NIETZSCHE TOWARD A GENERAL ECONOMY

Arkady Plotnitsky

> *The world, apart from our conditions of living in it, the world that we have not reduced to our being, our logic and psychological prejudices, does not exist as a world "in itself"; it is essentially a world of relationships; under certain conditions it has a differing aspect from every point; it presses upon every point, every point resists it — and the sum* of these is in every case quite incongruent.* — Friedrich Nietzsche, *The Will to Power*

> *Its having come apart makes an unfortunate difference for its beauty, its artistic value, but none for anything else. Its other value is just the same.* — Henry James, *The Golden Bowl*

Although the presence of evaluation in any creative or interpretive act, including literary criticism, is rarely denied, the relations between evaluation and interpretation as subjects of theoretical investigation have not been quite symmetrical in recent years, or even throughout the twentieth century. While the literary theorist has available at the moment a number of diverse and theoretically promising approaches to interpretation, the same by no means can be said about evaluation. If anything, one could detect a broad tendency to suppress the discourse on value. The reasons are mul-

---

* The reading of this word in Nietzsche's manuscript is doubtful.

tiple and persistent, and the situation is characteristic of both the European and Anglo-American scene.[1]

Heidegger, whose significance for the whole Western horizon in this century has been enormous, concludes his own negative "evaluation" of evaluation in *An Introduction to Metaphysics* as follows:

> How stubbornly the idea of values ingrained itself in the nineteenth century can be seen from the fact that even Nietzsche, and precisely he, never departed from this perspective. The subtitle of his projected magnum opus, "The Will to Power," is "An Attempt to Reevaluate All Values." The third book is called: "An Attempt to Establish New Values." His entanglement in the thicket of the idea of values, his failure to understand its questionable origin, is the reason why Nietzsche did not attain to the true center of philosophy. Even if a future philosopher should reach this center — we of the present day can only work toward it — he will not escape the entanglement. No one can jump over his own shadow.[2]

It is difficult to determine fully the extent to which Heidegger's devaluation of "the idea of values" in the *Introduction to Metaphysics* and elsewhere, particularly in the influential *Letter on Humanism*, shaped the negative attitude toward value and evaluation in twentieth-century intellectual history. At the very least, his critique is paradigmatic of that attitude. In Heidegger's case, the question of value is specifically related to his interpretation of Nietzsche's "philosophy." This is important, given an equal or perhaps even more significant presence of Nietzsche in modern theory. In general, as Derrida suggests, most specifically in his analysis of Heidegger, everything depends on how one reads Nietzsche, this crucial — "central" — margin of philosophy.

Although a great deal more might as yet be at stake, "everything" would refer above all to logocentrism or the metaphysics of presence, "a powerful historical and systematic unity," whose limits are identified and exhaustively analyzed by Derrida, "along with the project of deconstruction."[3] I shall not enter into the details of the Derridean project, and there is no need to do so as Derrida's discourse and language have become quite familiar — even all too familiar — by now. Perhaps (Derrida's) *deconstruction* of *logocentrism* demonstrates its critical force most powerfully in Heidegger's case and particularly in exposing the difference between Heidegger and Nietzsche. Derrida thus writes in *Of Grammatology*:

> Nietzsche has *written what* he has written. He has written that writing — and first of all his own — is not originarily subordinate to the logos and to truth. And this

subordination has *come into being* during the epoch whose meaning we must deconstruct. Now in this direction (but only in this direction, for read otherwise, the Nietzschean demolition remains dogmatic and, like all reversal, a captive of that metaphysical edifice which it professes to overthrow. On that point and in that *order of reading*, the conclusions of Heidegger and Fink are irrefutable), Heideggerian thought would reinstate rather than destroy the instance of the logos and the truth of being as *"primum signatum"*: the "transcendental" signified ("transcendental" in a certain sense, as in the Middle Ages the transcendental — *ens, unum, verum, bonum* — was said to be the *"primum cognitum"*) implied by all categories or all determined significations, by all lexicons and all syntax, and therefore by all linguistic signifiers, though not to be identified simply with any one of those signifiers, allowing itself to be precomprehended through each of them, remaining irreducible to all the epochal determinations that it nonetheless makes possible, thus opening the history of the logos, yet itself being only through the logos: that is *being nothing* before the logos and outside of it.[4]

Derrida goes on to expose (and to explore) in a nuanced and rigorous analysis, the fundamentally logocentric grounding of the Heideggerian project. Most significant for us is that the metaphysics of presence, either in its Heideggerian form or in any other, offers itself to analytic dismantling or deconstruction through the Nietzschean critical strategies and perspectives. Derrida thus speaks in *"Différance"* of "themes in Nietzsche's work that are linked to the symptomatology that always diagnoses the detour or ruse of an agency disguised in its *différance*: or further, to the entire thematic of active interpretation, which substitutes incessant deciphering for the unveiling of truth as the presentation of the thing itself in its presence, etc. Figures without truth, or at least a system of figures not dominated by the value of truth, which then becomes only an included, inscribed, circumscribed function."[5]

As this formulation suggests, however, these themes are, in the same deconstructive gesture, reinscribed through the thematics of value. To be sure, values appear and are inscribed in Nietzsche without the value of truth, perhaps even without the value of value (in its metaphysical sense). If, however, *both* evaluation and the critique of (metaphysical) values are conceived along these Nietzschean lines, then a theory of value and evaluation will have to erase (perhaps in Derrida's sense of taking under erasure, *"sous rature"*) the *metaphysical* possibility of permanent, universal, absolute, objective (or, conversely, subjective) values: in short, all *"present* values," all values of *presence* (or truth). Such a deconstruction, however, will be inseparable from the development of a theory accounting for "metaphysical" values; that is, precisely, for their *value* or necessity — historically, culturally, institutionally, psychologically, biologically, and so on.

One might suggest, then, that we should speak here of the "historical" character of all evaluations and values. Let us note in passing that this radical locality or relativity or, one could say, *différance* of value, has, like Derrida's *différance*, nothing to do with the subjectivity, especially the *conscious* subjectivity, of value. Values, in so far as they appear as "local values," are always interactive — therefore always social and political — products of the historical dynamics at issue in such an account. Values are also the effects of a complex (and always *inter*subjective) psychological play. The unconscious, therefore, will play a crucial role in this reinscription of value, as Nietzsche, anticipating Freud, was first to understand in full measure. What Nietzsche calls "perspectivism" is precisely this *perspective* on values as historically determined, socially interactive, and inhibited by the unconscious. Rather than viewing values as "given," existing in or by themselves, objectively, universally, or otherwise "present," as Heidegger seems to imply, Nietzsche would conceive of all values as produced *locally* under the conditions and constraints — psychological, biological, social, cultural, and so forth — of *specific, historical*, evaluative configurations. The evaluative play so conceived would, of course, also include the historical specificity of one's own *perspectival* evaluations of the perspectival evaluations of others.

The Nietzschean perspectivism demands thus a theoretical framework within which objective, universal, or otherwise "present" values, or other structures, can be theoretically considered and accounted for. For our local theoretical projects do, in most cases, include broader situations, long-term projections, and other expanded aspects and conditions of our interaction with the world, along with more comprehensive theoretical accounts of such interactions. The understanding of values and evaluation developed here, for instance, will in turn offer, from a historically local perspective, a *global* view of the problem. It will do so, however much locality, heterogeneity, perspectivism, difference, or dissemination of value will inform this understanding.

In this sense, in the place of absolute, universal, objective (or subjective) values, we can speak of local *value(s)* or, under certain conditions, the *necessity* of "universal" values; that is, of a local value of universal values and of the historical conditions and constraints of their production and inscription. Nor, conversely, can the concept of local value be exempt from a similar scrutiny: the fundamental locality of value, that is, the value or necessity of such a conception, in turn becomes an important theoretical issue.

Throughout his text, most specifically in *On the Genealogy of Morals*, Nietzsche was the first to approach critically the emergence of allegedly permanent values and value hierarchies — good (and evil), true (and false), moral (and immoral), beautiful (and ugly), and so on — as they have been locally or historically produced. Armed with this understanding, he was able to deconstruct the previous metaphysical understanding of these oppositions. The critical aspect of this deconstruction amounts to exposing the possible, and often historically actual, reversibility of their hierarchical structure. This reversibility results from the derivative character of the oppositions with regard to the radically non-oppositional — "beyond good and evil" — historical play where they emerge. But Nietzsche also performed his "deconstruction" of the historical system of morals as an interpretation, with a remarkable intuition of the historical locality of his own positions. Nietzsche's quotation marks — "we," "we immoralists," "our" values, and so on — are highly indicative of this attitude, however much he would have privileged "us" and "our values" over others.

In general, theoretical projects of this type will take into account that universal, permanent, absolute, or objective values (or the structures of consciousness or presence in general) will not quite disappear. Such values will continue to "exist" as universal, permanent, or objective for those who live with them or conceive of them as such, or who have done so in the historical past. From "our" perspective, however, such values require a historical and theoretical investigation as *local* values, as do the associated concepts of "objectivity," "universality," or "permanence." In this sense, the metaphysical (classical or traditional) values, at least some of them, will remain *valuable* or necessary for us as well. The — Nietzschean — question "who are we?"[6] will in turn be a part of the same theoretical investigation.

It has been the case, historically, that the damaging effects of logocentrist ideology are "first" felt in the logocentrist interpretations of *interpretation*, rather than evaluation. As Derrida maintains, analyzing the structuralist and/as Rousseauistic thematic (in a pointed parallel to his discussion of Heidegger and Heideggerian hope):

> There are thus two interpretations of interpretation, of structure, of sign, of play. The one seeks to decipher, dreams of deciphering a truth or an origin which escapes play and the order of the sign, and which lives the necessity of interpretation as an exile. The other, which is no longer turned toward the origin, affirms play and tries to pass beyond man and humanism, the name of man being the name of that being who, throughout the history of metaphysics or of ontotheology — in other words, throughout his entire history — has dreamed of full presence, the reassuring foundation, the origin and the end

of play. The second interpretation of interpretation, to which Nietzsche pointed the way, does not seek in ethnography, as Lévi-Strauss does, the "inspiration of a new humanism" (again citing the "Introduction to the Work of Marcel Mauss").[7]

Given Nietzsche's "entanglement in the thicket of the idea of value," one can suggest that a deconstructive interpretation of interpretation may be viewed, particularly in its *affirmative* (Nietzschean) aspect, as correlative to inscribing evaluation (as *locality* of value) in the interpretive process, while the other interpretation of interpretation — the dream of truth, origin (or end), presence, and foundation — acts so as either to suppress evaluation (and its study) or to establish metaphysical values as considered earlier, or, in most cases, in the same gesture, to do both at once.

A different inscription of the borderlines of interpretation will, of course, in turn imply a reinscription of value. Both — interpretive boundaries and values of any kind — will, in any given situation, appear as the historical effects of local conditions and the constraints of the interpretive process. This general difference in inscription, however, whether we speak of interpretation, evaluation or history, will also suggest a broader significance of evaluation in the whole process and, thus, of the question of value as the subject of theoretical investigation. As shall be seen presently, such an inscription must in fact connect evaluation to the limits and borderlines of interpretation.

A crucial aspect of interpretive dynamics in general is that, theoretically, an interpretation has no termination: that is, in principle, we can interpret any configuration forever. Nor, as Derrida shows, inscribing what he calls "trace," does interpretation have an absolute origin; the notion of trace is, in effect, introduced by Derrida in order to account for this structural, i.e., ineluctable, loss of origin.[8] Any element of text or meaning — a "mark" produced in an interpretation — is always already a trace of some preceding structures out of which such elements are produced, and, in principle, these chains of origin cannot be terminated either. But, of course, in every actual case we do terminate our specific interpretation at some point, as we do also begin them somewhere. That is to say, we always, however implicitly, mark the frames and limits of such beginnings or closures. Any given chain in the network of the traces that constitute and produce a text, meaning or interpretive inference, and that constantly refer to other preceding traces and generate new ones, is always abandoned somewhere, once we switch to a new chain.

Evaluation as structure is perhaps best seen in relation to this abandonment: that is, the limits of our interpretations are evaluative, or rather evaluation inscribes itself in relation to such limits. We begin or stop at some point and/or select one or another alternate trajectory of traces to follow because, under the constraints of the moment, it is "the best" we can do. The effect of constraints is crucial, for we constantly find ourselves under conditions that control our interpretations and establish or enforce the trajectories at issue. We simply cannot do anything else. It is also important to stress, in this context, that such a conception of evaluation, though enabling an account of the emergence of metaphysical values, including "present"values and the value of presence, does not claim that there *is* any "present" value. It is rather the structure of preference that is at issue, the preference that might, under certain conditions, be enforced and is, under all conditions, constrained.

Freud's distinction between terminable and interminable analysis developed in the great late essay "Analysis Terminable and Interminable" is useful here, particularly in relation to evaluation in theoretical situations. This distinction also plays an important role in Derrida's discourse. As Freud writes:

> This would mean, then, that not only the therapeutic analysis of patients but his [the analyst's] own analysis would change from terminable into an interminable task.
>
> At this point, however, we must guard against a misconception. I am not intending to assert that analysis is altogether an endless business. Whatever one's theoretical attitude to the question may be, the termination of analysis is, I think, a practical matter. Every experienced analyst will be able to recall a number of cases in which he has bidden his patient farewell *rebus bene gestis*.[9]

Utilizing psychoanalytic practice as a vehicle of theory, deconstruction points toward "the necessity of an interminable analysis."[10] But one must also account for the necessity of termination, for any analysis or interpretation is *necessarily* terminated at some point. At the very least, death of one kind or another — of analyst or patient, or of theorist — will terminate an analysis.

Defining man as *homo mortem*, Heidegger, in his perhaps most famous proposition, speaks of the finitude of *Dasein* in man that is more original than man. Analogously (but also in a radical displacement of Heidegger), Derrida writes: "Death is the movement of *différance* to the extent that this movement is necessarily finite" (*Grammatology* 143). *Différance* is also, in effect by the same token, "the history of life... as the history of *gramme*" (*Grammatology* 84). *Différance* itself, however (and perhaps death as well), must be distinguished from finitude. For "it would not mean a single step outside of metaphysics if nothing more than a new motif of 'return to finitude,' or of 'God's death,' etc., were the result of this move. It is that conceptuality and that problematics that must be deconstructed. *Différance* is also something other than finitude" (*Grammatology* 68). Rather, finitude (and terminability) is one of the effects of *différance*. "Infinity" (and interminability) would be another such effect. Displacing the Heideggerian (or, in general, metaphysical) finitude, such a psychoanalytic or deconstructive termination involves, as Freud seems to imply, an evaluation or certain pragmatics under given constraints. (The latter are inscribed, in Freud's essay, in specifically psychoanalytic terms.) In his recent essay on, among other things, Freud, psychoanalysis and literature, "My Chances," Derrida speaks of "analysis that [he] will call (with some circumspection) *pragrammatological*, at the intersection of a pragmatics and a grammatology."[11]

One could go even further in this direction and suggest that interpretation can produce no meaning (in the classical or traditional sense, such as the signified content of a text), but only *value*. A specific interpretive act, an interpretation of a literary text, for example, produces not a meaning but rather a *value*, something that is for the moment better than other possible effects of the given text. This latter, of course, is already — "always already" — produced as a certain value. One can in fact say, following Nietzsche (and, as shall be seen below, Valéry), that it is some value of such a product that makes one insist on its truth, presence, essence, and so forth. There can be no absolute origin here, but, as with terminations, only a provisional one, and thus, at least in part evaluative. Nor can one have only one origin or termination, so radically heterogeneous is the structure of the trace, the structure of history. In this irreducible *dissemination* of evaluative/interpretive chains, nothing, therefore, may at any moment have only one value.

We must then inscribe value through a radical difference, a certain *différance*, even though we can do so only within the limits of a "historical closure" of metaphysics and science and their "*incompetence*" (*Grammatology* 93). Like James's golden bowl, value is always broken; yet a value of one kind or another is always in place.

To say that the interpretation produces value is not to say much, however, unless we specifically account for evaluation as being different from other structures involved in the interpretive process (as value production), including its differences from the classical formation of meaning, or alternatively, unless we specifically redefine the whole interpretive situation in terms of value. Given this latter possibility, an interpretation of interpretation in which all interpretation is conceived as evaluation is, therefore, not unthinkable. Nietzsche perhaps implied as much. Nietzsche's interpretation of interpretation as "the 'active, moving discord of different forces, and of differences of forces'" (*Margins* 18) is also a confrontation — an unconscious confrontation — of values. This confrontation, moreover, is also seen by Nietzsche as taking place in nature as *physis* or matter. In effect it defines nature, as it becomes in Nietzsche's later works the will to power as nature and nature as the will to power. The necessity and desire of presence will appear within this scheme as the active positing of one's values and one's will to power. Let us briefly note that by inscribing the "names" and "concepts" of difference and force or power into the chain of evaluative reinscriptions of interpretation, one (Nietzsche, for instance) is already dislocating, through evaluation, such a reinscription: a single, unique, or final name is no more possible in this case than in any other.[12]

More axiological inscriptions of interpretation are possible then. I do prefer, however, to retain the name of "interpretation" (what Derrida calls *différance* or *writing*) for the process of the emergence of value, while reinserting the term or operator "evaluation" in order to mark the abandonment and transfer of the differential chains generated in an interpretive process. Inserted in this framework, evaluation will appear as the operative or structural limit of the interpretive process.

This reinscription of both terms — interpretation and evaluation — does imply their mutually defining relationship. In the regime of *différance*, the register of evaluation then operates so as to intercept or rechannel the chains in the unconscious flow of "always everywhere differences and traces of traces."[13] This regime, perhaps without a name, certainly with more than one name, designates the structure (*as process*) where values emerge and articulate themselves *as* values. Such values may be the products of explanations and theories (principles, formulations, theorems, axioms, corollaries, conclusions, etc.), commodities or financial investments, versions or lines (or words, or still smaller units) of a poem, specific interpretations of such units, poems, or any literary (or other) texts, and so forth. Any of these value formations, moreover, may, under given historical conditions (or by the force of a given set of historical constraints), pass into another.

Depending upon the historical conditions of their emergence, values may appear either as metaphysical, "present" values, including the value of presence, or as transformational, local values, making, for instance, *presence* into *a* value of presence as a local value. Under still different conditions, values may appear as non-values, as "meanings," for instance, or "texts" or "things" (though they still remain "values" from the perspective just delineated).

Let us reiterate that the locality of evaluation and (or without) values will by no means neglect, but rather accentuate, the social and historical exterior — the outside — of the interpretive process. In the Derridean discourse, "the exterior" appears — in complex interaction between the inside and outside of (within) *writing* and *différance* — as the "radical alterity" inaccessible to the dyadic structures of metaphysics and presence. In effect, this radical alterity (the exterior) plays a critical role in the structuring of constraints, whose operation in the evaluative process has been emphasized all along here. The constraints at issue operate by enforcing — or forcing out — the trace, transferring or suppressing the trajectories in various ways through the interpretive network, and imposing the margins and boundaries of interpretation. It should be noticed at this point that the role of unconscious operations — of what is termed by Derrida (importantly in its interaction with the radical alterity of the interpretive outside) the structural unconscious — will remain crucial in evaluative operations as well, in part, to be sure, because the latter can never be quite divorced from the operation of the trace, and, as Derrida insists through his discourse, "there are *no* 'conscious' traces" (*Margins* 21).

I cannot enter here into the details of the structural unconscious of evaluation, but shall emphasize that it will remain crucial for the theoretical matrix (of evaluation) under consideration in the present essay. It might even be said that without accounting for the unconscious — Freudian — effects (however they might be renamed and however much their classical theories deconstructed) no (valuable) theory is possible. Such an account will, among other things, suggest that certain differential chains — the fabrics of traces — will be "abandoned" by evaluative or constraining operations only provisionally; indeed, the interpretive process, the continuous production of new "values," will be overtaken by or suppressed in (exiled to) the structural unconscious. This is still somewhat crude, but I shall "terminate" here by adding that the concept of the unconscious is, of course, also central in the Nietzschean understanding of evaluation (and interpretation) as affirmative play — as *positing, actively affirming*, rather than selecting (by a *re*-active process) one's values or meanings.

It follows, however, that in so far as one reappropriates the Derridean matrix — the emergence of the trace — as the emergence of value, one then cannot claim that interpretation is primary, or precedes evaluation. For it is precisely this kind of theoretical logic — "first" this, "then" that, "before and after" — that is first to be given up. The (Nietzschean) point is that even though interpretation as conceived here is the emergence of value, or the production of whatever values emerge, it is nonetheless always evaluation; or, in Nietzsche's terms, it is always a positing of values, an affirmation and play without truth, presence, origin, or center. Evaluation, that is, will in turn, reciprocally, both produce and inhibit interpretation. The analysis of either will also be the analysis of the structure of this inhibition: values coming into play (of evaluation) in the emergence of the trace as interpretation without meaning; and the trace emerging in part through evaluation without ("present") values.

"This 'primacy' of inhibition is even more the inhibition of the Primary,"[14] Samuel Weber suggests, referring specifically to Freud's distinction between primary and secondary processes. More general theoretical implications of this formulation are unavoidable, however. "[Primacy] — in the sense of being theoretically and practically irreducible — [of] the notion of inhibition"[15] will imply precisely that our analysis of evaluation, as of interpretation, is interminable and indeterminate in the sense that there is no ultimate grounding structure or conclusive, true, universally applicable or "valid" theoretical explanation. Such an analysis instead will require continuous "interminable" investigations of historical configurations, some of which are also our own. That is, our account of evaluation — and (in) its relation to interpretation — will obey that very law of evaluation and its conditions that it attempts to account for: it will emerge and will be determined and (or) terminated as an account under the specific local conditions and constraints of the historical situation that is precisely our own.

The problem(s) at issue cannot therefore be reduced to a *simple* choice between "evaluation" and "interpretation," whatever their distribution or reinscription in "interpretive" or "evaluative" interpretations of interpretation might be. Nor can it be the question of a simple choice between the two interpretations of interpretation (and evaluation) with which I began here — the logocentrist and the transformational or deconstructive. The transformational interpretation of interpretation itself can, and historically must, be considered along a certain spectrum: from various logocentric conceptions of transformation, such as in Heidegger, to their simple reversal in the conception of interpretation as absolute discontinuity and randomness of meaning. The latter, like all unproblematized reversals, will "leave the previous field untouched."[16] The (deconstructive) transformational reinscription of interpretation and evaluation must be "comprehensive" with regard to both of these positions: logocentrism and the perspective of absolute locality are, in this sense, equally the faces or effects of transformations. As Derrida writes, again in juxtaposing Nietzsche's interpretation of interpretation to that of Lévi-Strauss:

> For my part, although these two interpretations must acknowledge and accentuate their difference and define their irreducibility, I do not believe that today there is any question of choosing — in the first place because here we are in the region (let us say, provisionally, a region of historicity) where the category of choice seems particularly trivial, and in the second because we must first conceive of the common ground, and the *différance* of this irreducible difference.[17]

Derrida seems once again to be concerned here with the specific historico-theoretical configuration — "which is also our own" — that forces one to think of the broader sense of the historical conditions and constraints that led to the possibility or necessity of both these interpretations of interpretation: Nietzsche's and Lévi-Strauss's (or logocentrists' in general). The choice (if "today there is any question of choosing") demanded by the present analysis is indeed that of conceiving first (if such a thing — "first" — is possible) of the common ground or *différance* that Derrida insists upon. That is, one must ask what could be the historical conditions under which either interpretation of interpretation (and their common ground and *différance*) emerged; what would be the conditions under which it was possible, preferred, abandoned, and so on. This question is in fact Nietzsche's question, directed specifically to Kant's interpretation of interpretation.[18]

A historical analysis of this type will in turn engage *our own* historical conditions. To be sure, this double-historicity emerges in part because the historical situation *under* analysis is also our own. But our theories are thus *historical* also in the more general sense of an explanatory double-bind. Every explanation, every interpretation, inherits the diachronic trace of the history of its own production, and of a theory — an interpretation of interpretation — always involved there.

As this configuration enters the scene of theory, it demands an analysis not only with respect to the question of choice and the constraints of the situation, but also the question of evaluation. For example, what makes the category of choice particularly trivial in the region of historicity that Derrida speaks about? And why is there no question of choosing under the specific conditions of the situation at issue? Both questions will, particularly in the Nietzschean context, involve the problem of evaluation: where do we place evaluation as the interpretation of interpretation, or as an aspect of it, or in its relation to the common ground or *différance* at issue?

It would follow from the analysis given earlier that the category of choice is indeed trivial in the sense that "we" (some of "us") cannot simply, by a throw of dice, as it were, choose either one or another of the two interpretations, nor the *différance* that Derrida offers us "to be conceived of first." Like Derrida's, our choice or its absence is mightily constrained indeed.

But the category of choice is also trivial in another sense, related to the first, but worthy of separate consideration, namely, in the sense that "we" cannot assume or accept that some of us can, strictly speaking, choose (though "some" nonetheless do) one interpretation and others another, while still others choose the *différance* of both, and so on through the spectrum of possible alternatives. That is to say, we cannot accept the coexistence of different theories or interpretations or interpretations as equally possible or acceptable within the institutional configuration where we and our theories belong, even though we recognize that different interpretations are accepted by others starting from a theoretical or ideological position different from our own. The issue here is not so much of theoretical fallacy (though the latter concept must in turn be analyzed) as it is one of institutional struggle for domination between theories and interpretations. It may be that these structures of domination are, in effect, equivalent to the structures or constraints of our "own" choice as just considered, the latter being in turn the structure of the institutional value, power and constraints necessarily inscribed in the questions at issue. By so contrasting a "war" of theories with theoretical differences without opposition, I have in mind only the points of intersection where a different theory infringes upon the power — whether institutional, theoretical (in whatever sense), or other — of our own explanation. It would be foolish not to recognize the general spectrum of theoretical difference operating within any given configuration, field, or discipline.

The category of choice becomes somewhat less trivial when Derrida does make his theoretical choice (in the absence of choice, as it were) advancing the necessity of the "common" ground and the *différance* of two interpretations of interpretation and thus raising the more general question of what he calls *différance* and *writing*, or still otherwise. It is worth pointing out that, while constituting a more general, i.e. comprehensive, theoretical question, neither *différance* nor *writing* can exist in general, outside the historically particular context and discourse of their inscription. In this sense, what Derrida speaks of here can be called an interpretation of interpretation only in a highly provisional fashion and within the metaphysical and historical closure constraining our language and discourse. Once this choice, or non-choice, is made, it follows then that a theory of interpretation (or evaluation) *must* investigate the structures, like *différance* or *writing*, that historically condition or produce specific interpretations of interpretation.

But why indeed does this "choice" become theoretically preferable or inevitable under "our" current conditions of theoretical discourse? This choice, in fact the choice of difference and the choice of *différance*, can be preferable or inevitable only under the specific conditions and constraints of the operation of *Derrida's* theoretical discourse. We might say that, in these specific cases of "choosing," the choice is under "the constraints of the differential-supplementary structure" that Derrida constantly uncovers in operations such as metaphor (displacement) and history (deferral) — in short *différance* — throughout the text of Western philosophy.[19] Such structures are themselves produced under comparable theoretical constraints, and in this sense are no different from any other structures or theories. They are neither primary nor originary. As was indicated earlier, all the way through such analytical technique the circularity or double-bind is at work, continuously requiring further analysis — why, for instance, do we or "must" we accept the constraints of the differential-supplementary structure? — and continuously preventing the ultimate termination of any interpretation or theory. This circularity is, of course, itself one of the constraints of the differential-supplementary structure at issue. (Why, i.e., under what conditions, do we or "must" we accept this constraint? Hegel, for example, certainly did not; neither, in the phenomenological shadow of Hegel, did Husserl. At this point, the law, the cruel law of the interminability of the analysis of theory and its institutions, begins to assert itself most powerfully.)

With this double bind or explanatory vicious circle in mind, we might, by way of our own analysis, add a few further remarks on the constraints of *différance*. One of the forces of its operation is indeed Derrida's deconstruction, i.e., the exposure of the operation at issue in the text of philosophy. But one might quite legitimately ask here, does not Heidegger also expose the presence and truth of Being in the "same" text? This is, of course, the question — "in the region of historicity" — to which Derrida's remark on the choice between Nietzsche and Lévi-Strauss refers and which could be forcefully applied; and here, as perhaps nowhere else, the question of a common ground, of *différance*, enforces itself. It is not, of course, that with Heidegger's powerful impact upon his discourse, Derrida himself has missed the chance to ask this question. Quite the contrary: *différance* is introduced as always already "comprehending" the Heideggerian question and is designed to comprehend the Heideggerian onto-ontological difference.[20] There is, as Derrida maintains, "no simple answer" to this question of the relationships between *différance* and *truth* of Being, including the truth of Being as onto-ontological difference between Being and beings (*Margins* 22). Nonetheless, it is possible to conceive of the Heideggerian structure as "comprehended" in this sense, and therefore our own discourse as "constrained" (against Heidegger, as it were) by this comprehension and by the constraints of the differential-supplementary structures. It is, in effect, by introducing this structure that the comprehension at issue occurs in the first place.

One of the fundamental theoretical preferences, values or, again, constraints thus emerging will be (in contrast to a transcendental signified of the Heideggerian type) a different inscription of the interpretive transformations in an irreducible differential play, such as *différance*, conceived within the closure but in a radical difference — *différance* — from metaphysics and logocentrism. At the same time, "logos," "truth," "presence," or "Being" will be reinscribed as the effects of this non-centered and non-originary play. This reinscription will be a part of the set or system of constraints enforced by the transformations of *différance*, while a theoretical reinscription of *différance* will itself be local and, unlike Heideggerian structures, will not be conceived teleologically, nor to constitute an epoch or stage in the history of revealing or concealing the truth of Being. The inscription of *différance* thus will not participate in any kind of progress of "thinking" or of philosophy. *Différance* is introduced above all strategically, and therefore locally in our sense, and Derrida maintains that, "by means of this solely strategic justification, I wish to underline that the efficacy of the thematic of *différance* may very well, indeed must, one day be superseded, lending itself if not to its own replacement, at least to enmeshing itself in chains that in truth it never will have governed" (*Margins* 7).

This replacement will never be governed by any original *différance*, included in any hierarchy or subordination, and the law of such replacement will therefore be quite different from the Heideggerian truth (and epoch) of Being. This history, the historicity of history, and the region(s) of historicity Derrida invokes, will therefore also be inscribed differently from the Heideggerian historicity of *Dasein*, which is thus exposed as metaphysical. This different historical inscription will, in turn, constitute a part of the constraint at issue, the constraint that compels our "choice," or, at least, that we feel compelled to take into account in "choosing" between interpretations of interpretation.

It appears, then, that under these (*structural*) constraints — in the absence of choice — Derrida does indeed make a theoretical evaluation and, I think, a correct one. It is significant at this juncture that, as in fact throughout Derrida's discourse, a preference is given to Nietzsche's interpretation of interpretation. Powerful theoretical structures and historico-theoretical configurations constrain this preference; but then no evaluation (and no interpretation) can occur outside structures that constrain it. If, in the final account — and there will be, once again, no final account — the inevitability of constraining structures renders the category of "choice" or "evaluation" trivial, it is only in so far as such terms are inscribed by some previous conceptual framework, theory, strategy or ideology. Derrida, in truth — and this is somewhat strange given his usual terminological precautions and precision — does not indicate which specific "trivial" category he has in mind. What I have suggested here is that in as much as evaluation always occurs under the constraints of the moment, one could reinscribe it as a procedure where constraints so reduce the range of alternatives as to eliminate the possibility of "choice" altogether, dissolving the latter as a category and thus making it trivial.

In this sense, the dynamics of choice and compulsion and those of evaluation and constraint are the same dynamics or, rather, they can be conceived as the same within the theoretical matrix developed in the present analysis. Other theories are, of course, possible. In fact they do continuously function, offer themselves to a possible integration in a given framework, and establish their authority. These other theories, and the historical conditions and institutions of their operation, can never be simply dismissed by a critical or deconstructive analysis. However, from the present perspective, their necessary analysis and interpretation — in so far as they are integrated, taken into account, deconstructed, dropped from consideration, and so on — are also evaluations. How evaluative and constraining dynamics dissolve each other under the conditions of particular historical configurations will, as was suggested earlier, constitute the ongoing task of a theory of evaluation.

In effect, such an investigation will be necessary, not only specifically for the question of constraints, but also for the interaction between evaluation and interpretation as a whole. No critique of evaluation, then, can eliminate the necessity of accounting for the conditions under which evaluation occurs. Rather, under the theoretical and historical constraints considered earlier, including, specifically, "the constraints of a differential-supplementary structure," a theory will formulate and analyze the question of how these conditions are accounted for and whether the terms "evaluation" and "value" will be retained or, for whatever theoretical and strategic reasons, removed from theory.

One reason for such removal might well be generated by the historical configuration of negative attitudes toward evaluation and, especially, toward the term "value." Others may be produced by fashions, which should by no means be discounted as conditions or constraints of theory. An effective account of evaluation, therefore, when it occurs, may very well avoid, suppress, or attack the term, or, following the current fashion, forget the name "evaluation."

In this context, it is a curious and perhaps also symptomatic fact of modern intellectual history that, for all Derrida's critiques and deconstruction of "the instance of the logos" in Heidegger, and in spite of his powerful effort to "save Nietzsche from a reading of the Heideggerian type," the question of value never actively enters the intellectual horizon of his own discourse (*Grammatalogy* 19).[21] This is particularly interesting in view of the extent of Nietzsche's presence in Derrida's thought. For, as suggested earlier, Nietzsche's contribution, to "the deconstruction of the instance of the logos and the related concept of truth or the primary signified, in whatever sense understood" (*Grammatology* 78), would have been impossible without his insistence on evaluation and without his specific concept of value.

The "Nietzschean affirmation of the play of the world"[22] is the affirmative of the play of *value*, while Derrida's reading of Nietzsche and his discourse in general seem to suppress the thematics of evaluation. Perhaps we find here an example of Heidegger's impact by way of his role in the critique of evaluation and value. Derrida's dependence on Heidegger is, by Derrida's own account, fundamental: "Heidegger's meditation," as he maintains, is "uncircumventable" (*Margins* 22).

The preceding analysis of evaluation, however, would also suggest that the whole conceptuality of value and evaluation must be radically reconsidered as a result of Derrida's — as well as Nietzsche's — critique of classical philosophy, and that it must be placed theoretically within what may be called a "general economy" accounting for *différance*, rather than the restricted economy of "economic," social and aesthetic value.[23]

Here, of course, one has to confront the extremely complex question and task of a more detailed and rigorous investigation of the relationships between the question of value and the question of "*différance* as the relation to an impossible presence, as expenditure without reserve, as the irreparable loss of presence, the irreversible usage of energy, that is, as the death instinct, and as the entirely other relationships that apparently interrupt every economy" (*Margins* 19). The interruption at issue ("of every economy") will also bear heavily on the critical analysis, deconstruction and reinscription of the concept of profit. For it would be equally mistaken to insist unequivocally and uncritically without interruption on "economies," "profits," and related concepts. These questions also relate to the question of the structural unconscious and associated Freudian themes — the pleasure principle and beyond the pleasure principle — in evaluation and the production or inscription of values.

It is, in this sense, not only a question of relating the theory of value to "the theoretical perspective, conceptual structures, and analytic techniques developed by Jacques Derrida... (especially in conjunction with the renewed attention to Nietzsche)," as Barbara Herrnstein Smith suggests,[24] but in general relating any such theory to the problematics of the structural unconscious, particularly "in conjunction with Nietzsche." Incorporating and indeed announcing the unconscious through value remains one of Nietzsche's greatest achievements. As I indicated earlier, without the unconscious, without "accounting" for the Freudian effects, a theory of value would remain only a restricted economy. This is not to say, of course, that such restricted economies have no theoretical *value*. Their analysis and inscription furthermore may crucially effect an inscription of general economies of value, including the transactions with the unconscious. Equally importantly, these questions also open, in the context of Bataille and in general, the problematics of the Marxist theory of value in its relation to the problems at issue in the present essay.

Although some of the considerations suggested here might be perceived as consequences and implications of Derrida's discourse, these consequences are neither made quite explicit nor fully explored by Derrida.[25] The inquiry into evaluation remains (as Nietzsche pointed out), or has become again, an urgent task of theory. As I indicated earlier, it is by no means impossible that, as one reinscribes the concept of value as the general economy or grammatology of *différance* and *writing* (in Derrida's sense), "the solution of the problem of value" urged by Nietzsche will imply a dissolution of the concept of value itself. The concept of value, that is, might dissolve, or rather might be differently reinscribed in a different metaphoric chain. As Derrida writes, in one of his numerous statements to that effect, in "White Mythology": "[The issue] is rather to deconstruct the metaphysical and rhetorical schema at work in [the] critique of [philosophical language], not in order to reject and discard them, but rather to reinscribe them otherwise, and especially in order to begin to identify the historico-problematic terrain on which philosophy systematically has been asked for the metaphorical rubrics of its concept" (*Margins* 215).

Since the name and the concept of value — along with all words and concepts comprising "the philosophical language" of the metaphysics of presence, above all the concepts of concept and, thereby, meaning — are thoroughly implicated in this schema, this metaphysics and this language, the very term "value" might rhetorically need to be given up. But we cannot give up all terms. For where do we find other — absolutely other — language? And the language of philosophy or theory in general cannot make itself independent from everyday (i.e., non-philosophical, non-theoretical) language. This opposition between two languages is the first to go, to be deconstructed, to be differently reinscribed.[26] Is *différance*, for example, Derrida's famous "neither word nor concept," a better name than "evaluation"? Quite possibly. But will it eliminate the theoretical necessity of differently reinscribing evaluation? Not at all, unless the latter is already reinscribed in the movements of *différance, trace, writing*.

Such a "solution of the problem of value" (dissolving values, above all historically, by way of exploring the conditions determining the concept of value) would, I think, be quite acceptable to Nietzsche; indeed it is very much in the Nietzschean style of "deconstructing the metaphysical and rhetorical schema" of classical philosophy. Devoid of value, theoretically unacceptable to Nietzsche, and to "us," would be the *metaphysical* negation of values, including Heidegger's dissolution of values and evaluation in the truth of Being. A critical account of evaluation will remove or deconstruct — "comprehend" — metaphysical or logocentric concepts of value, but, in the same movement, such an account will also remove or deconstruct the uncritical dismissal of values.

Nietzsche, it seems to me, inscribes value and evaluation along with what he called "appropriation," "affirmation" and "play," as an interpretation of interpretation, deconstructing truth, presence, and related metaphysical schemata. Value in Nietzsche refers above all to the conditions of historicity, difference and active discord of perspectives: in short, to *différance* in interpretation. Nietzsche's notion of value, then, is inseparable from and perhaps the condition of what Derrida calls, attributing the notion to Nietzsche, "*différance* in its active movement":

> Since the sense of being is never produced as history outside of its determination as presence, has it not always already been caught within the history of metaphysics as the epoch of presence? This is perhaps what Nietzsche wanted to write and what resists the Heideggerian reading of Nietzsche; *différance* in its active movement — what is comprehended in the concept of *différance* without exhausting it — is what not only precedes metaphysics but also extends beyond the thought of being. The latter speaks nothing other than metaphysics, even if it exceeds it and thinks it as what it is within its closure. (*Grammatology*, p. 143)[27]

How much then does metaphysics suppress along with evaluation, if the latter notion is taken in its Nietzschean sense and with Nietzschean implications? We should, therefore, adhere more closely to Nietzsche's pioneering and astonishing insight, which replaces truth-value with value without truth; and, utilizing along the way the more recent theoretical perspectives, we would move ahead, developing our understanding of the structure and dynamics of evaluation, rather than attempting to protect our theories and explanations from it. That all truth is perhaps only a mask of value — like truth-value, for example — has, of course, been no secret since Nietzsche at least, or perhaps long before. Valéry powerfully exposes this masquerade of truth in Descartes's case, interpreting Descartes against Descartes.

As Derrida writes in his essay on Valéry (Nietzsche's presence, however, is unmistakable, in both Valéry and Derrida):

> Philosophy is written — third consequence — as soon as its forms and operations are not only oriented and watched over by the law of meaning, though, and Being, which speaks in order to say I, and does so as close as possible to the source of the well.
>
> Of this proposition, as of its simulacrum, Descartes here is exemplary. Valéry does not cease to question him, never leaves him; and if his reading of Descartes at the very least might appear uneven to the historians of philosophy, the fact was not unforeseen by Valéry, who interpreted it in advance. We will concern ourselves with this for a while.
>
> What is the operation of the I in the Cogito? To assure itself of the source in the certitude of an invincible self presence, even in the figure — always paternal — Freud tells us — of the devil. This time a power is gained in the course of a movement in grand style which takes the risk of enunciating and writing itself. Valéry very quickly suggests that truth is Descartes's last concern. The words "truth" and "reality" are once again in quotation marks, advanced as effects of language and as simple citations. But if the "I think therefore I am" "has no meaning whatever," and *a fortiori* no truth, it has "a very great value," and like the style is "entirely characteristic of the man himself." This value is that of a shattering blow, a quasi-arbitrary affirmation of mastery by means of the exercise of a style, the egotistic impression of a form, the strategem of a mise en scène powerful enough to do without truth, a mise en scène keeping that much less to truth in its laying of truth as a trap, a trap into which generations of servile fetishists will come to be caught, thereby acknowledging the law of the master, of I, René Descartes. (*Margins* 295)[28]

Undoubtedly, the same type of analysis could be applied to Heidegger as well. Indeed, it appears that Nietzsche never pretended to take any philosophical discourse as anything other than a positing — as value and as style — of "the law of the master," or to be doing anything else himself.

Our (and Nietzsche's) analysis would, however, compel us to recognize and inscribe the plural and heterogeneous nature of both style and value: otherwise we will never leave the metaphysical limits of truth and presence.[29] The structure of this heterogeneity, however, and thus the structure of value, will require an explanation within a comprehensive theory of evaluation, along with and in interaction with a different interpretation of interpretation — as Nietzsche "perhaps wanted." This would indeed resist the Heideggerian reading of Nietzsche. Nietzsche, then, emerges — historically — as the central decentering figure who, with extraordinary power and insight, subjected both the logocentrist interpretation of interpretation and the logocentrist interpretation of value and evaluation to a radical theoretical scrutiny. Perhaps Heidegger is right, and Nietzsche is as yet too close to us, too close to "attain the true center of philosophy"[30] envisioned by Heidegger's hope or despair. But then again, from Nietzsche's prelude, the "Prelude to the Philosophy of the Future" (Nietzsche's subtitle to *Beyond Good and Evil*), we might want to move in a different direction.

Notes

1. Barbara H. Smith has analyzed this situation in relation to literary theory and the American critical scene in "Contingencies of Value," *Critical Inquiry* (Autumn 1983), 1-35, and in the earlier essay "Fixed Marks and Variable Constancies: A Parable of Literary Value," *Poetics Today* (1979), 7-23.

2. Martin Heidegger, *An Introduction to Metaphysics*, trans. R. Manheim (New Haven: Yale University Press, 1979), p. 199.

3. *Positions*, trans. Alan Bass (Chicago: The University of Chicago Press, 1981), p. 51.

4. *Of Grammatology*, trans. Gayatri C. Spivak (Baltimore: Johns Hopkins University Press, 1976), pp. 19-20. Subsequent references will be to this edition and will be given in the text.

5. *Margins of Philosophy*, trans. Alan Bass (Chicago: University of Chicago Press, 1982), pp. 17-18. Subsequent references will be to this edition and will be given in the text.

6. *The Gay Science*, trans. Walter Kaufmann (New York: Vintage, 1974), p. 285.

7. *Writing and Difference*, trans. Alan Bass (Chicago: The University of Chicago press, 1979), p. 292. On Heideggerian hope, see the conclusion of *"Différance"* in *Margins of Philosophy*, p. 27.

8. See his discussion in *Of Grammatology*, pp. 61-63, and *"Ousia* and *Grammè,"* in *Margins*, pp. 63-67.

9. *The Standard Edition of the Complete Psychological Works of Sigmund Freud*, ed. James Strachey (London: The Hogarth Press, 1964), v. 23, pp. 249-50.

10. Derrida, *Positions*, p. 42.

11. *Taking Chances: Derrida, Psychoanalysis, and Literature*, ed. Joseph H. Smith and William Kerrigan (Baltimore: The Johns Hopkins University Press, 1984), p. 27.

12. See Derrida's discussion in "Différance," *Margins*, p. 27.

13. Derrida, *Positions*, p. 26.

14. *The Legend of Freud* (Minneapolis: University of Minnesota Press, 1982), p. 39.

15. Weber, *Legend of Freud*, p. 39.

16. Derrida, *Positions*, p. 41.

17. *Writing and Difference*, p. 293. See also the remark in *Of Grammatology*, p. 62.

18. *Beyond Good and Evil*, trans. Walter Kaufmann (New York: Vintage, 1966), p. 19.

19. On the related question of metaphor as the condition of possibility of the discourse and the (allegedly non-metaphorical) language of philosophy, see, in addition, the essays "White Mythology" and "The Supplement of Copula" in *Margins*, and the essay on Levinas and Bataille in *Writing and Difference*.

20. See the discussions in "Différance" and *"Ousia* and *Grammè*," both in *Margins*; see also *Of Grammatology*.

21. *"Evaluation,"* let us point out, is, however, mentioned on the same page by Derrida as one of "the concepts radicali[zed]" by Nietzsche, along with *"interpretation, perspective,* [and] *difference"* (p. 19).

22. Derrida, *Writing and Difference*, p. 291.

23. On the relations between restricted and general economy, see Derrida's rarely discussed, but, in my view, essential, essay on Georges Bataille, "From Restricted to General Economy," in *Writing and Difference*, along with related remarks in "Différance," and the essay on Kant, "Economimesis," *Diacritics* (June 1981), pp. 4-25 (especially p. 5).

24. "Contingencies of Value," p. 7.

25. I am not saying that the concept of value is never touched in the Derridean discourse. An extremely suggestive, if dense and curtailed, account is offered — "very schematically," as Derrida himself says (*Margins*, p. 214) — of the metaphor of value as well as the value of metaphor, in "White Mythology" (*Margins*, pp. 214-19). It traverses the familiar "constellation" (p. 219) of Derrida's canon from Nietzsche to Mallarmé (via Freud and Saussure, supplemented here by Marx and Lenin) and the familiar Saussurean analogy, along the lines of the interaction between diachrony and synchrony, between political economy and linguistics, that is, the economy of the sign. Cf. also the suggestive passages in *Of Grammatology*, p. 142, and in the essay on Valéry in *Margins*. (I shall return to this latter text below.) Rather, the very concept seems to be marginalized — which it can be, of course, and which is the case in most texts to which Derrida refers. At the very least, however, the "fact" or history of evaluation would have to be accounted for.

26. On this question, see for instance Derrida's essay "Violence and Metaphysics" in *Writing and Difference.*

27. Cf. also the parallel passage in "Différance," *Margins,* p. 18.

28. The "source" in Valéry is given in Derrida's footnote in the text of the essay entitled "Qual Quell-Valéry's Sources." The absence of the reference to Nietzsche here is rather interesting in the context of the discussion above on the relationships between the question of value in Derrida's discourse and his reading of Nietzsche.

29. On the plurality of Nietzsche's styles, see also Derrida's essay in *Spurs: Nietzsche's Styles,* trans. Barbara Harlow (Chicago: University of Chicago Press, 1980).

30. Heidegger, *An Introduction to Metaphysics,* p. 199.

6

DIOGENES LAERTIUS *CONTRA* GADAMER: UNIVERSAL OR HISTORICAL HERMENEUTICS?

György Márkus

The hermeneutics of Hans Georg Gadamer is often charged, as far as its consequences and implications for a theory of interpretation in the narrower sense are concerned, with a relapse into the morass of an unchecked subjectivism. By rejecting in principle the question of *the* 'correct' interpretation as a misconceived and objectifying methodological ideal, and by replacing the problem of how to understand 'better' with the problem of why we always understand the same texts and manifestations of cultural life 'otherwise,' it represents — it is argued — a self-defeating relativism. Gadamer himself rejects these criticisms as misunderstandings of both the very task of a philosophical hermenuetics and also of the decidedly anti-subjectivist intentions and implications of his theory. The latter deals with what is common (in the sense of their conditions of possibility) to all modes and ways of understanding, with what happens to and with us when we understand. It discloses that understanding is not simply one of the possible cognitive relations of a subject to some objects, but the basic mode of our finite and temporal existence, encompassing the whole of our world experience. Such a philosophical investigation certainly has consequences for a theory and methodology of interpretation proper, since interpretation is the explicit, conscious, and self-reflective understanding of tradition under conditions when it becomes problematic or endangered. But it does not preclude the possibility of a normatively oriented methodology of interpretation, concerned with those rules which — at the present level of learning — should secure its reliability or scientificity.

I would like to suggest in this paper that such a happy compromise between the philosophical elucidation of an underlying, fundamental, facticity and the secondary, methodological problem of establishing its (currently) valid norms cannot be upheld, and is not in fact upheld by Gadamer himself. But in contrast to critics who find in his theory a limitless relativism, the danger of an 'everything goes,' I am troubled instead by the fact that his philosophy at least at some points seems to posit a historically and culturally specific and limited model of interpretation as its valid form, while at the same time it seems to suppress the normative force of this claim through its ontologization as a happening of effective history.

The problem-shift — from the question of what we should do when we interpret to the question of what interpretation does — is properly regarded as the decisive achievement of philosophical hermeneutics with respect to a theory of interpretation proper: the disclosure of the functions of the varying cultural practices of exegesis, historical reconstruction, canon-formation, criticism, etc., as forms of a 'productive' assimilation of tradition, in which they themselves are embedded while mediating it. But the step from here to an 'ontological' conception of interpretation which simply by-passes the problem of its normativity seems to me both illegitimate and unsuccessful. To the degree that it succeeds, it necessarily reduces interpretation to an actually effective mediation between the present and the past, and thereby obliterates its distinction from misinterpretation because this distinction cannot be treated as concerning a merely *post facto* ascertainable pragmatic effectivity. To view interpretation as conscious actualisation of the very 'productivity of time' means to miss its specific productivity, its character of a cultural *performance* which is always, at any moment, normatively regulated — not so much by the methodological rules of an explicit hermeneutics, which a given culture may or may not contain, but by the way its objects, functions, and procedures are (mostly unreflectively and partly in an institutionalised way) integrated into the on-going cultural practices of the time.

Fortunately, Gadamer does not proceed consistently in the above direction. But he breaks away from it only by positing a definite type of interpretative practice as its structural model in general. And insofar as he interconnects these two divergent lines of thought, he interconnects them in a problematically Hegelizing manner. He assumes the ultimate identity of "*An-sich*" and "*Für-sich*," i.e. silently maintains that only an interpretation which correctly recognises our own untranscendable temporality, and therefore the inherent embeddedness of all works of culture in 'effective history' (Wirkungsgeschichte), can be truly historically effective, and that it alone can truly preserve the continuity of history and 'save' a tradition from the danger of 'forgetting.' From this also follow his efforts to uncover an ultimate structural identity between a still pre-historical, 'naive,' and a truly historical hermeneutic consciousness.

In the following, I would like to show that Gadamar is unjustified when he claims universality for his conception of interpretation, i.e. for interpretation as an activity in the overarching medium of a tradition in which we participate and which determines our preconceptions, an activity through which a fusion of two historically distinct horizons is accomplished, by way of a hermeneutic circle that involves such a dialogic relation between question and answer as ultimately allows the question of the very text to emerge in our language, addressed to us, and thus providing the text with a hermeneutic application. This conception — and the rather directly regulative principles which follow from it, such as the supremacy of the text over the interpreter — can be criticised as to its universality from two opposite but, it seems to me, equally legitimate standpoints.

Firstly, insofar as this conception emphasizes participation in tradition as the precondition for the latter's interpretability, and regards interpretation as a structural constituent of the very tradition which it further develops by conscious appropriation, correspondingly demanding recognition of the supremacy of the interpretandum over the interpreter, and so forth, it has been and can properly be criticized as *archaizing and conservative*. This point is usually made by emphasizing the role that interpretation can and, at least under modern conditions, actually does play in breaking down the binding force of tradition, and in the critical emancipation from a past that has become a fetter for us in some way. Both this criticism and Gadamer's answer to it are well-known and I do not want to dwell on them.

I would rather mention another point. The aforementioned characterization of interpretation seems to miss one of its basic cultural functions under conditions of modernity: to *create* tradition where there was none, to transform mere documents of a past, whose cultural significance has either been lost or has been completely alien to our culture, into an effective tradition for on-going practices. The last hundred years of art history, with its 'discovery' of the Romanesque, of Mannerism, of the Oriental and the Primitive, can serve here as a telling example. The movement of primitive artifacts from museums of natural history (where they illustrated — mostly for children — the strange livelihoods of alien people) to museums of art, physically symbolizes this transformation.

Interpretation is certainly not the demiurge of this process. On the one hand, the documents of an alien past have to be available, and in this respect Gadamer's criticism of "historical consciousness" seems to be rather onesided. He only stresses its destructive effect upon the living tradition that it transforms into a mere otherness, an object, but he fails to appreciate its role in the accumulation of those documents of a truly alien past upon which the hermeneutic activities of interpretation today feed in their *search* for tradition. On the other hand, interpretation does not make mere 'documents' culturally relevant as tradition by its own power; it does so by linking them up with emerging and on-going practices that struggle for legitimacy against others well-embedded in the context of the effective tradition. Thus interpretation of this type is also intimately related to the shared effective tradition, but related to it not so much as to its supporting fundament, but rather as to its protagonist. Its positive content, the character of its selectivity and sensitivity, are essentially determined by that new practice which attempts through it to win a historical legitimacy. The connections between the 'discovery' of primitive art and the emergence of cubism or, as a matter of fact, between appreciation of the whole hermeneutic tradition and definite contemporary attempts at a 'reform' of philosophy, are obvious and unnecessary to elaborate.

There are, however, other aspects of the Gadamerian theory of hermeneutics which invite questions about its universality from an opposite direction, in the light of which it appears as a *modernizing* conception of interpretation. In the following, I would actually like to substantiate this second charge in a purely illustrative manner, by pointing to an example of the interpretation of philosophy that has been enormously effective historically, although perhaps it does not satisfy any of the conditions and characteristics laid down in general by Gadamer. My direct intent in employing this example is frankly historicist and relativist: I would like to indicate through it the dangers inherent in any *general* characterisation of interpretation. The character of the interpretation of texts is *historically and culturally specific*, that is, changing and divergent, and that not only in different *historical* periods but also in different *"cultural genres"* co-existing at the same time. The on-going cultural practices of the time to which the interpretandum becomes linked through interpretation always *preform*, essentially in an institutional and non-reflective way, what kind of interpretative procedures are regarded as appropriate. The question about the methodological correctness of interpretation can be raised meaningfully only in relation to, and on the basis of, this broadly and vaguely outlined normative background.

In order to get on with my task, I shall indicate some of the characteristic features of the interpretation of philosophy in late antiquity. For this I shall turn to a document which constitutes in the given respect at the very least the most extensive testimony: the history of philosophy of Diogenes Laertius. This is certainly both a problematic and mischievous choice. For a modern reader, who is not a classical philologist, but is nonetheless acquainted in an elementary way with Greek philosophy (and I myself certainly make claim to nothing more), *The Lives and Opinions of Eminent Philosophers* is a long series of misinterpretations, often verging on the absurd. And many classical scholars hasten to add that the book is the compilatory work of a rank amateur, equally lacking in discrimination and trustworthiness, definitely below the level of ancient scholarship. Nevertheless, the work has a significance beyond its encompassing character and hardly overvaluable historical influence. However mediocre the realization, it remains an ambitious syncretic attempt at the unification of the three basic ways and procedures in which antiquity dealt with the task of interpreting its philosophical past: doxographic, biographical, and diadochist historiography. In this respect, from a strictly hermeneutic view-

point, it is an important document — all the more so because its most
alienating features for us are, I think, demonstrably the consequences not
of the foolishness of its author but of the character of the shared inherited
procedures which he applies. It is perhaps appropriate therefore to examine what strike us as the most peculiar and distorted aspects of Diogenes.

One of the most often made derogatory remarks about the work concerns the absolutely inordinate place occupied in it by *biographies*, con-
taining, as it were, a lot of quite pointless information and anecdotes, largely
unreliable, clearly of folkloristic or legendary origin, arbitrarily ascribed
to this or that philosopher. All this, however, is not peculiar to Diogenes.
Not only does he follow well-established canons of philosophers' biographies, exploiting their materials, but he also acts in their spirit in simply
conjoining 'lives' to 'opinions' as seeming equivalents and parallels. In fact,
the *bioi* of Antiquity were not conceived as materials or stories of a purely
historical character, with relevance to the history of *philosophy* only insofar as some of the life-experiences of the authors can be used as explanations for some of the peculiarities of their doctrines. The relationship
between life and work was not conceived as one of a possible causal
ground, but rather as one of normative correspondence. The author's
character and conduct were regarded as the decisive *exemplum* that bore
testimony to the meaning and validity of the doctrine: biographies were
therefore part and parcel of a history of philosophy as such.

This is naturally intimately connected with the very meaning of
philosophy as a cultural activity in Antiquity. Since, in classical Antiquity,
philosophical knowledge was conceived not merely as an objectified system of true propositions, but also as a *habitus*, a disposition of the soul,
philosophy therefore meant not only a doctrine but equally a form of life.
It is their embeddedness in this tradition that determines the basic structural characteristics of biographies. In the first place, they are predominantly
either of apologetic or polemical character: either they attempt to affirm
the validity of a teaching by the moral excellence of its author as disclosed
in his conduct and death and by his various achievements and fame, or
else they intend to disprove a doctrine through sordid details from the life
of its creator. In both cases, however, they are conscious *stylizations* of
life through which the philosopher becomes transformed into a (positive
or negative) 'culture-hero.' From this follows the very strange and inorgan-
ic combination of a wealth of arid data, intended to give verisimilitude,
with certain legendary or purely concocted stories designed to bring the
intended moral characteristics clearly into focus and to invest the
hagiographically construed figure of the author with an exemplary significance and effectivity.

In all these respects, therefore, Diogenes stands firmly in an unbroken
context of tradition-transmission, organically connected with the character of the tradition itself. But it is equally important to see how far he bowd-
lerizes this tradition. After all, even allowing for what has been said, his

biographies seem to be mindless. It is precisely the meaningful, paradigmatic correspondence between lives and opinions that seems to be practically lost with him. Careful philological research can often establish the original 'point' of a story or anecdote that he reproduces, i.e. the way that it originally reflected back on the character of the doctrine; but this is never even intimated by himself. This, however, is not merely the result of his indiscriminate culling of materials from all kinds of courses, perhaps even of opposed intent, but is intimately connected rather with the basic hermeneutic end of his whole work, which is certainly not untypical of his own epoch. Diogenes Laertius has a generally apologetic, laudatory-eulogistic relationship to the *totality* of the Greek philosophical heritage. From this viewpoint, however, the meaning-relation which connects life as an exemplum with the *specific* character of a doctrine becomes unarticulable. If *all* philosophers represent a norm of excellence, then their excellence cannot be connected with the characteristic *contents* of their doctrines which make up their differences. In this respect, Diogenes breaks with the basic intent of the tradition in which he stands and which he directly continues.

This same paradox appears if we move to a second and even more alienating feature of his historiography, connected with its *doxographic* part. The Laertian descriptions of philosophical doctrines are not only fragmentary and unreliable, reading back ideas arbitrarily into the text, sometimes without any imaginable foundation. He also misrepresents and misinterprets the philosophical tradition in a deeper sense, owing to a seemingly absolute lack of ability to distinguish between the essential and the inessential, between what is characteristic of and what is purely accidental in a given philosophy. The modern reader finds a bewildering arbitrariness in what Diogenes regards worth mentioning and what he leaves out of his accounts. Such arbitrariness destroys the possibilities of meaningful unity in the views under discussion; philosophies are transformed by Diogenes into a collection of unrelated assertions, a catalogue of diverse opinions. He is only interested in answers, in the 'solutions' that philosophers have given to a seemingly senseless variety of problems, and he pays no attention to the *rationale* of these answers nor, generally, to the method of philosophy. He actually misses and destroys, therefore, precisely what is philosophical in the philosophies: their argumentative-demonstrative character. He retransforms rational and justified knowledge into unsupported *doxai* regarded for some reason as authoritative. In this way, an antiquarian interest in the preservation of the tradition actually finishes it off.

This almost inevitable impression evoked by reading Diogenes is misleading in one respect, however: his doxographic procedures are certainly not arbitrary. On the contrary, he proceeds on the whole according to a rather rigid method. He has a strict view of what philosophy is, based on its stoic division into three parts, and he has a long, ordered list of questions related to each of these great branches for which he searches for answers in his (mostly derivative) sources. Views concerning the nature of the universe, attitudes toward the 'miraculous,' philosophemata relating to elements and principles, then to matter, cause, and motion, and lastly to life, soul, and body — such is, for example, his basic 'catalogue of problems' as far as physics is concerned. The impression of a bewildering arbitrariness emerges because his ultimate sources in the majority of cases do not contain direct answers to all these questions, much less in this particular sequence, because the questions are not theirs but those of Diogenes. Even when he follows an original source relatively closely, e.g. Plato's *Timaeus*, he quite senselessly therefore 'modernises' it; in the given case, reads it through stoic spectacles.

But then again, his catalogue of topics and problems is certainly not peculiar to him. The lists with which he operates go back at least two centuries, allegedly to the *Placita* of Aetius. And this latter is related to an even earlier legacy, which it would certainly be senseless to accuse in misrecognition of the basic intentions of classical Greek philosophy: that is, the immediate followers of Aristotle, and ultimately Aristotle himself. Actually, in the above mentioned list of basic questions related to natural philosophy, one can readily recognise the basic topics that Theophrastus had allegedly treated in his *Physikon doxai*, which directly derives from the famous historiographical parts of the Aristotelian *Metaphysics* and *Physics*. And it naturally comes to mind at this point that, if one is to believe such philological authorities as Mondolfo, Cherniss, or McDiarmid, there is not much difference between the interpretative methods of Diogenes and Aristotle himself. Aristotle's first "histories of philosophy" were also completely dominated by his own systematic interests. Aristotle, too, treats all earlier philosophies as if they were attempts to answer his own questions, so that he too concentrates illegitimately on separate philosophemata isolated from their contexts and arbitrarily, often contradictorily, interpreted by him. It would seem, therefore, that the loss of the basic philosophical meaning of the tradition, so undeniable in Diogenes, is ultimately not the result of a specifically antiquarian attitude to it, but paradoxically of its precise opposite: an essentially ahistorical consciousness allegedly characterizing the *whole* of antiquity, i.e., that hermeneutic *naïveté* about which Gadamer speaks — in short, a simple inability to conceive any historical distance between the past and the present.

But it is certainly very difficult to speak of a hermeneutic *naïveté* in respect to Aristotle himself. If he "modernizes" the views of his predecessors, he does so, not because he is as yet unconscious, but precisely because he is completely aware of the problems of historical distance. His first fragmentary overviews of the history of philosophy — which, it should be added, actually consummate and make explicit its differentiation as a cultural activity *sui generis* and first clearly constitute it as a separate 'cultural genre' — are based on clear and sophisticated principles of interpretation which receive justification within the framework of his whole philosophy.

Precisely because philosophy for Aristotle is the science of *truth*, an understanding of its history cannot be simply a reproduction of earlier *opinions*. To interpret these latter as *philosophies*, one has to relate them to truth, and therefore to go beyond the confused, obscure language and the partial or mistaken intention of their authors — beyond the "stammer" with which first philosophy begins (*Metaph.* 993a11). One has to relate them to their veritable subject-matter, which expresses itself in these opinions often without the knowledge of their authors. To understand an author better than he did or could understand himself is the basic principle of an Aristotelian hermeneutics. This is accomplished when he discovers the place of a definite view in the logical space of all the possible answers to a problematic — as he does, for example, in his discussion of the question of *archai* in *Physics* 184b. Correspondingly, even that which is wholly false can be seen as related and contributing to truth, i.e., in its philosophical meaning and significance. As a result of this interpretative method, the past itself is made philosophically productive for the present: history delineates the problem situation, the "difficulty" which contemporary thinking has to solve, and at the same time allows the most elementary truth to emerge, because for Aristotle *consensus gentium et philosophorum* is a reliable index of truth.

Nor is this hermeneutics arbitrary. It is firmly based in the conviction that everyone makes some contribution to truth, that man stands to it in an original relation (*Eudemian Ethics* 1216b 30). The ultimate problems which men face are eternal and always the same, and essentially the same is the path which leads to their solution, from the simplest questions (like those about the material cause with which philosophical speculation begins) to the most complex and highest ones (like those about the final cause). It is only cyclically recurring natural cataclysms which again and again make knowledge once acquired lost, though not without confused and enigmatic remnants in myths, proverbs, and poetic wisdom, from all of which philosophy slowly emerges to begin its progress anew.

In this way, Aristotle offers a definite method for interpreting the philosophies of the past, by construing the history of philosophy as an approximation to truth, from confusion to clarity, and from one-sided and partial views of it to the encompassing totality represented by his own doctrine as the *telos* of the whole progress of knowledge. As a result of this totalizing effort, history becomes the reproduction of the unchanging configuration of truth, and each "opinion" can be understood in its true philosophical meaning through its place in this configuration, as a confused, one-sided aspect of its totality.

The beginnings of a doxographic history of philosophy immediately after Aristotle are still firmly rooted in this sytematizing effort and the conceptual scheme to which it gave rise. The history of ancient doxography, on the other hand, is the history of the dissolution of this framework. The list of questions addressed to past philosophies becomes autonomous, independent from the attempt to discover the unity of truth in the variety and contradiction of doctrines. Now it evokes merely the discord and the irreducible variety of opinions collected according to definite pigeon-holes. This clarifies just how unjustified is any comparison between Diogenes Laertius, who stands at the end of this process, and Aristotle, although seemingly they may be accused of committing the same hermeneutic sins, and Diogenes clearly follows procedures that can be traced back to Aristotle. But with Diogenes, these procedures have lost both their relevance to, and their justification through, the living practice of a philosophy.

It seems relatively easy to explain this whole process of degeneration. The peripatetic synthesis of the history of philosophy simply collapses as a result of the very openness of history. Only one generation after Aristotle's death, the doctrines of Epicurus and the Stoics emerge and achieve enormous significance. This fact makes the philosophy of Aristotle and his followers simply one among many diverse schools, and refutes in practice their synthesizing claim. From their great syncretic effort there remains only a dead, increasingly involuted schema of cataloguing the past according to a list of pre-given questions which themselves now have a merely traditionalistic justification. All this is a typical phenomenon of the routinization of a culture which has lost its original creativity and which has become epigonistic and solely emulative.

This explanation, however, fails to explain anything. History itself may have discredited both the concrete results and the form of realization of a peripatetic hermeneutics of philosophy, but it surely has not automatically refuted the validity of its principle: to understand the true meaning of the diversity of past philosophies through their synthesis in the present. As a matter of fact, such efforts were constantly renewed during late Antiquity. Already, in the New Academy, Antiochus of Askalon attempted, through a moralizing interpretation of the philosophies of the past, to demonstrate the essential unity of the doctrines of Plato, Aristotle, and the Stoics. And ancient philosophy essentially ends with a final great effort to demonstrate the identity of truth in the aporetic multiplicity of past opinions: in Plotinus, who thought of his own philosophy as mere exegesis of the ancient doctrines, and who disposed of a sophisticated method of interpretation based on a philosophical construal of the very history of philosophy as a dialectical, double movement, consisting of progress in the clarity of exposition and argumentation, accompanied by a substantive regress in the very grasp of the truth, i.e., a process of forgetting its originally given intuition. The real question is why these constantly renewed syncretic attempts, which gave a *philosophical* sense to the past tradition, remained in late Antiquity essentially marginal and sectarian affairs, while the seemingly mindless doxographic compilations enjoyed an uninterrupted continuity and enormous popularity. Routinization of a culture merely describes this process from the viewpoint of its end as known to us, but it does not answer the question as to what kind of *cultural sig-*

nificance and function such a transmission and interpretation of tradition could fulfill in its own time.

It is from the perspective of this question that the basic hermeneutic attitude to the past embodied in the practice of doxography in general, and in Diogenes Laertius in particular, appears most puzzling and paradoxical. Diogenes's attitude to the *whole* of Greek philosophy is that of a eulogist. He never tires of emphasizing the vital importance of philosophy for human life and its superiority to everyday knowledge and to all other forms of cultural activity. The value-character and the validity of the whole of this material which he attempts to demarcate, preserve, and defend is never in question for him and for that reason requires no justification; at best, it is attested by the excellence and eminence of the various authors as demonstrated in their biographies. Interpretation is completely uncoupled here from the question of validation and relevance, because these latter are posited as self-evident properties of definite types of texts regarded as intangible authorities.

Such a decidedly dogmatic attitude to the past as authority *per se* clashes, however, at least in our understanding, with the equally prominent emphas laid on the irreducible multiplicity of philosophical doctrines and the contradictions between them. Philosophy is for Diogenes a finite set of *controversial dogmas* represented by competing sects. His exposition does not simply lay bare this plurality, the *dissensus philosophorum*, but specifically accentuates it, because he makes the idea of a competitive relation between the various philosophies the basic principle for constructing their history. This is the point where Diogenes follows and incorporates into his work the third and latest tradition of the ancient historiography of philosophy: that of the diadochists. The essence of this latter is a personification of the relation between philosophies, conceived in the complementary terms of either a relationship of succession within one school, or rivalry between the different schools, both often bogus and concocted. Diogenes takes over this schema for organizing his whole material (allowing him to interconnect, at least formally, its biographical and doxographic constituents); and he takes it over in its most extreme form, as initiated perhaps by Sotion. According to this, the essentially opposed dual origins of Greek philosophy, the Ionian and the Italian, give rise to two separate lines of succession and development. In this way, the whole history of philosophy is transformed into a symbolic and unresolved system of competition which constantly takes on ever new forms. Originally, to be sure, there may have been some genuine philosophical intent and justification behind this schema — either a skeptical one, or an atomist Epicurean view of history as the incessant and accidental creation-process of new material and social organisms fighting, with various degrees of success, for their self-preservation (on the analogy of which are then conceived the schools of philosophy). In any case, this background is certainly lost in Diogenes, since the history of philosophy is a story now closed once and for all for him: philosophy had begun and has ended with the Greeks. This last remark, however, perhaps indicates already in what direction to search for the cultural meaning and function of this baffling dogmatism that makes do without any dogmas, except a belief in the supreme importance and validity of a tradition which in its content seems precisely to invalidate itself. The only part of the work where Diogenes develops and argues a view of his own at some length is to be found in its *proemium* and concerns the question of the origin of philosophy. Here he provides a polemic against the peripatetic view that the beginnings of philosophy are to be found among the barbarians. This conception is far from accidental in Aristotle: it is intimately connected with the way in which he solves the contradiction between the eternity of truth and the historicity of opinion within a conception of a cyclical development of knowledge. Diogenes goes to great lengths to refute this opinion (accepting, e.g., the legendary poets Musaius and Linus, but not the allegedly Thracian Orpheus, among the precursors of philosophy); he insists upon the purely Greek character of philosophy. To defend the Greek legacy of philosophy against the admixture of foreign elements of any kind is perhaps the only clear-cut purpose that one can explicitly find in the book. As a whole, it is permeated with a spirit of cultural separatism which, through the fixation of a given tradition, aims to maintain an endangered unity and individuality. The emergence of this spirit is readily understandable under the conditions of a vast empire whose *de facto* ruling elite has become increasingly heterogeneous with respect to geographical and social origin, actual background, and conditions of life. Philosophy is offered and, in fact, treated by Diogenes (and, in this respect, he is certainly not original) as the means and the core element of a cultural unification through which an elite can maintain its self-identity.

The transformation of philosophy into culture-goods to be acquired and possessed, which underlies the whole direct tradition in which Diogenes Laertius stands, necessarily involves a basic change in its very understanding, as against the classical model that this whole practice allegedly attempts to preserve intact. The first element in this transformation is a process of the growing "objectivation" of philosophy. From a search for the truth about Being and the Good, undertaken in a dialogue of questioning and answering or in an open-ended research by the like-minded, philosophy now becomes a *doctrine* that the teacher transmits to the disciples. Already in Alexandrian times, when the relevant terms of *didache* as doctrine and *paideuma* as discipline also appear, philosophy becomes conceived and articulated as a fixed content through this pedagogic triangle. The original, essentially anthropological concept of knowledge, as designating primarily an attitude, a *habitus* of mind, becomes to a degree reified: it now means essentially a set of propositions as a possible possession to be transmitted and appropriated, and conferring practical and spiritual excellence upon its owner. Hand-in-hand with this process of the doctrinalization of philosophy goes, however, the opposite process. As philosophy becomes in practice treated as a means to establishing a secondary, cultural unity, it also becomes increasingly homogenized with respect to other elements of the cultural tradition that can fulfill similar functions. From the Hellenistic period onward there is a constantly intensifying trend toward the amalgamation of philosophy with poetry, mythical and proverbial lore, and theosophic speculation — all under the supremacy of rhetoric. As a result of this "re-rhetorization" of philosophy — the theoretically most influential advocate of which is Cicero — its specificity as a cultural endeavour *sui generis* becomes increasingly lost. The main hermeneutic instrument of this cultural levelling process is the practice of allegoric interpretation which, first applied to Homer, then to the classical poets in general, is in ascendancy from the first century on, and invades philosophy itself with the neo-Pythagoreans and neo-Platonists. The distinction between *sensus literalis* and *sensus spiritualis*, which to a large extent determines the later history of hermeneutics, serves in this first historical form of its appearance not only to overcome, or more strongly, to liquidate the historical distance dividing the canonical texts of the past from the present, but also to liquidate the distance between the various cultural genres, to reconcile them all in their ultimate meaning, and thereby to make all of them valid and authoritative sources of a cultivated eloquence.

Now, it would seem that Diogenes stands in clear-out opposition to this trend. Certainly, his aim is precisely to demarcate the tradition of philosopy as such, and he constantly reaffirms the distinction of this latter from, and its supremacy over, poetry, rhetoric, or religious speculation. He also resorts to allegoresis most sparingly, essentially only in the early parts of Book I. Nevertheless, it is precisely the hermeneutic practice of Diogenes that clearly demonstrates just how far the real meaning of this demarcation has already been eroded. This can be seen, not only in his concentration on rhetorically employable philosophemata, neglecting their argumentative interconnections, but, even more explicitly, in the way he treats the whole question of argumentation in philosophy. Since dialectic constitutes one of the three recognized subdivisions of philosophy, Diogenes provides cataloguing overviews of the logical views of philosophers, as well. But, in addition, he has a pronounced interest in the "famous arguments" attributed to philosophers. He treats these arguments, however, even in such obvious cases as the Achilles of Zeno, without the slightest attempt to connect them with the character of the doctrine that makes use of them. In other words, in practice, Diogenes is interested in philosophical argumentation only insofar as it is a source of rhetorical tropes, and he treats them — to quote Quintilian — as "storehouses of trains of thought," applicable on the most diverse occasions, or as building-blocks for a rhetorical *probatio*. It is, therefore, not surprising that he himself constantly violates the principle of the cultural demarcation of philosophy which he espouses. As his references demonstrate, he does regard Euripides, Callimachus, minor historians and comic poets, as completely permissible sources and authorities, for instance on questions of "physics." In this respect he is a typical example of what Aristotle defined as the want of philosophical culture (*Eudem. Ethics* 1217a): the "inability in regard to each matter to distinguish reasonings appropriate to the subject from those foreign to it." For Diogenes, the separation of philosophy from other forms of cultural activity does not mean conceiving it as an endeavour with a specific, unique aim and method; he merely gives prominence to one type of text against others that can serve the same function, but with less excellence.

All these transformations, one could maintain, actually turn the practical significance to which classical philosophy had aspired into its direct opposite. As an endeavour to shape the soul by reason in search of truth alone, philosophy achieved its constitution as an independent cultural genre *sui generis* through becoming the dominant factor in a new concept and practice of civic education: it was historically the first, perhaps to this day the most daring, attempt at a purely secular rationalization of life-conduct (in the Weberian sense). However, with the disappearance of its life-basis, the democratic polis, philosophy first becomes privatized, and then finally takes on an opposite meaning. It retains the function of practical rationalization — if anything, late Antiquity overemphasizes its edifying role — but rationalization in the negative sense: as mere *post facto* justification and legitimation of already made, given choices and styles of life. Reunified with rhetoric, which equally had lost all its direct, juridico-political relevance, philosophy really becomes a mere rhetoric of reason: a common language of reasonableness through which the actual divergences in life-forms can be brought into a unity of cultivated talk and discussion which finds for each of them equally valid grounds in a hallowed and unique tradition. The perfect orator is the wise and the good man, Quintilian tells us. And it is precisely because philosophy is an irreducible plurality of competing sects nonetheless unified by the criss-crossing lines of descent and dispute that it can serve as the paradigmatic element and core content of this cultivated eloquence. The fact of disagreement among philosophers does not force one to take an ultimate stand in truth, invalidating all other views as mere opinions in error, and even less does it skeptically disprove the relevance of philosophical doctrines. It is exactly this variety in unity that confers a cultural validity upon philosophy.

In its general cultural context, the most alienating features of the interpretative practice of Diogenes Laertius seem therefore to appear specifically appropriate to the function posited for the object of interpretation within the framework of the actual cultural practices of the time. It is the latter that determine the specific appropriateness of interpretative practices themselves, forming a normative background which questions about the methodological correctness of interpretations always silently presuppose. In this respect, Diogenes is certainly a most unsatisfactory author. But in his own historical context, a 'better' interpretation would not have meant one that was more successful in giving a unified sense to the texts (a criterion completely alien to the spirit of doxography), but rather one that operated with its list of questions in a more systematic way, related the alleged answers to questions in a more motivated way, elicited more and more detailed answers from the same texts, etc.

To emphasize once again: it is not so much the idiosyncratic features of the *Lives and Opinions*, but the generally shared presuppositions of the inherent method that emerged historically in an uninterrupted process of tradition-transmission, that make the work for us completely unsatisfactory as an interpretation of ancient philosophy. And certainly — I take this as rather self-evident — these principles and interpretative practices do not exhibit any of the characteristics posited by philosophical hermeneutics as general features and conditions of interpretation. The method applied by Diogenes violently breaks the hermeneutic circle, precisely because it does not allow any dialogic relation between questions and answers to develop. By rigidly fixing the anticipatory prejudices of the interpreter in the form of a set of questions quite independent from the concrete character of the doctrine or text under discussion, it permits this latter to speak — or rather to stammer — only to the degree that it can be related to these prejudices directly. To be sure, these prejudices belong to the effective continuity of the tradition, but in their unreflexive immobility they disrupt its immanent sense-connections. Such an interpretative practice does not allow, therefore, for any fusion of the two historical horizons to be accomplished, since the horizon of the text does not emerge at all. The historical distance between the tradition and the present is not bridged, but coercively abandoned by forcing the former into the mould of the latter.

It might seem, however, that in this way at least that feature of interpretation is preserved which Gadamer explicitly designates as its most fundamental precondition and universal characteristic: the unity of explicative understanding with hermeneutic application. Even this, however, proves to be false — a fact which, incidentally, also demonstrates that to take legal (and biblical) hermeneutics, as Gadamer does, for the paradigmatic cases of interpretation in general is rather problematic. Legal validity belongs to the very concept of law in a way that cognitive (or practical, or whatever else) validity cannot belong as an unproblematic precondition and simple *datum* to the concept of philosophy — at least as long as this latter encompasses a plurality of possible standpoints and doctrines, and is not assimilated to the concept of religious revelation. Therefore, if application is understood, to quote Gadamer, as "bringing an opinion to validity" with respect to the present concrete situation of the interpreter, then the hermeneutic practice of Diogenes is radically non-applicative. From any modern standpoint, the most peculiar characteristic of his work is precisely that it completely divorces the explication of a doctrine from the question of its cognitive or practical validity. Hermeneutic application is posited here as an act separated from, and subsequent to explication, an act not of the interpreter but of the recipient, of the reader/listener who chooses from among the variety of philosophical opinions that or those which permit raising his own life-attitudes to the level of a cultivated, reflexive articulation and eloquence.

What is, however, the moral of this case? The hermeneutic principles underlying the work of Diogenes, though perhaps appropriate to their own cultural context, do not satisfy any of the allegedly universal characteristics or preconditions of interpretations. So what? Is it not self-evident that they do not satisfy them because any attempt to understand the philosophical legacy of the past in accordance with these principles would necessarily result in its radical misinterpretation? And would it not be an unpermissible, even mindless, relativism to say: misinterpretation *for us*, from our own standpoint? No, such a hermeneutics results in misinterpretation *from the viewpoint of philosophy itself*, philosophy as a living, ongoing, continuous cultural activity. That is, one of the basic presuppositions of a hermeneutic of this type is precisely the effective *end* of philosophy which is treated as a mere tradition of the *past*. And truly, a person who understands philosophical texts in the way implied by Diogenes can be a philosophically cultivated person according to cultural criteria valid at a given age, but certainly *cannot* be a practising philosopher.

The only problem with this remark or objection, however self-evident it seems; is that it is certainly false, *if* interpretation is conceived as an event, a happening (*Geschehen*) in the transmission of tradition as effective history. In its actual historical effect, the work of Diogenes did precisely what it so clearly could not do at all: it contributed most significantly to the creative appropriation and assimilation of the legacy of Greek philosophy by the living philosophical practice of the early modern age. The *Lives and Opinions* is — as to its actual influence — in all probability the most important single work of a historic-interpretative type in the whole history of Western philosophy. Knowledge about the Pre-Socratics, the Stoics, and Epicureanism was transmitted to post-fourteenth-century philosophy largely through and on account of this book, and it is unnecessary to say how much modern philosophy is obliged to the resurrection and revival of these traditions. (In this respect, the publication by Gassendi of the Xth book of Diogenes can be seen almost as an act of symbolic significance.) Furthermore, the work of Diogenes served as more than an absolutely irreplaceable *source*. Up to the first half of the eighteenth century, actually till Brucker, it also constituted the *paradigmatic model* for all histories of philosophy. Its disposition and method in many respects determined the first form in which post-medieval philosophy has given account of its own historicity.

Now there is no question that this factually fulfilled role is largely a result of accidents, i.e. the chance conservation of manuscripts during the intervening millenium between the third and thirteenth centuries. Nevertheless, I would like to argue — though certainly in a merely tentative way — that if the question concerns not just the individual peculiarities of the work of Diogenes, but the general characteristics of his hermeneutical practices, then these latter, so clearly distortive of the original meaning of the interpreted heritage, were at the same time important factors allowing this legacy to be *preserved and saved* in spite of and throughout processes of enormous socio-cultural dislocation and change. That is, the case can at least be made that the whole grafting of the Greek philosophical legacy on the body of the Judeo-Christian heritage was made possible, or at least was significantly facilitated, by the availability of interpretative methods and, more generally, cultural attitudes which, by obliterating the constitutive distinctions between *episteme* and *doxa*, between philosophy and rhetoric, certainly debased philosophy, but at the same time offered a hermeneutic *instrumentarium* that could be employed for the sake of such a reconciliation.

To put the matter bluntly: classical philosophy, with its claim to be the sole way to truth and to making human conduct both right and reasonable, necessarily stood in a relation of irreconcilable competition with any universalistic religion of salvation that made the same claim on its own behalf. The development of a cultural attitude which ascribed an enormous prestige to philosophy as a cultural good, but put its original relation to truth, as it were, in parentheses — an attitude which we find embodied, among others, in Diogenes — arguably opened the way toward the possibility of a certain type of reconciliation. In any case, it is a fact that the actual annexation of Greek philosophy to the Scriptures as a propaedeutic to the latter was accomplished through the use of exactly those interpretative methods which were elaborated in late Antiquity and which we encounter in Diogenes. Already Alexandrian Judaism (Philo, above all) employed them fully, for example by elaborating a typical *bios* of Moses which identified him with Musaius and, in this way, in a typically diadochist manner, transformed him into the true archaget of Greek philosophy. And the early Christian apologists and fathers of the Church, like Clement of Alexandria, Origen and Jerome, used the whole hermeneutic arsenal of late ancient doxography, with all its antiquarianizing and allegorizing methods of interpretation, applied both to the Bible and to pagan philosophy, to establish essential correspondences between the two, and to transform philosophy into a preparatory introduction into the true doctrine of the Church bestowed by God upon the Greeks.

If there are any conclusions to be drawn from this account, they seem to be rather destructive for hermeneutics as a philosophical enterprise in general. Conceived as a science answering the question of what makes an interpretation true or correct, a general hermeneutics seems to be impossible, since the sought-for criteria are relative and dependent upon a changing cultural framework which ascribes definite functions to interpretation and may ascribe them in radically different ways for different epochs and different cultural genres. But neither does this recognition of the inevitable historical perspectivity or *Standortgebundenheit* of interpretation open up the way to its ontological understanding as an event in effective history. To the question of what interpretation does in this latter sense, again no general answer is possible. Even such (at first glance) frighteningly relativist generalizations as the Gadamerian "to interpret means to interpret always otherwise," are not relativist enough. Interpretations are not simply spontaneous outcomes of changing life-situations; they always take place according to culturally defined normative standards, and whether a given culture has one such standard or many, and whether they are posited as stable or changing, depend on the character of the historical culture in question. Interpretation of tradition may demonstrate an enormous stability or it may have the character of a pseudo-organic growth over long periods of culture-history, as, for example, in rabbinical interpretations of the Bible in post-exile Jewry or interpretations of Confucianism during long periods of Chinese history. The plausibility of a general, ontologizing characterization of what all interpretations share in common is, it seems to me, based in Gadamer on an implicit identification of the question of the continuity of the transmission of cultural tradition with that of overall historical continuity and social identity. These two, however, are not identical. Precisely because of this fact, because the historical productivity of interpretation is not ontologically fixed, interpretation can do various things 'with us,' too. It certainly can be an important element in the maintenance of social identity, but equally it can transmit tradition in spite of significant disruptions in historical continuity, as well as create traditions between historically unrelated cultures, or else emancipate from a binding tradition within the processes of an essentially *continuous* social change.

This purely destructive result with respect to hermeneutics as a philosophical enteprise is, however, perhaps an outcome of the fact that both the methodological and the ontological conceptions of hermeneutics seem to mischaracterize the way and the sense in which interpretation becomes a problem for philosophy. It is perhaps worth mentioning that the well-known three stages in the development of a philosophical hermeneutic — the Romantic, the *geisteswissenschaftlich*, and the contemporary — refer to periods when, initially completely independently from any hermeneutic endeavour, the methodology of the historiography of philosophy also became quite suddenly a matter of lively discussion (from Garve and Reinhold to Ritter and Ast; with Renouvier, Riehl, Windelband, etc. and lastly, with Gueroult, Erhardt, J. Passmore, etc.). Both discussions, moreover, have taken place within an explicitly recognized *crisis in philosophy*. In general, it seems to me, the question of interpretation emerges in philosophy at times when it becomes deeply and generally problematic whether, our forms of interpretation and what we actually do and are able to do in interpreting the cultural legacy of the past, as it is normatively determined by our own contemporary cultural practices, are genuinely able to capture what is truly creative and significant in this legacy. In this sense, the philosophical problem of hermeneutics is always related to a critical questioning of the *meaningfulness of contemporary cultural life*. It is, and ought to be, part and parcel of a critical theory of culture which cannot, however, solve its own problems by merely hermeneutic means.

Notes

An earlier version of this article appeared as: "Interpretations of, and Interpretations in Philosophy," *Critical Philosophy*, I.1. (1984): 67-85. (Editor: Paul Crittenden, Dept. of General Philosophy, the University of Sydney, Sydney, N.S.W. Australia).

Secondary Sources

Bollarck, J. "Vom System der Geschichte zur Geschichte der Systeme." *Geschichte — Ereignis und Erzählung*. Hg. von R. Koselleck and W.D. Stempel, (München, 1973).

Braun, L. *Histoire de l'histoire de la philosophie*, (Paris, 1973).

Charrue, J.M. *Plotin lecteur de Platon*, (Paris, 1978).

Curtius, E.R. *European Literature and the Latin Middle Ages*, (London, 1979).

Didhle, A. *Studien zur griechischen Biographie*, (Göttingen, 1956).

Eon, A. "La notion plotinienne d'exegèse. *Revue Internationale de la Philosophie*, vol. 24 (1970).

Gigon, O. "L'Historicité de la philosophie chez Aristote." *La Philosophie de l'histoire de la philosophie*, (Paris-Rome, 1956).
"Das Proemium des Diogenes Laertios: Struktur und Problem." *Horizonte der Humanitas: Ein Freudesgabe für Prof. Dr. W. Wili*, (Bern-Stuttgart, 1960).

Guthrie, W. K. C. "Aristoteles als Philosophie-Historiker," *Aristoteles in der neueren Forschung*, (Darmstadt, 1968).

Hadas, M. *Hellenistic Culture*, (New York, 1959).

Hope, R. *The Book of Diogenes Laertius*, (New York, 1930).

Passmore, J. "The Idea of a History of Philosophy," *History and Theory*, suppl. V. 5, (1965).

Rahn, H. *Morphologie der antiken Literatur*, (Darmstadt, 1969).

Wehrli, F. "Von der antiken Biographie," *Theoria und Humanitas*. (Zürich-München, 1972).

7

CECI TUERA CELA: GRAFFITI AS CRIME AND ART

Susan Stewart

> *The law permits me to write; it asks only that I write in a style other than* my own! *I am allowed to show the face of my mind, but, first, I must give it a prescribed expression... Prescribed expressions mean only* bonne mine à mauvais jeu. — Marx, "Remarks on the New Instructions to the Prussian Censors." (1842)

Method and Situation

I have taken my title from Victor Hugo's self-conscious diversion in *Notre-Dame de Paris*: "le livre tuera l'édifice." In this little essay Hugo contends that the mechanical reproduction of print will destroy the monumental architecture of the Middle Ages, that the innovations of the press will thereby kill the solidity of the Church, and that a change in mode of expression is a change in human thought. Here Hugo takes as his subject the inverted teleology of certain loss: "L'homme qui a écrit ce mot sur ce mur s'est effacé, il y a plusieurs siècles, du milieu des générations, le mot s'est à son tour effacé du mur de l'église, l'église elle-même s'effacera bientôt peut-être de la terre."[1]

If for Hugo history is a progressive erasure, from another perspective — that of postmodernism — history is a progressive, and self-contradicting, accumulation. This accumulation of subjectivities, practices, goods and rationalities appears within the framework of a commodity system which can take up even its own negation and re-inscribe it within the discourse of novelty. The capacity for the re-inscription of negation as novelty is evident in a variety of postmodern cultural forms — "la mode retro"; kitsch; the "functional" ornamentation of postmodern architecture[2] — but it is particularly evident in the axiological premises shaping graffiti as writing, painting, dirt, and crime.

These premises, formulating the boundary between practices and artifactuality, continue a debate as old as the *Phaedrus* regarding a conflict between a divine and transcendent writing and a "bad" writing — laborious, human, and literal.[3] But more dramatically, such premises center on a current crisis in the situation of the artwork — a crisis modulated between the ephemeral and the classic, between the vernacular and the Law, between the brand name and the signature, and between commodity production and artistic practices. If modernist aesthetic theory suffered from the disjunction between spirituality and sensuality,[4] postmodern aesthetic theory suffers from a disjunction between intention and necessity erupting in the relations between artistic reproduction and reception. For it is the nature of the commodity system, of its compelling systematicity *per se*, to substitute labor with magic, intrinsicality with marketing, authoring with ushering.

Explanations or descriptions of axiological premises should take as their point of departure the locations of contradiction within those premises. Because at the present time graffiti is both outlawed and venerated, it provides such a point of departure. Radically taken up as both crime and art, graffiti has, in recent years, been the site of a conflict regarding the status of the artist and the art work in contemporary culture. The production and reception of graffiti show how the articulation of the art object proceeds according to certain axiological practices. It is not that the dismissal and veneration of graffiti are two oppositional gestures: rather, these gestures are part of a reciprocal and interdependent system of axiological practices tied into the larger values of the commodity culture. The "criminal art" of graffiti could only arise in its present form from a crisis in the situation of art objects as commodities: while graffiti emerges as a statement of this conflict on the level of the culture of the street, we see the same crisis outlined in "high" art's inversion of art's commodity status through recent developments in environmental, conceptual, and performance art. We can here specify a process whereby consumer culture, which is literally in the business of inventing arbitrary value and of circumscribing intrinsicality, takes up what is "not valuable" precisely to reinforce the structure of that gesture of articulation.[5]

In this sense the divergent attitudes toward graffiti are not only a matter of the interests of one social group or class posited against another, but can be seen as parts of a complex relationship between authority, power, institutions, and artistic production in the broadest sense. The intensity of the struggle for space and resources within an urban environment makes the conflicts centered on graffiti particularly illuminating of a discussion of such artistic production. Surrounded by violently oppositional valuations, graffiti pushes us to a limit where the postmodern emergence and disappearance of such notions as quality, integrity, and taste may be described historically and specifically, without necessarily valorizing the *a priori* status of such terms under modernism proper.

To focus on a sense of art as commodity here rather than, say, a sense of art as play, or art as experiment, or even art as expression, fiction, or the beautiful, enables us to examine how such categories as play, experiment, expression, invention, and the beautiful are summoned in the very process of canonizing this "crime" as "art." Methodology here must begin at a point where any intrinsic notion of the artistic is put into question or bracketted by social practices, rather than at a point where the phenomenon is already framed as art: in the latter case, the method can only reinscribe the conditions of its own attention. Obviously, this method is in conflict with any method that takes on a liberal pluralism of aesthetic judgments. And this is at least in part a matter of the questions raised by the topic. The responses to graffiti make clear that, in practices of production and apprehension, aesthetic valuation is a process of repression and emergence, erasure and reinscription. Thus it is also necessary to put into question any account of axiological practices that is transcendent and equivocal — if only because such a model itself is tied into notions of the classic and assumptions of transcendent consciousness.

The goal here is to account for the *presentness* of the phenomenon at hand. Hence it is necessary to take into consideration the specificity of contemporary consumer culture. And it is also necessary to take into consideration a set of manipulations and resistances to that culture, by which the culture's very structure marks off a closed arena of consumption. The theme of access — access to discourse, access to goods, access to the reception of information — has import for the creation of such a methodology in a profound sense, calling into question the relations between a micro- and a macro-analysis: the insinuating and pervasive forms of the mass culture are here known only through localizations and adaptations. Graffiti as a phenomenon vividly takes on the form and thematic of that tension as it addresses the relation those cut off from consumption bear to consumerism and as it addresses the ways the consumer culture absorbs and reinscribes all other forms of cultural production.

It is not necessarily the intention of graffiti writers or artists to point to the paradoxes of consumer culture; rather, the paradoxes inherent in the production and reception of graffiti are paradoxes that are shaped by the contingencies of this historical conjuncture. Thus there is a certain risk of "trendiness," or just the same, a risk of datedness, in taking graffiti as a subject, but it is the very ephemerality of graffiti that is of interest here. For this sense of ephemerality, the sense that one's subject may disappear by morning, serves the interests of exploring a continually novelized economy.

Such a study, moreover, summons the spectre of "bad taste," for graffiti pushes us to a point which breaks down the very usefulness of the notion of taste and thus calls for the relocation of *taste* within its historical (liberal/democratic) milieu.[6] Even the primacy of the senses in this relocation becomes historicized, for as Baudrillard and Rubert de Ventos have shown us, the facility for "good taste" in the post-Puritan upper classes is a facility for the suppression of the sensual and the emergence of fine discrimination and careful mutability.[7] More importantly, the axiological model that depends upon the exercise of taste amid a panoply of objects no longer is suited to an object of study that takes as its very point or focus consumerism's patterns of suppression and emergence with regard to art objects. Whereas Wordsworth, in a famous passage in the 1800 *Preface*, called for a more active exercise of the faculty of taste and a rejection of the merely habitual, we here find the necessity of rejecting an axiological model in which elements have equivocal standing, mutuality, and reciprocity as items for consumption.[8]

Who Is John Scott?

> There is therefore a good and a bad writing: the good and
> natural is the divine inscription in the heart and the soul;
> the perverse and artful is technique, exiled in the exteriority of the body. — Derrida, *Of Grammatology*, p. 17.

Since the 1960's teenagers, mostly boys, in cities such as Philadelphia, New York, and Los Angeles (the *loci* of this strongly local essay) have engaged in a practice of graffiti writing which is public and exterior and which has a particular focus. Using markers, pens, and/or spray paint, they have written their names, in the form of nicknames or special graffiti names called "tags," on subway cars, public buildings, walls, and many other exterior surfaces — for example, several early Philadelphia writers earned their legendary status by writing their tags on a jet at the airport and on an elephant at the Philadelphia zoo. Graffiti writers have distinctive codes of style and behavior, both individual (one's particular style of writing) and local (New York style, for example), which are readily recognized by those who practice graffiti. This style has only occasionally to do with the referent or legibility of graffiti. In fact, the term "wild style" is used for letters that cannot be read as anything except as the mark of an individual's (now past) presence at the scene.

I will outline more specifically these practices below, but it should be clear from the outset that I am not concerned here with the more hidden forms of graffiti writing, such as bathroom graffiti, which have often been the focus of psychological studies. Nor am I concerned with the writing one finds often prior to this development, like the mark of a high school prank ("Class of '58") or graffiti of the "John loves Mary" type. My point is not that there is no relation between these forms, but rather that the public and institutionalized production of the kind of graffiti I address, and its consistent emphasis upon the *name*, make it of quite different interest to us here. Perhaps a counter-example will help clarify my neglect for now of the earlier forms; for whereas such forms are anonymous messages to an abstract public, the forms I will discuss are the personal signatures of an individual style, designed to be read by a particular audience in particular ways.

A Philadelphia madman named John Scott has, over the past ten years or so, placed red bumper-stickers printed with black letters reading "Who is John Scott?" in hundreds of locations throughout the city. If we juxtapose the practice of John Scott with the practices of contemporary graffiti writers, we might conclude that the key to John Scott's madness lies in the mass production, the distanced compulsion, of his question; for John Scott has no style, no handwriting, coterminous with a private body. The question of John Scott's identity is a social question, an anterior question, which Scott is compelled to recapitulate, virtually to map, as the ephemeral trace of his journeys across town — the radical alienation of Scott's gesture lies in its perfect merging, its perfect identification, with that anteriority. Scott's body is an extension of the machine that poses the question; the *himself* is the always deferred place or location of the question's posing. The fame of Scott has no referent other than the surface of its own repetition.

My point is to contrast this gesture with the practice of the graffiti writer (graffiti "artists" call themselves "writers," so to avoid further confusion the native term will be used). The graffiti writer's goal is a stylization inseparable from the body, a stylization which, in its impenetrable "wildness," could surpass even linguistic reference and serve purely as a mark of presence, the concrete evidence of an individual existence and the reclamation of the environment through the label of the personal. Who is this graffiti writer? The "victims" of graffiti project a graffiti writer in the mode of John Scott, singular and disturbed. Yet ethnographies, perhaps in their own village, and village-making, tradition, characterize graffiti in contemporary urban environments as an indigenous or folk form carried out by a community of writers relatively homogenous in age (9-16).[9] This community is structured by an explicit hierarchy: beginners (called "toys") work with master writers as apprentices. The toy generally progresses from writing simple "tags" (signatures made with markers or spray paints) on any surface to writing "throw-ups" (larger tags thrown onto inaccessible surfaces or the outsides of subway cars) to writing "pieces" (short for masterpieces: symbolic and/or figurative works such as landscapes, objects, letters, or characters drawn on a variety of surfaces).[10]

Given this social background to the practice of graffiti, the function of graffiti appears repeatedly, nevertheless, in the emic or native scheme of things as a matter of individuation. One of the principle rules of the graffiti writer's code of ethics is that a writer cannot copy or "bite" either the tag or the style of another writer without instigating a cross-out war, or, more directly, a first-person fight. The reputation of the writer depends upon the recognizability of his or her style, but even more importantly upon his or her facility for "getting up" — that is, a facility for making one's mark as frequently and in as dispersed a fashion as possible. Although writers with "messy handwriting" are spoken of with contempt, the sloppiest writer whose name appears frequently throughout a city will have far more status than the most polished writer whose work is limited to just a few examples. Thus the honorific titles "King of the Line," "All City — Insides," and "King of the City," are bestowed, regardless of style, on those writers respectively whose tags appear in every car of a certain subway line, or on the insides of every subway car, or in as many locations as possible.

There is no question that graffiti's investment in frequency of production borrows from the methods of commodity advertising and publicity; the writer is his or her own "agent" and here agency as artistic expression is a tautological process of self-promotion miming the reflexive signifiers of fashion and "packaging." But as will become more and more apparent, this borrowing of advertising methods is a matter of adaptation, manipulation, and localization. "Fame" becomes "fame" as celebrity and appreciation are closely restricted to the esoteric codes of the folk community. Writers frequently mention the thrill of seeing their "tags" on the TV news as a backdrop to an event being filmed and this is a particularly apt metaphor for graffiti's interstitial relation to the structures of the culture in general.

Because writing graffiti is illegal and quite specifically dangerous, the aesthetic criteria at work in the writers' schemes of evaluation are a matter of conception and execution more than a matter of judgments regarding the qualities of a final artifact — writers will often make evaluative comments part of their "pieces," leaving a history of the constraints on their work: "Sorry about the drips," "It's cold," "Cheap paint," "Too late. Too tired," etc.[11] Graffiti writers plan larger pieces, and practice smaller ones, in sketch books which they call "black books" or "piece books," and the execution of a large piece depends upon "racking up" or "inventing" — that is, stealing — sometimes hundreds of cans of spray paint and hundreds of markers before a piece can be begun.[12] The graffiti writer often must be an accomplished thief, athlete, and con artist; thus "personal" style itself is a matter not simply applied to the artifact, but to many aspects of the graffiti writer's everyday behavior. These obstacles to production are a major factor in the evaluation of graffiti by the folk community of writers and a special weight is thereby given to frequency of production when such evaluations are made.

It is important to re-emphasize that the art of graffiti is an art of the autograph; the tag is a signature adopted from the writers' given names, from nicknames, or from a name chosen for its sound or appearance. For example, a Philadelphia writer chose the name PARIS, but decided after making a few tags that the "S" did not offer good visual closure and so added an "H" because he felt that the block letter of the "H" gave the name a more finished quality — hence his tag PARISH.[13] And black books serve as autograph books as well as sketch books — writers ask more accomplished writers to autograph their books; toys especially prize such collections and study the autographs to determine how individual effects are accomplished. In this sense, contemporary graffiti's antecedents would not seem to be only the privatized anonymity of indoor forms of graffiti, but also the slam books or autograph books that have been long a tradition of American adolescents — books used to define emerging identities within the adolescent social group, as teenagers collect the signatures, written in the most stylish handwriting, of their friends.

Finally we should note that the function of individuation, stylization, and uniqueness would also seem to be served by the appropriation of the metaphor of the robot in both graffiti and its sister art, break dancing. The distinctly geometric letters called "Robot Style," or styles such as "Computer" and "Mechanical" style[14] find their complement in the mixture of freeze-frame stopping found in break dancing and its accompanying hand-made "scratches" (moving a record back and forth on a turntable by hand).[15] This mixture of body movement and the imitation of mechanical action is mirrored as well in the home-made innovations that diversify the function of the graffiti writer's materials: improvised spray can tops, improvised inks, and transformations of marker tips[16] all demonstrate the imposition of individualized style upon mass forms, tools, and identity. Writers do not conceive of their role as one within a larger narrative or historical structure than this specific tradition of graffiti writing; rather, they place their arts within the interruptions and interstices of social life, marking off a physical space for a time and inscribing it within an individuality both unique and ephemeral. In this way graffiti resembles the "cut" frame of cinema, refusing metonymy, refusing — here negating — an "outside" in favor of an "inside out": a focus on the separation.

Graffiti As Dirt

It is easy to see how graffiti becomes dirt once we consider, in the mode of much recent cognitive anthropology, dirt to be something in the wrong place or wrong time and consequently something ranked at the bottom of a hierarchical scale of values.[17] It is of course the fixity of the scale and the arbitrariness of its contents at any given point which provide the scale with its particular power. But more specifically, graffiti can be seen as a *permanent* soiling of the environment simply in its constant replicability, its emphasis upon repetition and replacement. Graffiti is widely considered to be a *defacement*: an application that destroys the significance of its material base just as the defacement of coins invalidates their worth, their face value, and proves a threat to the monetary system as a whole.

The analogy to the defacement of money is particularly apt, for graffiti is considered a threat not only to the surface upon which it is applied; it is considered a threat to the entire system of meanings by which such surfaces acquire value, integrity, and significance. Thus we find former New York mayor Lindsay saying that he and his staff had never really wondered whether graffiti was "anything but defacement."[18] The Philadelphia City Ordinance banning the sale of spray paint to minors states that graffiti "contributes to the blight and degradation of neighborhoods, and even discourages the formation of business." And the head of the police-gang control-unit in Los Angeles declares that "graffiti decreases property value and signed buildings on block after block convey the impression that the city government has lost control, that the neighborhood is...sliding toward anarchy."[19]

This is graffiti as non-culture. Linked to the dirty, the animal, the uncivilized, and the profane, contemporary urban graffiti signifies an interruption of the boundaries of public and private space, an eruption of creativity and movement outside and through the claims of street, facade, exterior, and interior by which the city is articulated. Graffiti makes claims upon materiality, refusing to accept the air as the only free or ambiguously-defined space. In fact the practice of graffiti emphasizes the free commercial quality of urban spaces in general, a quality in contrast to the actual paucity of available private space. In this, graffiti hearkens to what is a much older, and perhaps mostly Latin, sense of the street. For example, Helen Tanzer, in her study of the graffiti of Pompeii, notes this tradition: "one reason why shops were tolerated in a residential district is that in the genial climate of Campania most of the time was spent out of doors, as is the case today, and the houses faced inward in the fashion familiar in the patio type of house throughout the Latin countries. The peristyle gave freedom and privacy to the household."[20] We may extend Louis Kahn's contention that "the street is a room by agreement" to include the street as playground, ballfield, and billboard by agreement — or by conflict, subterfuge, and the exercise of power and privilege.

To think of the street in this way is to confront the interior world of domestic genres — the still life, the window display, the arrangement of consumable objects — with a radical exteriority; an exteriority characterized by movement and direction, a body set into motion like a machine — but as we noted above, a machine made singular, stylized, and individual. The accoutrements of lettering in graffiti — the characters and arrows — serve as heralds to the name, pointing to its fluidity and speed. This characteristic sense of motion arises in part, no doubt, from the necessity of working quickly under terrific constraints and it is a matter of a thematic arising from graffiti's hounded scene of production. But it is also a sense of motion that relates to the mobility of the name and the sense of an author who traverses the city. The subway car is the perfect surface for graffiti — a moving name is set into motion by this travelling billboard. A name that "gets around," that "goes places," must be seen against a background of the fixed society it traverses and that society's continually deferred promise of personal mobility.

Graffiti writers often argue that it is ethical to write on spaces which have been abandoned or poorly maintained; it is considered a sign of amateurism, moreover, to write on churches, private homes and automobiles, and other clearly "private" property. Writers sometimes extend this argument to a complaint regarding the "emptiness" or lack of significance characteristic, in their opinion, of public and corporate architecture overall.[21] To these buildings characterized by height and anonymity, the graffiti writer attaches the personal name written by hand on a scale perceptible to the individual viewer. In this sense, the graffiti writer argues for the personalization of wall-writing and for the appropriation of the street by those who primarily inhabit it. Here the presence of the writer is posited against absenteeism and neglect; graffiti writers espouse an anti-monumental politics, contrasting to the monument's abstraction and stasis the signature's personality, mobility, and vernacular, localized, audience.

We might note that, despite the implicit sexual metaphor of "getting up" one's name, contemporary exterior graffiti is rarely, if ever, obscene, since the entire practice and valuation of graffiti among writers centers upon the importance of the tag or name and its frequent appearance. Yet the public and the law often declaim the obscenity of graffiti and we might conclude that in a general sense the obscenity here is an utterance out of place. All display is a form of exposure and just as the spaces of reproduction in society are maintained through the regulation, by means of taboo and legitimation, of places and times for sexuality, so, in this case, do writing and figuration in the wrong place and time fall into the category of obscenity. In fact the more illegible, or "wild style," the writing, the stronger is the public's assumption that the message must be obscene.[22]

Unlike other forms of dirt, graffiti, as a kind of vandalism, is intentional; and, even worse in the eyes of the law, graffiti is not in any physical sense ephemeral. In fact, for durability of surface and materials, graffiti is a far more permanent art than, say, painting on canvas. Yet city governments must make the claim that graffiti is, as are other pranks, reversible or erasable in order to legitimate the vast resources the state has expended on "graffiti maintenance." The New York MTA alone has spent up to ten million dollars a year in what it calls "normal graffiti maintenance" and has been willing to experiment with toxic chemical paint removers that provide clear threats to the health of MTA workers and residents of neighborhoods bordering on the train yards.[23] Of course, graffiti does not exist in the singular work, but rather in a process of rampant reproduction. Through such maintenance programs city governments have simply cleared more space for writing and thereby provided a needed service to the writers by creating such additional free surface space.

The intentionality of graffiti is accommodated by attributing graffiti's production to gangs, criminals, and the insane (for the public, not always mutually exclusive categories). On August 19, 1972, in the *New York Times*, Mayor Lindsay claimed it was "the Lindsay theory that the rash of graffiti madness was 'related to mental health problems.'"[24] This claim amended an earlier statement by the mayor that graffiti writers were "insecure cowards."[25] The Los Angeles government, in anticipation of the Olympics, violated standard constitutional rights regarding evidence and trial by jury in forcing gang-members to clean up graffiti or go to jail — regardless of whether they could be proven to be guilty of writing the graffiti.[26] And the Philadelphia police have adopted the phrase "hard-core graffiti writers" to describe those apprehended in recent "sweep" arrests.[27]

These responses to graffiti may seem extreme in light of prevailing social values, yet liberal approaches to graffiti writing are even more insidious if we consider them in light of the values of writers themselves. For the predominant liberal solution to the "graffiti problem" is the demand that 1) the writers "erase" or paint over their own work or that of others, usually with white or beige paint, and thereby "whitewash" their work or 2) that the writers become art *students*, that is, work with brushes on static materials in a figurative style, thus subjecting themselves to a form of realism that would hardly be demanded of most contemporary art students proper.

This "encouragement" of the writer's creativity is in effect a matter of disciplinary punishment, a punishment that takes as its thematic a generalized representation and simultaneous suppression of the signature which had been at the center of the graffiti artist's work. The project of erasure offers a replication of the liberal position of presenting categories without the hierarchical determinations that are the work of history. Here erasure is a powerful metaphor for liberalism's dependence upon forgetting. For example, the director of the Philadelphia Anti-Graffiti Task Force has announced that graffiti writers will be asked to go to "vacant housing projects and paint venetian blinds, flowers, or figures of human beings on boarded-up windows."[28] Thus the *trompe l'oeil* of the middle classes, the facade of civic values, is to be maintained as a punishment by those whose initial project was the destruction of such an illusion — the graffiti signature, which marked in unmistakable color the truth of desolation and abandonment, is here replaced by the mere illusion of presence and a remarkable sense of "public appearances."

Foucault has taught us that the function of discipline after the pastoral innovations of the Reformation is to individualize the subject and thus to individualize a continual self-surveillance.[29] Yet in the contemporary practice of graffiti writing, a public and publicized subjectivity is the point or focus of the illegal act; reformist efforts hope that the redemptive and penitent activity of erasure or cleansing will produce such self-surveillance or that the anonymity and subjection of apprenticeship to an alien tradition will check the writer's ego and prepare him or her for the long hierarchical process of becoming an artist via institutions. It is also an effort to distance the writer from his or her own production — to force the writer to see graffiti from the viewpoint of a mediating discourse hitherto unavailable to him or her: the history of the tradition (and not as it is presented in the black books).

In a profound sense, the current "crisis" regarding graffiti is symptomatic of a crisis in the status of the body. On the one hand, there is the inappropriate display of the body and its reproductive power implicit in graffiti's signifying practices. The affront to the facade in graffiti writing might be considered as an extension of the tradition of the criminal's self-marking and self-mutilation. Here one rebels against the imposed environment by inventing a new surface — the body's exterior — for the inscription of one's identity, writing upon that surface a set of social relations denied by one's imprisonment: lovers, family, the names of exotic places, the mottos of one's value system.[30] The criminal's assertion of the tattoo offers some consolation thereby for the state's confiscation of his fingerprint and for the insult of the mugshot.[31]

On the other hand, there is the threat of graffiti, articulated by its "victims" as an attack or form of violence. Here, the facade which graffiti inscribes is clearly a projection or externalization of the private body of the middle classes. It is private property that has maintained appearances, that has put its best face forward, and graffiti's confiscation of the urban environment, its relentless proclamation that what is surface is what is public, poses the threat to exchange, to business as usual, noted in the ordinances and police statements above. Here graffiti's emphasis upon elegance, speed, grace, and the sensuality of the body must be contrasted to the abstractions of wage-labor and mechanical production represented by the surfaces it inscribes. Graffiti writers have put their subjectivity in the wrong place and it must be properly reassigned by disciplinary measures. As Marx noted in *The German Ideology*, "The exclusive concentration of artistic talent in particular individuals and its suppression in the broad mass which is bound up with this, is a consequence of the division of labor."[32] Such reforms are designed in a true sense to find for the graffiti writer "a place in life," where he or she can make, in most circumscribed fashion, his or her "mark."

Graffiti As Art

We do not find the current fashion of venerating graffiti as gallery art far from these reformist efforts. The avant-garde here appears as a quarrel in the house of the bourgeoisie and, whereas the appropriation of graffiti by the art establishment has meant the retention of the signature, the mode of execution and reproduction, equally essential to the graffiti aesthetic, have been dropped. For the point is to make graffiti a commodity, and to do so one must clearly define its status as a unique object. One must invent a self-conscious intentionality which places the artist intertextually within the tradition as it is defined by critics and the art establishment in general.

Let me clarify this point by emphasizing once more that graffiti writers themselves explain their tradition in terms of individual and regional styles; and the apprenticeship and black book aspects of their work commit them to a certain linear and even patriarchal view of their place as writers. Further, the writers readily recognize their debt to the iconography of billboards and other forms of advertizing; comic strips; logos; and commercial calligraphy. But this iconography quite literally points to the writer's name in the configuration of the "piece," and the pointing is another gesture of localization within the graffiti aesthetic. Thus the graffiti writer's sense of the tradition here is not the same as the tradition of the Tradition, not the same as Sidney Janis's introductory remarks in the catalogue of his Post-Graffiti Show: "urban-bred, the graffiti artist continues the tradition of Pop Art which he admires."[33] Thus this show announces the death of graffiti proper (hence "post-graffiti") and the rejuvenation of the Pop Art tradition which the Janis Gallery was instrumental in presenting in the first place.

A dominant number of the most successful graffiti artists, moreover, are in fact art students proper, often middle-class adolescents who have had contact with and befriended street artists. As Calvin Tompkins suggests in the *New Yorker*, "Crude as it may be in execution, the work of these artists (Keith Haring, Kenny Scharf, Jean-Michel Basquiat, Ronnie Cutrone) has a certain sophistication — an awareness of such antecedents as Dubuffet's 'art brut,' Cy Twombly's elegant scribbling, and the comic-book imagery of pop artists. The graffiti artists lack this sort of reference — when they spray paint on canvas, it does not look like other art. Nor does it much resemble the work they used to do on trains."[34]

Tompkins's remarks make clear that the two complementary axes of the art establishment's appropriation of graffiti are tradition and adaptation. But the claiming of tradition in this much-documented case has skipped the track of graffiti's own history. This history might move from the graffiti of the Athenian agora, Pompeii, and Arabic traditions of place marking and camel brands, to medieval cathedral inscriptions, through the whole history of public, anonymous, generally political forms of art.[35] But in an important sense, the tradition should not be dated before the late 1950's and the early 1960's when this kind of autograph graffiti and the community of writers sharing its legibility specifically arose. In Tompkins's account, this tradition is derailed onto the track of art history, specifically the history of painting as institutionally canonized — that is, as a progression of individual artifacts worked by individual masters.

Thus graffiti is continually linked with the spontaneous, the primitive, the real of this tradition — a real located in nature and the body. Here the invention of a tradition for graffiti, particularly as a form of "folk art," is the invention of both nostalgia and currency. Graffiti is valued as a dying art form, the romantic heir to abstract expressionism and pop art; and it is also valued as the newest and most fashionable art form: hence its thematics are often ones of youthful tragedy. Despite the facts of an ongoing practice, a technological sophistication, and a rather rigid apprentice system, graffiti is appropriated by a discourse applauding its "fresh and spontaneous" nature (Dolores Neumann in the Janis catalogue) or, as Norman Mailer describes it, "the impulse of the jungle to cover the walled tanks of technology." Claes Oldenburg's famous description of subway-car graffiti as a "bouquet from Latin America" equally contributes to this process of naturalization and primitivization. The widely-held assumption on the part of graffiti's opponents that graffiti is practiced by those of Afro-American and Latin descent is probably a matter of racism. Martha Cooper and Henry Chalfant have noted the complicated mixture of cultural backgrounds found among New York writers: for example, the "crew" or team of writers known as "The Vamp Squad" has members of Peruvian, Scottish, Italian, African, Jordanian, Puerto Rican, and Albanian descent.[36] The dean of the Moore College of Art in Philadelphia announced at the opening of a show by Lady Pink at that institution that "the art world has domesticated a formerly feral animal."[37] And the popularity of graffiti art in Europe may be attributed, certainly in part, to European notions of the American frontier, the American city, and the high-tech romance of a contemporary colonial culture.

The movement of graffiti to canvas and gallery space continues the process of substitution by which historical contingency is mythologized; mediating figures such as art students become the new graffiti artists and thus enable the street artists to "die off"; social workers and photographers become spokespersons and publicists for graffiti writers;[38] acceptable, readable, and apprehensible in scale, graffiti painting is enclosed within a proper space and time and delimited for consumption as a singular artifact, an artifact which now *stands for*, is metonymic to, an infinity of wild-style tags that would have been previously available only to a simultaneous consciousness that is the quintessential urban daydream. Thus what was formerly a matter of desecration and even violence is now modulated to a matter of domestic consumption — enter *taste*, for one likes the individual work or one doesn't. If the case is the latter, the work, like any other consumer good, can be left for someone else to take up. The virtues of the good are, of course, assumed by the consumer, for the commodity's magic always lies in the substitution of the "labor" of consumption for the labor of production.[39]

Graffiti on canvas, graffiti as art work or art object, clearly is the invention of the institutions of art — the university, the gallery, the critic, the collector. And it is an invention designed to satisfy the needs of those institutions to assert their own spontaneity, classlessness, flexibility, and currency — all qualities that can only emerge through a self-consciousness which negates them. We might ask why the commodity system has taken up graffiti writing as painting, for this transformation provokes some interesting problems. Here graffiti is moved from a permanent surface, the granite of the bank or the metal of the subway car, to the far less durable background of canvas. Here graffiti is transformed from something indelible calling for erasure to something eternal calling for curating. Here graffiti is halted in its self-perpetuating and rampant motion and framed quite literally as a static object.

Cooper and Chalfant note that "a subway car is sixty feet long and twelve feet high. To do a top-to-bottom (to paint the whole train) in the yard, where there is no convenient platform to stand on, a writer must climb up the side of the car and hang on with one hand while painting with the other; or, if his legs are long enough, he can straddle the distance between two parked trains."[40] Thus the writer never sees the entire "piece" until, and if, it pulls out of the train-yard. The motion of writing, constrained by these conditions, forecloses the possibility of a far view. Here such absorption is translated into the contemplation and distance of gallery art. The valuation of graffiti is an effort to accommodate through adaptation a novel threat to the status of the art object in general. To the extent that graffiti writers move off the street and into the gallery, the threat will be met. But of course there is no room in the gallery for that many writers and thus we arrive again at graffiti's most intimidating aspect: its sheer numbers.

Brand Names

It is important to remember that the crime of graffiti is a crime in mode of production. Unlike pornography, graffiti is not a crime of content. Paradoxically, in graffiti that sign of proper training, discipline, and Puritan control over the body — good handwriting — is elevated to a dizzying perfection, a triumph over the constraints of materials and surface. And certainly the high tradition of art has long recognized the ascendence of the signature which has made graffiti possible; we have only to think of the secular's encroachment upon the triptych, and, later, of de Kooning and Rauschenberg's collaborative erasure.

Part of the threat of graffiti is its claim that anyone can be an artist. Graffiti's system of masters and apprentices is theoretically available to anyone. But, unlike other forms of mass creativity from "*proletkult*" to "lifestyle," graffiti promises and indeed depends upon a dream of the individualized masses. It has borrowed from the repetitions of advertizing and commercial culture an anti-epitaph: the name's frequent appearance marks the stubborn ghost of individuality and intention in the mass culture, the ironic re-statement of the artist as "brand name." Graffiti celebrates the final victory of the signature over the figure, the sign over the referent, by making claims on the very subjectivity invented by consumerism. In this sense it has overgone pop art, which always took on the abstractions of the exchange economy solely as a matter of thematics.[41] For graffiti has re-enacted, within a vernacular setting, that culture's style of simultaneous distribution, erasure of authenticity, and insistent superficiality. Thus graffiti has borrowed from consumer culture not simply an iconography, but an entire rhetoric. And in the localization of that rhetoric is its resistance to its own absorption into the larger commodity system. The discourse of graffiti is a discourse, thereby, of euphemism: the ornament covering the surface appears not simply in the pieces themselves, but also in the graffiti writer's presentation of self and in his or her anti-language which substitutes the tag for the proper name, and phrases like "nasty," "the death," "vicious," "bad," and "dirty" for the standard terms of approval in evaluation.[42]

But the larger threat of graffiti is its violation of the careful system of delineation by which the culture articulates the proper spaces for artistic production and reproduction. As suggested above, those who call graffiti a form of violence are not only invoking the process by which all violence penetrates the materiality of the body; they are also calling our attention to graffiti's disregard of the boundaries of all materiality. It is not so much that graffiti is, after all, a public art; rather, graffiti points to the paradox of a public space which belongs to no one, and to the paradoxes of privacy and face, presentation and display, by which surface, space, and the frontal view are gestures of respectability and respect toward a generalized order for its own sake.

Graffiti's own emphasis upon insides and outsides, differentiating the kinds of tags and pieces that can appear on various kinds of interior and exterior surfaces, underline the ways in which graffiti works toward turning commodity relations inside out. For graffiti attempts a utopian and limited dissolution of the boundaries of property. Within the manufactured environment of the city, it points to the false juxtaposition by which the artistic is made part of the private and domestic while its figure or referent stands outside in nature.[43] Furthermore, it elaborates upon an earlier cultural moment where, in a gesture perhaps slightly less desperate than that of the criminal's tattoo, the "personal" space of the body became a site of creativity and innovation during the mid-to late-1960's. In this elaboration, it is the city itself which now appears as a body — not an artifactual body held in common and available for display, but a body known, as our own bodies are known: piecemeal, fragmented, needing an image or signature.

Graffiti may be a petty crime, but its threat to value is an inventive one, for it forms a critique of the status of all artistic artifacts, indeed a critique of all privatized consumption, and it carries out that threat in full view, in repetition, so that the public has nowhere to look, no place to locate an averted glance. And that critique is paradoxically mounted from a relentless individualism, an individualism which, with its perfected monogram, arose out of the paradox of all commodity relations in their attempt to create a mass individual; an ideal consumer; a necessarily fading star. The independence of the graffiti writer has been shaped by a freedom both promised and denied by those relations — a freedom of choice which is a freedom among delimited and clearly unattainable goods. While that paradise of consumption promised the transference of uniqueness from the artifact to the subject, graffiti underlines again and again an imaginary uniqueness of the subject and a dissolution of artifactual status *per se*.

It is the style of the writer, relentlessly and simultaneously appearing across and through the city, that is graffiti's triumph over property and history. It is precisely graffiti's mere surface, repetition, lack of use, meaninglessness, and negativity that give us the paradox of *insight* with regard to the billboard of commodity culture. And this is exactly the point: that graffiti has no lasting value, no transcendent significance. If my project here has been the redemption of methodology from such larger and ahistorical assumptions, it has also been to emphasize the fleeting and vernacular nature of such a redemption.

Notes

1. Victor Hugo, *Nôtre-Dame de Paris* (Paris: Librairie de L. Hachette, 1869), vol. I, p. 2. The essay, "Ceci Tuera Cela," is in the same volume, pp. 255-74.

2. See Fredric Jameson's "standard" formulations regarding the postmodern affinities for pastiche, the image, and a commodified history in his interconnecting essays, "Postmodernism and Consumer Society," in *The Anti-Aesthetic: Essays on Postmodern Culture*, ed. Hal Foster (Port Townsend, Washington: Bay Press, 1983), pp. 111-25, and "Postmodernism, or The Cultural Logic of Late Capitalism," *New Left Review* 146 (1984), 53-92.

3. "Only in principles of justice and goodness and nobility taught and communicated orally and written in the soul, which is the true way of writing, is there clearness and perfection and seriousness." "Phaedrus," *The Works of Plato*, trans. B. Jowett (New York: Tudor, n.d.), p. 447. See also Derrida's discussion of the *Phaedrus* in *Of Grammatology*, trans. Gayatri Chakravorty Spivak (Baltimore: The Johns Hopkins University Press, 1976), p. 15: "the writing of truth in the soul, opposed by *Phaedrus* to bad writing (writing in the 'literal' [propre] and ordinary sense, 'sensible' writing, 'in space'), the book of Nature and God's writing, especially in the Middle Ages; all that functions as *metaphor* in these discourses confirms the privilege of the logos and founds the 'literal' meaning then given to writing: a sign signifying a signifier itself signifying an eternal verity, eternally thought and spoken in the proximity of a present logos."

4. See T.W. Adorno, *Aesthetic Theory*, trans. C. Lenhardt, ed. Gretel Adorno and Rolf Tiedemann (London: Routledge & Kegan Paul, 1984), pp. 14-22, 128-47.

5. Michael Thompson has made a valuable analysis of this process in his book, *Rubbish Theory: The Creation and Destruction of Value* (Oxford: Oxford University Press, 1979). And more recently, Barbara Herrnstein Smith has extended the discussion of reclassification as a matter of a facility for adaptation: "It may be noted here that human beings have evolved as distinctly opportunistic creatures and that our survival, both as individuals and as a species, continues to be enhanced by our ability and inclination to reclassify objects and to 'realize' and 'appreciate' novel and alternate functions for them." See "Contingencies of Value," *Critical Inquiry*, 1001 (Sept. 1983), 13.

6. See, for example, Paul Rabinow, "Representations are Social Facts," in *Writing Culture: The Poetics and Politics of Ethnography*, ed. James Clifford and George Marcus (Berkeley: University of California Press, 1986), p. 248: "I would add that if it arose in the 1960's in part as a reaction to the academic canonization of the great modernist artists, post-modernism, moving quickly, has itself succeeded in entering the academy in the 1980's. It has successfully domesticated and packaged itself through the proliferation of classificatory schemes, the construction of canons, the establishment of hierarchies, blunting of offensive behavior, acquiescence to university norms. Just as there are now galleries for graffiti in New York, so, too, there are theses being written on graffiti, break dancing, and so on, in the most avant-garde departments."

7. See Jean Baudrillard, *Le Système des objects* (Paris: Gallimard, 1968), p. 43, and Xavier Rubert de Ventós, *Heresies of Modern Art* (New York: Columbia University Press, 1980).

8. William Wordsworth, "Preface to the Lyrical Ballads," (1800), in *The Complete Poetical Works of William Wordsworth* (Boston: Houghton Mifflin, 1904), p. 794. See also Raymond Williams, "Taste," in *Keywords* (New York: Oxford University Press, 1976), pp. 264-66.

9. Information in this section is abstracted from Craig Castleman's important and comprehensive study, *Getting Up: Subway Graffiti in New York* (Cambridge, Mass.: MIT Press, 1982); from Martha Cooper and Henry Chalfant, *Subway Art* (New York: Holt, Rinehart, 1984); and from a series of radio interviews conducted by Terry Gross at WUHY, Philadelphia, on the following dates: Interview with "Cornbread" and "Parish" and interview with Henry Chalfant, February 10, 1984; Interview with "Lady Pink," April 11, 1984; Interview with Madeline Smith, Henry Chalfant, and call-in show, May 3, 1984. I am grateful to Danny Miller and Terry Gross of WUHY for providing me with recordings of these programs, and to Sally Banes for her comments on graffiti and break dancing when a preliminary version of this paper was delivered at the Xth International Congress on Aesthetics, Montreal, August, 1984.

10. A striking example of graffiti's obsession with the name is an ongoing masterpiece along Philadelphia's 30th Street Station's main incoming commuter train tunnel. Here a series of ornamented tombstones have been drawn, each marking the death of a celebrity (the Kennedys, Marilyn Monroe, etc.). A new death in the evening paper will inevitably show up as a new tombstone on the morrow.

11. See Cooper and Chalfant, p. 38. General, 1977, p. 71.

12. Castleman records the term as "racking up." Norman Mailer's earlier work, *The Faith of Graffiti* (New York: Praeger, 1973), records the term as "inventing" (n.p.; see Section 2).

13. Radio interviews with Parish by Terry Gross, February 10, 1984.

14. See Castleman, pp. 25-26 and 55-65, for comments on style names. Cooper and Chalfant quote Kase 2, a "King of Style" as follows: "Wildstyle was the coordinate style and then computer. That's what I brought out. Nobody else can get down with it cause it's too fifth-dimensional. I call it the fifth dimensional step parallel staircase, 'cause it's like computer style in a step formulated way. It's just sectioned off the way I want. Like if I take a knife and cut it, and slice you know I'll slice it to my own section and I'll call it computer style." (p. 71)

15. See Robert Palmer, "Street Smart Rapping Is Innovative Art Form," *New York Times*, February 4, 1985, p. C13.

16. Cooper and Chalfant, p. 33, display a photograph showing the difference between "fat caps" and "skinny caps" and describe the way nozzles are fitted onto spray paint cans to achieve different effects.

17. See Mary Douglas, *Purity and Danger* (London: Routledge, 1966); Edmund Leach, "Anthropological Aspects of Language: Animal Categories and Verbal Abuse," in William Lessa and Evon Vogt, eds. *Reader in Comparative Religion* (New York: Harper and Row, 1972), pp. 206-20; and Thompson, *Rubbish Theory*, which explores the hierarchical aspects of these systems of classification.

18. Quoted in Mailer, n.p., Section 4.

19. "Clamping Down on the Gangs in the Graffiti Fight," *The Philadelphia Inquirer*, November 21, 1982, p. 2-A.

20. Helen H. Tanzer, *The Common People of Pompeii, A Study of the Graffiti* (Baltimore: The Johns Hopkins University Press, 1939), p. 4.

21. Call-in show on graffiti, conducted by Terry Gross, WUHY, Philadelphia, May 3, 1984.

22. A passage from Donald Preziosi's *Architecture, Language, and Meaning* (The Hague: Mouton, 1979), p. 39, provides an interesting gloss on the illegibility of graffiti: "Artifactual markings must satisfy requirements which seem, on the face of it, to be at cross-purposes. On the one hand, a mark must be sufficiently enhanced perceptually so as to be palpable to members of a group and to speak clearly to outsiders of passage and settlement claims. On the other hand, it should maintain sufficient opacity so as to be, to a certain extent, enigmatic; it may be necessary under certain conditions not to reveal too much about a group and its habits. In effect, architectonic objects may need to balance properties of synechdochic *caricature* and *camouflage*.

23. See Castleman, pp. 150-57.

24. Edward Ranzal, "Ronan Backs Lindsay Anti-Graffiti Plan", *New York Times*, August 29, 1972, p. 66.

25. Quoted in Mailer, Section 4.

26. See "Clamping Down on the Gangs."

27. See, for example, "Ten arrested in City War on Graffiti," *Philadelphia Inquirer*, July 26, 1986, p. B-2, and "Eleven Arrests in Graffiti Probe, "*Philadelphia Inquirer*, June 25, 1986, p. B-4.

28. Edward Colimore, "Vandals Fire Back in Graffiti War," *Philadelphia Inquirer*, January 25, 1984. In a complex, and ironic, development, graffiti writers hired by the Anti-Graffiti Task Force for such painting have finally received their pay for such work after months of protest, and even demonstration on their part. Embezzling and financial irregularities characterized the administration of the program, now under investigation. See *Philadelphia Inquirer*: "For Youths, City Jobs Turn Sour," August 25, 1986, p. B-1; "Graffiti Workers Go Unpaid," September 4, 1986, B-1; "Graffiti Workers To be Paid Today, Officials Decide," September 5, p. B-7.

29. Michel Foucault, *Discipline and Punish*, trans. Alan Sheridan (New York: Vintage, 1979).

30. For a variety of accounts of these practices, see Floyd Salas, *Tattoo the Wicked Cross* (New York: Grove Press, 1967), a novel set in a reform school where young Mexican- and Afro-Americans are incarcerated; Sylvia Ann Grider, "Con Safos: Mexican-Americans, Names, and Graffiti," in *Readings in American Folklore*, ed. Jan Harold Brunvand (New York: Norton, 1979), pp. 138-51; and A.J.W. Taylor, "Tattooing Among Male and Female Offenders of Different Ages in Different Types of Institutions, "*Genetic Psychology Monographs*, 81 (1970), 81-119, a study of tattooing among New Zealand criminals, borstal boys and girls, and some Maori analogues.

31. I am grateful to Bill Van Wert for this point.

32. Reprinted in *Marx, Engels, on Literature and Art*, ed. Lee Baxandall and Stefan Morawski (New York: International General, 1977), p. 71.

33. Post-Graffiti, Sidney Janis Gallery, New York, 1983, unpaged catalogue.

34. Calvin Tompkins, "The Art World: Up From the I.R.T.," *The New Yorker*, March 26, 1984, p. 101.

35. See, in addition to Tanzer: *Graffiti in the Athenian Agora* (Princeton: American School of Classical Studies in Athens, 1974); Henry Field, *Camel Brands and Graffiti from Iraq, Syria, Jordan, Iran, and Arabia* (Baltimore: The American Oriental Society, 1952); and Violet Pritchard, *English Medieval Graffiti* (Cambridge: Cambridge University Press, 1967).

36. See Cooper and Chalfant, p. 50.

37. Ann Kolson, "Subways Were Her Canvases, A Spray Can Her Brush," *Philadelphia Inquirer*, April 13, 1984.

38. Henry Chalfant interviews with Terry Gross, February 10, 1984 and May 3, 1984. For a discussion of the social worker Hugo Martinez's involvement with the United Graffiti Artists in New York, see Castleman, pp. 117-26.

39. A patron of graffiti writers in Great Neck, New York, who had her children's room covered with graffiti murals, told the press: "It's individual, it's very personal. It's spontaneous." The individual she has in mind is, not surprisingly, herself — the consumer and the personality she exercises through choice, taste, and eclecticism. Yet we might also note that, as is frequently the case in the adaptation of primitive and working class cultural forms, the children's room is the repository of savagery here. See Dinah Prince, "The New Chic in Decorating? Graffiti in the Home." *Philadelphia Inquirer,* December 23, 1982, p. 3-D.

40. Cooper and Chalfant, p. 34.

41. For a discussion of the theme of money in pop art, see Nancy Marmer, "Pop Art in California," in Lucy Lippard, ed., *Pop Art* (New York: Praeger, 1966), pp. 139-61, pp. 156-57.

42. See Castleman, p. 25. Chalfant and Cooper provide a glossary of terms on p. 27, noting: "Writers have a specialized vocabulary, often metaphors for war and violence, such as 'bomb,' 'hit,' and 'kill.'" The euphemistic and sublimating aspects of this vocabulary become foregrounded when one considers the graffiti writer's generally antithetical relation to gangs (see Castleman, pp. 91-115, for a discussion which contrasts the gang member's vested interest in territory with the graffiti writer's vested interest in mobility) and often pacifist politics (cf. the "Fabulous Five's" Lee Quinone's famous "Stop the Bomb" whole car masterpiece).

43. I take this point from Rubert de Ventós, *Heresies of Modern Art,* p. 134: "When our entire environment is a manufactured one, we cannot pretend that the 'artificial' activity of the artist can and should remain restricted to the private domestic sphere, as in periods when privacy was synonymous with 'culture' and environment with 'nature.'"

8

PANIC VALUE: BACON, COLVILLE, BAUDRILLARD AND THE AESTHETICS OF DEPRIVATION

Arthur Kroker

1986 was the 350th anniversary of the publication of Descartes's *Discours de la méthode* and, with it, the creation of the epistemological *récit* for the emergence of the modernist, geometrically centred perspective of the "thinking subject" framed within the discursive space of the liberal body. Which is just perfect. Because all of contemporary French thought of the post-liberal variety — from Michel Serres's bleak vision of *Le Parasite* (where the positions of host and parasite are the regulatory poles of hypermodern experience) and Bataille's meditations on the "solar anus" and the "pineal eye" (as the privileged signs of the general economy of excess) to Michel Foucault's tragic reflections on transgression (as working only to confirm the "limit experience") and, finally, Jean Baudrillard's hologram of the ultramodern scene — all represent the *fatal implosion* of the Cartesian subject. No longer the Cartesian thinking subject, however, but *fractal subjectivity* in an ultramodern culture where panic science is the language of power: no longer ratiocination to excess, but *parallel processing* as the epistemological form of postmodern consciousness (where Mind is exteriorized in the structural paradigm of telematic society); no longer the geometrically-focussed and self-regulating body, but *technologies for the body immune* as key features of a libidinal economy that produces toxic bodies and designer aesthetics as its necessary conditions of operation; and no longer univocal (grounded) perspective, but the fatal implosion of perspective into the *cyberspace of virtual technology*. And this is as it should be when we are already living beyond gravity (in hyperreal bodies) and beyond representational space (in the mathematical reality of fuzzy sets where individual particles have no meaning apart from the patterning of the larger totality). For the Cartesian self no longer exists — except perhaps as an optical afterimage of the present condition of the post-Cartesian body as the dangling subjectivity in a quantum reality.

In his recent schizo-biography, *L'Autre par lui-même*, Baudrillard, writing parodically in the tradition of *Barthes by Barthes* and Sartre's *Words*, has produced a brilliant hologram of the postmodern scene, that rupture where the representational space of modernist perspective dissolves into the detritus of fractals, fuzzy sets, and bodies without organs. Noteworthy less as critical theory of the reflexive and subordinated sort, *L'Autre par lui-même* is a fascinating account of how the fractal subjects of the *fin-de-millenium* think their (disappearing) selves in relation to exterminism as their public destiny. The text is itself symptomatic of the postmodern fate as *our* implosion into the density of the schizoid sign which suffocates. Indeed, the title of the book (*The Other by Himself*) parodies the postmodern fate as a schizoid time in which inner subjectivity bears no relationship to the external condition. In his essay, "The Uses and Abuses of History," Nietzsche had intimated the same:

> In the end, modern man drags around with him a huge quantity of indigestible stones of knowledge, which, then, as in the fairy tale, can sometimes be heard rumbling about inside him. And in this rumbling there is betrayed the most characteristic quality of modern man: the remarkable antithesis between an interior which fails to correspond to any exterior and an exterior which fails to correspond to any interior.[1]

Nietzsche's "remarkable antithesis" has always been Baudrillard's starting-point. *L'autre par lui-même*, like Baudrillard's other texts, from *L'Échange symbolique et la mort* and *Pour une critique de l'économie politique du signe* to *Simulation* and *Amerique* is about the fractal existence of post-Cartesian subjects who live indifferently between the poles of the pleasure of catastrophe and the terror of the simulacrum. The menacing quality of postmodern times (dangling subjectivity in quantum reality) is caught perfectly in the chapter headings: "Why Theory?" "Metamorphosis, Metaphor, Metastasis," "From the System of Objects to the Destiny of the Object," and "Rituals of the Transparent." This text is like an artistic probe to the extent that it is a supine, mimetic reflection of the postmodern mood: fragmented *hyper-parole* which actually compels the grammatical order to implode with all of the intensity, speed, and transparency of the hyper-modern condition.

Yet what is important about *L'Autre par lui-même* are not its refusals. In Baudrillard, these are always the same: the theoretical refusal of the subordination of thought to an ideological reflex of the commodity-form; the refusal of *all* theories of value, particularly the Marxian theory of surplus-value as obsolescent, both in the Bataillian general economy of excess and a *trompe l'oeil* deflecting attention from the question of value itself as immanent to the logic of the technological dynamo; an aesthetic refusal of the geometrically configured space of the Cartesian subject (in favour of a reflection of "virtual space"); a refusal of the signifier of the social as nothing more than a "piling up of ventilated remainders"; a refusal of the *grand reçit* of History, except in its last imploded side as a *"stratégie fatale"*; and, finally, a refusal of theory itself because of its residual function as a screen-memory, blocking from view the violent metastasis of fractal subjects.

As in all of Baudrillard's writings, what is significant about this book are its *blindspots*. As a brilliant decipherer of the postmodern mood, Baudrillard's blindspots are paradoxically his major theoretical strength. Like art in the age of ultra-capitalism, fascinating *only* to the extent that it is an immanent screen for the designer logic of estheticized recommodification, Baudrillard's writings are, themselves, a deep and direct readout of the scanner logic of the hyper-modern condition. Consequently, if Baudrillard's *psychological blindspot* is that he has no theory of the subject, that is because subjectivity itself has only a schizophrenic quality in which the subject is split between an internal condition surplus to the requirements of telematic society and an external condition of the designer self. If Baudrillard's *aesthetic blindspot* is his refusal of a theory of value, that is because Baudrillard has drunk deeply of Nietzsche's insight that "value" is the dynamic discourse of nihilism, and to speak of the "recovery of the question of value" is only to assent to the language of deprivation. If Baudrillard's *political blindspot* is his failure to maintain a critical distance from the postmodern (or Baudrillardian?) scene, that is because his writings are allergic to self-deception, and alert to the mirroring of the contemporary triumph of liberalism in theoretical reflection that never seeks to exceed the limits of progressivism and pragmatism. If Baudrillard's *existential blindspot* is his failure to develop an adequate theory of political resistance, this may be, not only because the language of resistance is recuperative of the logic of the simulacra that feed parasitically on "challenge and resistance," but also because the rhetoric of resistance in ultramodern societies falls silent in the face of cynical history, cynical sex, and cynical power. And, finally, if Baudrillard's *theoretical blindspot* is his failure as a systematic (scientific) theorist because of his privileging of the poetic imagination, this may be because his writing is an artistic strategy in which words are probes into the immanent logic of *panic science* — words that need to work hysterically in order to *exceed* the desperate logic of hyperrealism.

To dismiss Baudrillard would be to foreclose remembrance on theory itself which, like art in the age of estheticized recommodification, only remains interesting to the extent that it catches up with the disappearing masses as the missing matter of the social, and when it manages to evoke the postmodern mood in all its moments of sacrifice, waste, and loss. To resist Baudrillard would be the residual strategy of modernists nostalgic for the logic of the dialectic, the transgression that only confirms. If, as Charles Levin has written, Baudrillard is fascinating as a "sign, a talisman, a symptom" of the postmodern scene, then to really resist Baudrillard would be *to exceed* his intellectual project, to push it to its point of immanent collapse in a final burst of cultural dyslexia: where we could read the artistic edge (a fusion of pop realism and electronic art) between deprivation and creation, between fatalism (with its *stratégies fatales*) and the new world of ultramodernism. Indeed, this is Baudrillard's challenge: an invitation to thinking anew about ultramodernism which embraces "intimations of deprival" as its most dynamic logic, but also contains new possibilities for post-Cartesian subjects in a waiting time at the end of history. To be dangling subjects in quantum reality is our fate now: like the ancients, to have consciousness of much, but the ability to do nothing about it.

And so, how to *exceed* the bitter Nietzschean edge in Baudrillard's lament, "Why Theory?"

> And if reality, under our eyes, suddenly dissolved? Not into nothingness, but into a real which was more than real (the triumph of simulation)? If the modern universe of communication, the space of hypercommunication through which we are plunging, not in forgetfulness, but with an enormous saturation of our senses, consumed us in its success — without trickery, without secrets, without distance? If all publicity were an apology, not for a product, but for publicity itself? If information did not refer any longer to an event, but to the promotion of information itself as *the* event? If our society were not a "spectacle," as they said in '68, but, more cynically, a *ceremony*? If politics was a continent more and more irrelevant, replaced by the spectre of terrorism, by a generalized taking of hostages, that is to say, by the spectre of an impossible exchange? If all of this mutation did not emanate, as some believe, from a manipulation of subjects and opinion, but from a logic without a subject where opinion vanished into fascination? If pornography signified the end of sexuality as such, and from now on, under the form of obscenity, sexuality invaded everything? If seduction were to succeed desire and love, that is to say, the reign of the object over that of the subject? If strategical planning were to replace psychology? If it would no longer be correct to oppose

truth to illusion, but to perceive generalized illusion itself
as truer than truth? If no other behaviour was possible than
that of learning, ironically, how to disappear? If there were
no longer any fractures, lines of flight or ruptures, but a
surface full and continuous, without depth, uninterrupted? And if all of this were neither a matter of enthusiasm
nor despair, but fatal?[2]

Exceeding Baudrillard

Maybe, Baudrillard's "Why Theory?" is too conservative in its subordination of the subject to the reign of the object. For what is the dark,
imploded side of the Cartesian self if not our positioning as dangling subjects, spectactors to our own fate, in bodies that alternate between the frenzy
of the schizoid ego and the inertia of hermeticism? That question is what
two contemporary painters, Francis Bacon and Alex Colville, intimate in
their haunting, painterly descriptions of the schizoid ego and the hermetic body as parallel, reverse mirror-images of the hypermodern self at the
fin-de-millenium. In Bacon and Colville's artistic productions, the body
alternates between its suspension in an infinitely imploded and inertial state
of pure hermeticism (Colville) and its dispersion *en abyme* in the exploding detritus of the schizoid ego (Bacon). Here, the pain of the external condition is so overwhelming that the gaze turns inward as the body implodes
into the density of a sign with no referent; and there the body is turned
inside out — actually peeled open — as its organs are splayed, like negative photographic images, across the field of a dead, relational power. To
be buried alive in the perspectival fictions of their own skins, or splayed
across the postmodern scene with all their organs hanging out: these are
the alternative images presented by Bacon and Colville of panic bodies
at the *fin-de-millenium*.

This deep complicity between Colville's and Bacon's visions of the postmodern body may be because they both realize that the Cartesian body
does not exist anymore, that, like a fuzzy set in mathematical theory, it
always was only a perspectival illusion: a panic site where only the pattern
is real; and onto which are inscribed in the space of an absent presence
all the anxieties, myths, and fantasies of the simulacra. The body imploded (Colville) or the body exploded (Bacon), the hermetic self and the schizoid ego as indifferent poles configure the fate of the post-Cartesian self
in the age of estheticized recommodification.

The Hermetic Self

For example, Colville's *Two Boys Playing* is a study of the implosion
of the body into the dark but transparent density of a floating sign: disem-
bodied in space; the product of a perspectival simulation; faces turned in-

Alex Colville, *Two Boys Playing*

ward as marks of cancelled identies; the very *technique* of the painting a parody of the colours and tone-lines of the aesthetics of seduction (from the muted colour of the water to the paint strokes which, in their striking similarity to the cut strokes of Egyptian sculpture in the classical period, also satirize permanence); and everything patterned according to the topological rules of hyper-symmetry (from the curvature of the bodies to heads that actually grow out of each other). But what gives away the privileging of designer artifice — artifice as a perspectival simulation — is that there is brilliant light, but no shadows; body positions without depth (the boys hover over water and land); and though the painting is titled *Two Boys Playing*, the dominant psychological mood is not play, but mourning and loss. *Two Boys Playing* is, in fact, about a logic without a subject, designer subjectivity; the body an essential topological aspect of the artifice. And if the painting can convey so vividly all the signs of the aesthetics of seduction, it is only to emphasize that the boys playing — with neither eyes, ears, faces, nor discernible identities — are also buried alive in the catastrophe of their own skins: hermetic bodies fit for ultramodernism.

And likewise with Colville's *Man, Woman and Boat* and *Four Figures on a Wharf*. These paintings (reminiscent of de Chirico's Turin meditations) are metaphysical because they illustrate the ontology of hyperrealism: our disappearance into the fascinating, and relational, topology of a measured and calculative universe. Here, everything has been reduced to perspectival relations of spatial contiguity (the mummy-like figures of *Man, Woman* and the symmetry of the classical statuary); the water, in both paintings, does not represent an edge, but the opposite — the dissolution of all borders; the mapping of which is sidereal and topographical. We might say, in fact, that these paintings figure the double liquidation of classical mythological space (*Four Figures on a Wharf* is a hologram for the world as a fuzzy set), and modern panoptic space (for there is no disappearing viewpoint in *Man, Woman and Boat*). As the immolation of classical and panoptic space, they also work to provide the internal grammatical rules of the intensely mathematized space of ultramodernism: folded in time, more real than the real, always topological and fractal. Consequently, the ultra-symmetry of colours, figures, and textures in *Man, Woman and Boat* and *Four Figures on a Wharf* are real because their very perfection indicates their *hyperreal* existence as sliding signifiers in a topographical and aestheticized surface of events. In space as a designer, mathematical construct, the boat floats on the water, the classical statuary is geometrically abstracted, and the designer environment is superior to any original because its ontology is that of excessive *hyper-nature* .

The metaphysical experiment in Colville's art is most explicit in *Nude and Dummy*. David Burnett has said about this painting that

> *Nude and Dummy* reflects measurement, a point made explicit when he replaced one of the figures with the dressmaker's dummy. The purpose of a dummy is wholly contained in the notion of measurement and the painting represents an interlocking scale of measurement. First that between the woman and the domestic architecture, second, between the woman and the dummy. The picture is concerned with standards; it responds to the way we orient ourselves to the world through the structures and conventions we use. Painting, too, in its ordering of illusions, has its conventions of measurement.[3]

This is incorrect. In mathematized space, the body is only understandable cabalistically: a topographical filiation *en abyme*, a perspectival simulacrum, a fractal figure with no (hyperreal) existence except as part of a large holographic pattern, the product of the folded space of culture as a fuzzy set without depth. In aestheticized reality, the Nude is the table of values of the measured Dummy. But what lends the painting an eerie and stylized sense of absence is that the table of values has lost its referential significance:

Alex Colville, *Man, Woman and Boat*

no periodicity, no hierarchy, no immanent *difference*, and no point of comparison between Nude and Dummy except as negative, refracted terms in an internal spiral of aesthetic catastrophe. *Nude and Dummy* paints the end of the (modernist) space of the *trompe-l'oeil*, and the beginning of the implosive terror of the simulacra.

Like a Descartes in reverse image theorising the implosive space of ultramodernism, Colville paints the burnout and decomposition of the periodic table of values. His artistic imagination begins at that moment when ratiocination (to excess) flips into its opposite sign-value: the collapse of calculative measurement into the indeterminacy of fractal subjectivity; and the dissolution of the periodic table of values into the hyper-density of a fungible, instantly reversible and random, sign-system. Colville's metaphysical insight suggests not that the "ordering of illusions" and the "conventions of measurement" have fled the painterly canvas and been installed as the deep logic of ultramodernism, but, rather, that the real is a cyberspace without depth or fracture: fractal subjectivity in designer environments linked only by the pleasure of the aesthetics of catastrophe.

Francis Bacon, *Studies from the Human Body*, 1975.
Gilbert de Botton, Switzerland

Like static background radiation from the Big Bang, all of Colville's paintings represent the massive aesthetic fallout from his primary metaphysical deduction: ratiocination to excess mutates into the parasiting of the historical event by the estheticization of space; and the aesthetics of seduction is predatory in its internal coding of all the disappearing elements of culture. Colville's world is hermetic: here everything is a matter of suffocated speech, of (external) frenzy as a sign of (internal) inertia, and of the gaze turned inwards into the dark, and surplus, space of dangling subjectivity.

Colville's world, then, is the horizon of cynical power, panic sex, and dead history. A vision of life on the beach after the catastrophe, this is a world that can only be spoken in the languages of indifference (*Snow*), vertigo (*Taxi, Two Pacers, At Grand Pré*), cancelled identities at the end of time (*Pacific, Morning, June Noon, To Prince Edward Island*), and intimations of deprival before the technological dynamo (*Horse and Church, Horse and Train, Woman in Bathtub*). Colville's world is a site of visual frenzy to the point of excessive stillness, like the fashion photography of Man Ray, in which the scene of the lips on the wall bears no relationship, except as counterfeit to the counterfeit, to the beckoning arms of the wom-

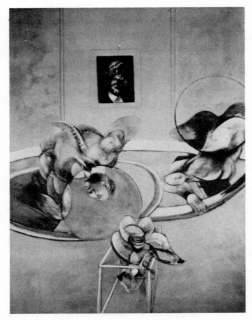

Francis Bacon, *Figure Writing Reflected in a Mirror*, 1976.
Private Collection

an reclining on the couch, a dark absence into which can be read all of the fear and panic mythologies of pestilential culture. Parallel to Colville's bleak vision of the hermetic body are the desperate writings of Bataille, another parody on the redoubling of the body in an endless labyrinth of images: "Beings only die in order to be born, in the manner of phalluses that leave bodies in order to enter them" (*The Solar Anus*).

> In bed next to the woman he loves, he forgets that he does not know why he is himself instead of the body he touches. Without knowing it, he suffers from an obscurity of intelligence that keeps him from screaming that he himself is the woman who forgets his presence while shuddering in his arms. They can well try to find each other; they will never find anything but parodic images, and they will fall asleep as empty as mirrors. (*The Solar Anus*)

Francis Bacon, *Three Studies of the Human Head*, 1953.
Private Collection

The Schizoid Ego

> *I would like my pictures to look as if a human being had passed between them, like a snail, leaving a trail of the human presence and memory traces of past events, as the snail leaves its slime. I think the whole process of this sort of elliptical form is dependent on the execution of detail to show how shapes are remade or put slightly out of focus to bring in their memory traces.* — Francis Bacon, *The New Decade*

Studies from the Human Body leaves a trail of human presence in triptych form: carcasses; muted screams; and specimens imaged on experimental medical slides.

Bacon's postmodern body is the reverse image of Colville's. In Bacon, Colville's hermetic body, where the pain is so intense that identity is cancelled, has been turned inside out: a corps morcelée, mutilated by all the signs of excremental culture as the essence of a society typified by the *predatory* exploitation of the vulnerable by the powerful, by the bleak exchange of host and parasite as the emblematic sign of *parasitical* culture, and by all the detritus of liberalism. Where Colville's body traces an inward pattern in search of the upturned orb of the pineal eye, Bacon's body is peeled open: organs exteriorized, central nervous system splayed across the field of power relations; and its dominant — the screaming head.

Bacon has said of his artistic practice that it represents the direct inscription of his nervous system onto the canvas. But he was too modest to note as well that his work is a visual recitative of a more general condition of cultural afterimages, where the mind is on its way to being exteriorized in a processed world and the externalized nervous system is the key cultural principle of spatial contiguity. There, where television is the real world, the subjectivity of increasingly technical beings atrophies into the frenzy of inertia, the reality of which can be caught, as Bacon does, in all of his work, by smearing photographic and cinematic trace images to draw out the real.

In the same way, movies today (e.g. *Blue Velvet, Brazil*) capture perfectly the spirit of pestilential culture. In *Blue Velvet* only the parasites like Frank have energy and can make things happen; everyone else is a passive host — either as the victim of sexual parasitism at the level of sadomasochism, or a spectator sinking into self-parody and kitsch like the detective. The movie alternates like a phasal shift between life as a 1950s advertising scene and violent excess, between frenzy and inertia. The movie *Brazil* provides a chilling vision of life as a *vis mediatrix* — with us as the social remainder of a processed world.

Similarly, Bacon's artistic vision is about postmodern bodies as X-rayed afterimages of technological society at such a point of excess that it becomes a site of excremental loss. As Foucault suggested in *The History of Sexuality*, when life is wagered on its technological strategies, human beings are reduced to ventilated remainders: *objects of torture* (the sacrificial image of the Crucifixion is everywhere in Bacon's art); *vultures (Portrait of George Dyer Crouching)*; *vagina dentata (Lying Figures with Hypodermic Syringe)*; exploding torsos and screaming heads (Bacon's Pope); or just quick images of the solitary agony of a human being dying, vomiting his sickness into a toilet bowl.

Bacon's postmodern body is a relentless alternation between the pleasure palace (an object of seduction as in *Study of Nude with Figure in Mirror*) and the torture-chamber (*Three Figures* and *Portrait*). In these paintings, the thermodynamics of sexual voyeurism slide silently into their opposite number: human beings with supine vertebrae twisted like fit specimens for the medical laboratory.

If Bacon can express so well the voyeuristic sadism of a world where de Sade's sexual thermodynamics are the reverse side of Kant's categorical imperative, and by smearing X-ray images to draw out the hyperreality of *our* devolution into servomechanisms of science as the language of power in a processed world, this is because Bacon is one artist who expresses in haunting images what Nietzsche meant by "winter thoughts."

In *Thus Spake Zarathustra*, Nietzsche said of our existence that it would be a "homeless time": "The human earth became to me a cave, its chest caved in, everything living became to me decay and moldering past."[4] Not an unhappy time, but a time of the triumphant emergence of nihilism, suicidal and passive, as the North American culture. The nihilists for Nietzsche?

> Fundamentally, they want one thing most of all: that nobody shall do them harm. So they steal a march on everyone and do good to everyone. We have set down our chairs

in the middle — that is what their smirking tells us — and as far away from the warriors as from the contented swine. This is mediocrity.[5]

But Nietzsche also murmured: "Even what you omit weaves at the web of mankind's future; even your nothing is a spider's web and a spider that lives on the future's blood".[6]

Meditating on the "body as a bridge suspended over the abyss," Nietzsche might have been writing in advance on Bacon's grisly world of the body peeled open when he reflected:

> That you have despaired there is much to honour in that. That you have despised that makes me hope, for the great despisers are the great reverers. For you have not learned how to submit, you have not learned the petty prudences.[7]

That is exactly the art of Francis Bacon and Alex Colville: they have not learned the "petty prudences." Allergic to self-deception, and working aesthetically to probe the hypermodern condition, their artistic productions are a reflection from another "wintry" time: the end of the twentieth century as a time of cluster suicides, cultural dyslexia and forms of schizophrenia, as the postmodern mind runs down to random disorganization and burnout, where hermetic bodies and schizoid egos become panic sites at the *fin-de-millenium*. Colville's imploding self and Bacon's exploding bodies are violent edges of resistance and excess; cuts, existing midway between the ecstasy of catastrophe and the decay of the simulacrum, as indifferent poles of ultramodernism. In their artistic visions, Baudrillard's lament about postmodern reality that suddenly dissolves into a "real which [is] more than real" has been confirmed, and then exceeded.

Notes

1. F. Nietzsche, *Untimely Meditations*, trans. R.J. Hollingdale (London: Cambridge University Press, 1983), p. 78.
2. Jean Baudrillard, *L'Autre par lui-même* (Paris, 1987), pp. 53-54.
3. David Burnett, *Colville* (Toronto: McClelland and Stewart, 1984), p. 77.
4. F. Nietzsche, *Thus Spake Zarathustra*, trans. R.J. Hollingdale (Harmondsworth, England: Penguin, 1969), p. 236.
5. *Ibid.*, p. 190.
6. *Ibid.*, p. 191.
7. *Ibid.*, p. 297.

Contributors

JAY M. BERNSTEIN: Philosophy, Essex. *The Philosophy of the Novel: Lukacs, Marxism, and the Dialectics of Form*. (Minnesota, 1984).

JOHN FEKETE: English, and Chairman of Cultural Studies, Trent. *The Critical Twilight: Explorations in the Ideology of Anglo-American Literary Theory from Eliot to McLuhan*. (Routledge, 1978). Ed. *The Structural Allegory: Reconstructive Encounters with the New French Thought*. (Minnesota, 1984).

ARTHUR KROKER: Political Science and Humanities, Concordia. *Technology and the Canadian Mind: Innis, McLuhan, Grant*. (New World Perspectives [Montreal] and St. Martin's, 1984). With David Cook, *The Postmodern Scene: Excremental Culture and Hyper-Aesthetics*. (New World Perspectives and St. Martin's, 1986).

CHARLES LEVIN: Ph.D. Program in Humanities, Concordia. Candidate at the Canadian Institute of Psychiatry in Montreal. Trans. *For a Critique of the Political Economy of the Sign*, by Jean Baudrillard. (Telos, 1981). Journal essays on French thought and psychoanalysis.

GYÖRGY MÁRKUS: Philosophy, Sydney. *Marxism and 'Anthropology': The Concept of Human Essence in the Philosophy of Marx*. (Humanities, 1978). Numerous books in Hungarian, German, and French.

ARKADY PLOTNITSKY: English, Pennsylvania. Journal essays on continental criticism.

BARBARA H. SMITH: Braxton Craven Professor of Comparative Literature and English, Duke. *Poetic Closure: A Study of How Poems End* (Chicago, 1971). *On the Margins of Discourse: The Relation of Literature to Language*. (Chicago, 1978).

SUSAN STEWART: English, Temple. *Nonsense: Aspects of Intertextuality in Folklore and Literature*. (Johns Hopkins, 1980). *Yellow Stars and Ice* (Princeton, 1981). *On Longing: Narratives of the Miniature, the Gigantic, the Souvenir, the Collection*. (Johns Hopkins, 1984).

Index of Names

CultureTexts

Arthur and Marilouise Kroker   General Editors

CultureTexts is a series of creative explorations in theory, politics and culture at the *fin-de-millenium*. Thematically focussed around key theoretical debates in the postmodern condition, the *CultureTexts* series challenges received discourses in art, social and political theory, feminism, psychoanalysis, value inquiry, science and technology, the body, and critical aesthetics. Taken individually, contributions to *CultureTexts* represent pioneering theorisations of the postmodern scene. Taken collectively, *CultureTexts* represents the forward, breaking-edge of postmodern theory and practice.

Titles

The Postmodern Scene: Excremental Culture and Hyper-Aesthetics
Arthur Kroker/David Cook

Life After Postmodernism: Essays on Value and Culture
edited and introduced by John Fekete

Body Invaders: Panic Sex in America
edited and introduced by Arthur and Marilouise Kroker

Forthcoming

Panic Science

Forgetting Art

Liberal Burnout